Nice Girls and Rude Girls

SOCIAL AND CULTURAL HISTORY TODAY

Published and forthcoming:

Nice Girls and Rude Girls

Women Workers in World War I

———⟶⟵———

Deborah Thom

I.B.TAURIS PUBLISHERS

London • New York

Paperback edition published in 2000 by I.B. Tauris & Co Ltd
Victoria House, Bloomsbury Square, London WC1B 4DZ
175 Fifth Avenue, New York NY 10010
website: http://www.ibtauris.com

First published in 1998 by I.B. Tauris & Co Ltd

ISBN 1 86064 477 5

A full CIP record for this book is available from the British Library

Designed and typeset by Dexter Haven, London

Printed and bound by SRM Production Services Sdn Bhd, Malaysia

Contents

Acknowledgements

I started writing about the women workers of the Woolwich Arsenal as the beginning of my academic career and during a period living in South-East London, where the questions which I wanted to answer had been generated. I wanted to understand the history of a community, and the role that women played in historical change. Many of these pieces reflect the dual motives for which they were written. The history of local lives, related to some of the participants through the Workers' Educational Association class on 'The People's History of Woolwich', which I taught briefly, was thus given an airing to a critical audience which knew the social and physical geography of the area very well and often had illuminating examples and incidents to relate. The other place where these ideas were discussed early on was at the London Women's History Group, where women members of a group which ranged very broadly in age and academic experience battled over the historical issues of the day: in particular, the question of how far it was possible to describe a history of women or of some women was extensively discussed, as an issue with live political implications. Sometimes the questions about political organisation and the notions of power used in these essays written over 15 years read very oddly. They all have their origins in academic summaries, when I studied first at Warwick University in 1975 for an MA thesis and then at Thames Polytechnic, in the old buildings in the centre of Woolwich itself, where I did my PhD. I did not at the time publish either as a whole, and had intended never to do so, because I felt that the issues raised by my findings did not make a book. Then a copy of my PhD thesis was stolen from the Library of Thames Polytechnic, and I kept having letters from people who wanted to follow up some section of the PhD, and I decided that the scattered articles would work together after all.

The originality of these studies lies, I hope, in the emphasis on the relationship between workers' own organisations and changes at work, and thence the emphasis in the sources on the records kept by Gertrude Tuckwell of the Women's Trade Union League.

This remarkable collection of press clippings, pamphlets, letters and minutes has been kept at the Trades Union Congress Library, and is now available on microfiche. The second substantial source I have used is the Women's Work collection of the Imperial War Museum, whose trustees provide and support a remarkable library and associated collections of diaries, letters, objects and photographs, which includes the Women's Work Collection among its records. I am very grateful to these two great institutions which continue to recognise the significance of public memory and provide so valuable a resource for the historian.

Many people have given me help, guidance and support during the 20 years for which I have been thinking, with greater or lesser attention, about the subject of this collection. Feminist scholars working on this topic welcomed me when they found out we were interested in the same things and shared generously their time, sources and insights, and I am particularly obligated to Marion Kozak, Gail Braybon and Antonia Ineson. The women of the London Women's History group and my Workers' Educational Association class often provided an invaluable sense of intellectual community which made up for the difficulty of being a graduate student at the Poytechnic where I worked as a part-time teacher, and thus not having the institutional resources I see around me now in my third academic insitution, the University of Cambridge. In particular, Angela John gave unstinting advice and help as an editor, colleague and friend. Numerous people found books, suggested sources and help but I benefited especially from Andrew Crozier's aid, Ian Patterson's bibliographic expertise and the everhelpful staff of the Greenwich Local History Library. The then Social Science Research Council supported me while I was doing some of the research for the two dissertations and the pieces republished in this book, without which much of the primary research would have been impossible.

I am grateful to all the publishers of the pieces here reproduced for permission to reissue them, and to the editors of these collections who helped in many ways to make them clearer, even if I now take this opportunity to make the pieces longer again.

Since coming to work in Cambridge I have received both intellectual stimulus and moral support from my colleagues at Robinson College, in the Family Research Group, at History and Philosophy of Science, and in the group which teaches the course on gender in the history faculty. Dr Gillian Sutherland has been supportive throughout, although my lingering in the First World War has delayed other work in which she has an interest. My three sons have given me distraction and an interest in questions of gender which endures. Like their father, Ian, they have given emotional interest which has both sustained and distracted me; to this, Ian has added a rigorous and critical scholar's eye, for which I have mostly been very grateful. My brother Martin has provided a rivalry and a model which has been most helpful, as has his frequent help with babysitting; my parents have always supported me and given me that invaluable resource, the capacity to believe that there was nothing I could not do if I wanted to do it enough.

List of Abbreviations

AEU	Amalgamated Engineering Union
ASE	Amalgamated Society of Engineers
ASL	Anti-Sweating League
BLPES	British Library of Political and Economic Science
DORA	Defence of the Realm Act
ELFS	East London Federation of Suffragettes
EMP	Ministry of Employment
GFTU	General Federation of Trade Unions
GMWU	General and Municipal Workers Union
GTC	Gertrude Tuckwell Collection
HMWC	Health of Munition Workers Committee
IWM	Imperial War Museum
LSE	London School of Economics
MM	Ministry of Munitions
MMOH	Ministry of Munitions Offical History
MOH	Medical Officer of Health
MUN	Ministry of Munitions
NFWW	National Federation of Women Workers
NUR	National Union of Railwaymen
NUWSS	National Union of Women Suffrage Societies
PP	Parliamentary Papers
PRO	Public Records Office
RECON	Ministry of Reconstruction
SJCWIO	Standing Joint Committee of Women's Industrial Organisations
SUP	Ministry of Supply
TGWU	Transport and General Workers Union
TUC	Trades Union Congress
WCG	Women's Co-operative Guild
WIL	Women's Industrial League
WLL	Women's Labour League
WSPU	Women's Social and Political Union
WTUL	Women's Trade Union League
WU	Workers' Union

Chronology

Battles are in capitals, and indented

1906	Formation of National Federation of Women Workers, to provide a union for women excluded by trade unions in their trade; Sweated Industries Exhibition organised by the *Daily News*
1908	Trade Boards Act
1911	Great unrest
1912	Chain-workers strike; adult suffrage league formed

1914

August

4	War declared: army mobilisation
5	War Emergency Workers National Committee set up 'to safeguard workers' interests'
8	Defence of the Realm Act (DORA) gives Government general powers of regulation
2	Women's Employment Central Committee set up to organise work for unemployed women
23	MONS

September

6-9	MARNE

October

20	YPRES

1915

January

14	Dilution agreement in Sheffield between ASE and local employers; skilled men withdrawn from army for munitions work

February	Strikes in Dundee (jute), Clyde (engineers), London (docks)

March

4	Shells and Fuses agreement between engineering employers and TU allowing unskilled workers and women on skilled men's work

September

October

December

1917

January

February

June

July

21	Ministry of Reconstruction set up
October	Maximum hours for munition workers to be 65-67 for men (over 16), 60 for rest

November

7	Soviet Revolution
26	Coventry strike over recognition of shop stewards agreement begins

December

3	Coventry strike over recognition of shop stewards agreement ends

1918

January

14	General increase in women's wages of 3s 6d for women, 1s 9d for girls

February

6	Vote for women over 30, all men over 21
18	Demobilisation arrangements announced

March

2	Treaty of Brest-Litovsk signed between Germany and Russia
21	GERMAN OFFENSIVE ON SOMME

April

9	LYS

May

27	GERMAN OFFENSIVE ON CHEMIN DES DAMES

July

1	Embargo order prohibiting any additional employment of skilled labour
15	GERMAN OFFENSIVE ON RHEIMS AND MARNE
23	Embargo strikes in Coventry, Birmingham, Rugby, threat of national unofficial engineering strike

August

8	BRITISH OFFENSIVE ON SOMME
17-23	Strike of London tram and bus workers gains 5s for women on men's work
25	Tube strike in London gains equal war wages for men and women
30	Strike of metropolitain police secures wage increase of 13s

September

7   Women munitions workers awarded wage advance: 5s women, 2s 6d girls

20-27   Unofficial strike of railway workers fails to increase wages rise to 10s, but wins 5s

November

7   Demobilisation: workers allowed to leave munitions work

11   Armistice

25   Out-of-Work Donation scheme: 24s for men, 20s for women (plus allowance of 6s for first child, 3s for next), 12s for boys, 10s for girls; paid for 26 weeks for forces, 13 for civilians

December

5   General Election

6   Special branch of Ministry of Labour set up to provide training or re-employment for women

17   Special scheme for domestic economy training for soldiers' wives or fiancees

1919

January

25   Belfast strike for 44-hour week

27   Clyde and Forth workers strike for 40-hour week

May   First refusal of unemployment donation for 'unreasonably refusing work' on domestic service; high levels of industrial unrest, continuing in June and July

1   National Industrial Conference proposal for minimum wage and 48-hour week accepted in principle

September Report of War Cabinet Committee on Women in Industry

26   Railway strike, national emergency proclaimed, ends new wage rates

October

5   Railway strike ends

25   Scheme to use private employment agencies and labour exchanges to increase supply of domestic servants

December

23   Sex Disqualifications Removal Act allows women into trades and professions; Restoration of Pre-war Practices Act reimposes trade practices, ie rescinds dilution agreements

1920

February

7   Women's Training and Employment Committee to promote employment and training for unemployed and those adversely affected by war

1921

April

1   Ministry of Munitions ends

1924   Merger of NFWW into GMWU; WTUL effectively becomes part of the TUC

Source: mostly from N.B. Dearle, *Economic Chronicle of the Great War*, London, 1924

Chapter 1
Introduction

In 1916, Jennie Randolph Churchill wrote in her book *Women's War Work,* 'It is one of the virtues of war that it puts the light which in peacetime is hid under a bushel in such prominence that all can see it'.[1] Her sense of war bringing women's contribution into the light, making women visible, was widely shared. The metaphor is even more useful than that because it raises the question of agency. Who hid their light? Did they do so themselves? In addition, the coincidence of the end of the war with the granting of the vote to women over thirty made contemporaries see wartime occupations as intrinsically emancipatory, because they had previously been done by men. Mrs Fawcett, a leading suffragist, wrote in 1919, 'The war revolutionised the industrial position of women. It found them serfs and left them free'.[2] Her contemporary, the trade-union leader Mary Macarthur, shared her belief in profound change:

> Of all the changes wrought by the War, none has been greater than the change in the status and position of women, and yet it is not so much that woman herself has changed as that man's conception of her has changed.[3]

There is a question here that continues to echo in the literature of war and social change since it was first framed in the attempt to find some productive outcome after so much death, so much loss and so much dramatic change in personal relationships as well as public lives. Many have hoped for some benefit, even some recompense for that loss. Some historians alongside these women activists have looked for a beneficial restructuring of gender relations for the female sex as well as a conceptual shift in the construction of gender. Histories have been more than usually judgemental about the First World War, debating whether it was necessary at all, whether it produced any progressive change, whether it can be described comparatively. Whether, as Auden wrote of a war which occurred because of forces set in motion in Europe deriving in part from 1914-1918, the 1936 civil war in Spain, 'History to the defeated, Can say alas but never pardon'; it is unclear in the many accounts of the experience of World War I whether for women talking of 'victory' or 'defeat' ever serves any useful purpose except to expose the inadequacies of a history which replaces wars between combatants with wars between the sexes. The battle was far more abstract if one looks, not to biological sex mapped on to social gender, but to the construction of gender itself affecting the lives of men and women equally strongly. In the past, the analytical use of gender roles has been seen as used of men in the world of work, for women in the world of home and reproduction. The two rhetorical categories, the woman worker and the mother, existed in many of the workers of the First World War side-by-side and together, since many workers were both mother and worker. But sex, in the sense of sexuality and sexual behaviour, has also affected the history of gender relations, in that the workplace was a place where sexual morality was seen as operative, although how it might be affecting people's behaviour has not been much examined.

The theory of gender being used here accords with arguments others have put forward about how they find the essential nature of the 'incontrovertibility of difference,' to use Marilyn Strathern's phrase, useful in examining social categories.[4] Difference is at the heart of this story, in which a woman's work is defined upon entry by her relationship to a man who, fictionally in many cases, was doing the work she now does. Although I do not find the notion of patriarchy analytically useful because it takes one difference, that between men and women, and lays it on top of all the others, providing a very crude map of social relationships, there are some examples of a sexual hostility based on that fundamental difference which nothing else will explain, except some term such as mysogyny. My definition of patriarchy can be summed up in Judy Lown's description of 'patriarchy as a form of power, characterised in terms of organising and rationalising social relations based on male superiority and female inferiority'.[5] Hence part of this book is about the way in which work is constructed with an eye to relations of power, and I have aimed to get away from the naturalisation of gender relations involved in assuming either female subordination or a separate and distinctive social life for women.

The most significant body of work in English on women workers in Britain in the First World War has been written by Gail Braybon, who has produced two books, *Women Workers in the First World War* in 1981 and *Out of the Cage* in 1987 with Penny Summerfield. She has investigated connections between the ideas that shaped shifts in the labour market, male assumptions about women's nature and the history of their employment. Her work has emphasised the contribution of ideology to the shaping of a labour market and the many ways in which that ideology was made visible in wartime social commentary. In the second of the two books she has used much testimony material to give a wide range of women's reactions to the war period. This valuable body of work has made evident the very profound sense of reflexivity in writing about women and war. People have wanted to make sense of the experience and to preserve some value in it ever since the war first started and was seen as likely to last more than a few weeks. There were numerous books written by journalists, political commentators, even novelists, on women and war. Many of the earliest titles play with the relationship between the two ideas. The histories of women and the First World War have themselves reflected profound changes in feminism, social policy and publishing.[6]

At the end of the twentieth century, the questions about how working people constructed social change for themselves and the centrality of the workplace to their sense of identity seem to be extremely unfashionable ideas. A search through the index of periodicals revealed virtually nothing written in journals about women workers in the First World War in the 1990s, and when those words appeared at all they were with reference to middle-class women welfare workers, not manual workers. The issues of work, how it was changed by war and how the workers changed the work does primarily relate to the women of the working class, as they were defined at the time. For women of the middle class the war was far more productive of progress than it was for those who worked on manual tasks in factories. Women's history has, as I shall argue in my conclusion, gone through several phases, but more recent developments have tended to place the author of a piece of women's history at the centre of her own story. As a result there is a risk of history becoming more and more descriptive of people who are most like historians. The questions raised by the experience of the factory worker are often far removed from that of women whose workplace is differently organised, who have greater constructive control over both their pace of work and its content and whose labour, although it may be repetitive, is never as repetitious as work on mass production. In short, the meaning of work is different for the industrial worker and the academic. The questions of the different meanings of work for the privileged beneficiaries of innovation, and those for whom the world of domestic labour has meant most in their working lives, have thus been marginalised by questions of reproduction and sexuality. They do, however, remain pertinent.

There is also a phenomenology of manual labour which means that understanding the experience of war requires more than documentary evidence, rich though that is. The questions about how it felt to be a manual worker have often been argued on the basis of the accounts of observers, or of participants themselves many years later. The participants can often provide in their old age a re-enactment of that work experience, showing how deeply it became established in bodily memory, but photographs can show the nature of the experience too. In other words what is reflected by visual evidence is additional, and complementary to the comments of contemporary observers. Experience needs to be understood differently when it is shown in the body than when it is described by others or people themselves.

The relationship between the state and the labour market for women has always been complicated by questions of whether the state intervenes to regulate birth, motherhood and sex, and if it does, how far the intervention is constructed differently in a democracy under stress of war. Pedersen sees the state intervention of dependants' allowances creating 'a new direct relationship between the State and the working-class wife,' but also argues that this concern for private activities, particularly their role in reproduction, was 'of concern to the state only in the absence of men'.[7] The account of workplace regulation which follows suggests that Pedersen ignores the contribution of women both to political rhetoric and to policy. Women workers were of concern for the state as workers, and in some respects that concern did involve intrusion into the private world of home and family, particularly through the role of factory welfare, with its concern for women's time-keeping. I shall argue that the state did have an interest in the woman worker as a worker before the war and that it was not purely male absence that created state intervention, but partly the interests and representations of organisations of working women reflecting their growing political consciousness.

After war broke out, Government was influenced by the general concern for women as industrial workers. It was not until 1917 that motherhood became a major governmental or philanthropic concern in ways which were specific to wartime. Mrs Churchill's son Winston occupied the role of Minister of Munitions briefly in the penultimate year of war, and it was characteristic of his rhetoric that he claimed at the time that the Ministry was revolutionary in its introduction of new working methods and unusually directive in its ordering of a speedily-expanded labour market. He called this innovation 'an experiment in state socialism'. The question I posed in writing the third chapter was then one about industrial work itself, how the state created a new mobility for women's labour; I also asked how far wartime designations affected the experience of factory labour. Chapter 3, '"A Revolution in the Workplace"?', attempts to set the debates about the labour market, the state and equal pay in the context of vigorous contemporary debates about dilution.

Gerald de Groot recently wrote in *Blighty* that substitutes replaced skilled men and dilutees did not; that dilution was more common than substitution.[8] Both these assertions are incorrect. In fact both sorts of worker (not all of whom were women) replaced men, but the substitutes were those who did so on unskilled work, some of which was women's work before the war, the dilutees replaced skilled men, all of whom had been doing work described as men's work, and their work was then subdivided sometimes so that a semi-skilled or unskilled worker could do the tasks. Because there were more unskilled or semi-skilled workers in factories before the war there were more women replacing them during the war. There was certainly more public discussion about dilution. Dilution was the issue which most agitated Government and men's trade unions, because it meant that trade-union power to protect their members' interests was seen by them as greatly limited if workers not only abandoned the right to strike but also could allow anyone, non-union or unskilled, to do their jobs. That is why trade unions insisted that dilutees were paid at the same rates for the job. They feared that novice workers would accept less through ignorance and inexperience, and thus conscripts would not only face death at the front but the loss of their jobs and protection for their working conditions on return as well.

My original naive question had been one which asked whether Lenin, following Engels, had been right to see a major transformation in women's lives, particularly their family ties, when they engaged in waged labour in a wartime factory. 'When women work in factories the result is the dissolution of family ties.' The crudity of the question was quickly superseded when I was doing the interviews, which illuminated documentary study through questioning about the meaning and experience of factory labour and the recognition that work itself was highly differentiated within the factories and very differently perceived by women, who shared the belief that they were working class but felt very differently from each other about manual labour, about morality and, of course, about politics.

Women have often been described as if their contribution to factory life was neutral. They created new weapons, using new chemical explosives, adapting American machinery and raising output to startlingly high levels. Yet much of the discussion about war factories has left the women's contribution on one side, as if they were, like the machines they used, without historical agency, and most innovation was created only by the factory management. That initial impulse to investigate what it had meant to women to be described always in relation to the men whom they replaced, either as dilutees or substitutes, was supplemented by a desire to investigate how far they had in fact created new forms of labour in war factories.

In all the pieces in this collection the voice to which I have given priority has been the voice of women witnesses, and the impression which these many voices give is of great contrasts. The contrasts that are offered here are designed to address the debate about speaking in the name of women which has generated so much elegant historical writing by people who wish to argue that to speak for all women after the granting of the franchise disrupts the shared agenda – of a total lack of citizenship – and replaces it with a dissolution of feminism.[9] The arguments about discursive evidence and empirical objective evidence of 'experience' is an extremely important one. I write further in my conclusion about the necessity of comparing the two to assess the amount of stability in the 'identity' of the woman worker. Throughout, I have argued that women never speak with one voice and to suggest that they do or have any interest in so doing is itself a piece of historical condescension of the most damaging kind. Feminism has been described by several scholars as 'failing' after the First World War.[10] To have won the vote, as organised feminism had succeeded in doing for women over 30 in 1918, was not failure but success. What these historians see is the discontinuity in women's organisations which shared a belief that the entry of women into parliamentary politics would bring the benefits to public life that women had already brought to education and the poor law through the local franchise. Once that single common principle had been superseded by the varied interests that brought women into political agitation in the first place there was neither so much unity nor so much agitation. However, there continued to be large numbers of women in diverse groups with a common interest in extending the franchise to all adult women and in using it to benefit women, or society.

Women trade unionists, those who claim most directly to represent the interests of the factory worker, are particularly relevant to the discussion about the relationship between general social attitudes, public opinion, legislation and regulation. Their views of the dilution process are thus extremely interesting in exposing the ways in which the mobilisation of some women in the first spring of the war created new images of the working woman. It becomes very important to explain the steps which were taken to create a new workforce, and the extent to which Government, rather than employers or trade unions, made a constructive effort to create the new workforce, administer it and ensure that the over-riding imperative of high, expanding output was kept up. The sources for chapter 5 on trade unionism, '"The Bundle of Sticks"', are the evidence of trade-union newspapers, membership figures and contribution to national debates by people who spoke on their behalf.

The literature on women and war has generated substantial critical commentary by historians of women's labour in general. The First World War has been seen as a period which demonstrates the relationship of women to male workers, and demonstrates theories about a dual labour market and a segmented labour force. Heidi Hartmann has seen the war as providing a theatre of war for contest between the sexes over the privileges of artisanal status in the labour market. The cadres in the battle to impose male supremacy were the trade unions of skilled men who routed the women who had been replacing them once the war was over and the labour market was to be reconstituted.[11] My account of the trade-union agitation among women demonstrates how far this account of the processes of inclusion and exclusion seems to detract from the historical experience of women who constructed their own trade unions. They had policies about union organisation before and during the war, some of which they shared with their male contemporaries, some of which were designed to placate them but which represented a distinctively female construct of an old ideology, labourism. The two trade unionists who form the central figures of the account of women's trade unionism, Mary Macarthur and Julia Varley, could have been added to by discussing Susan Lawrence, who subsequently went into local government, and Margaret Bondfield, who was to become one of the first women MPs to hold ministerial office. One of the reasons that Varley and Macarthur dominate this account is that they were the two whose life work was most directly expressed in wartime organisation.

The history of women's labour in twentieth-century Britain is bound up with the history of their participation in politics at a national level. Women were provided with sex-specific legislation to protect maternity and reproductive health, and to control social life in general. Legislation in practice is powerfully influenced by class, since women of the working class have far more of their lives affected by both permissive legislation allowing local authorities or employers to provide protective officials (as in the factory inspectorate, health visitors and midwives) and in controlling their behaviour on the streets and in public places (as in public order legislation, policing practice and licensing of drink and entertainments). This is an obvious and banal point since part of the class distinction worked out through gender distinction lies precisely in the idea of where a respectable person can go without jeopardising respectability. The workplace for women remains as tightly regulated in some respects as the public space of the streets. Historians of women have increasingly rejected a dual public-private picture of society for both genders, pointing out that work is done at home and that family life is not left behind at the factory gate. War particularly encourages speculation about civic and communal responsibility, and particularly stimulates discussion about morality.[12] The First World War saw a large expansion of such debates about where women could go safely and where they should be allowed to share all the experiences of men, including risks and hardships. Where the public interest could be identified, there were many contradictory impulses involved in thinking about women who were, if expressing their views, wanting to participate more in public life, yet whose contribution to the nation remained in part to produce the next generation.

8

The history of women's wartime contribution is one therefore powerfully affected by the changes in state power and the debates over militarism. The Imperial War Museum, which has been an invaluable source for me as well as many other historians of women's labour, started its life in 1917 in the commemorative impulse of the time as the National War Museum, becoming imperial when the empire protested against its exclusion. Women's labour was included in the project from its outset.[13] Historians have been too busy writing about general attitudes to sexual difference to recognise the impact of state power on the female citizen. Contemporaries were not always so naive about the impact of wartime legislation on citizens' rights, and constitutional suffragists did not always share the historians' disinclination to assess state power. Mrs Fawcett's belief in the emancipatory experience of war was quickly moderated when she recognised the limits of access to it enjoyed by women. Martin Pugh has described the process by which women ended up with a limited parliamentary franchise in 1918, calculated to exclude enough women to ensure that they were a minority in the electorate, and thus excluding the majority of women war-workers.[14] In looking at the history of women's labour in wartime, we should be clear that the processes which directed it, shaped it and ensured that it was affected by pre-war understanding about women's labour were those introduced by Government, those called dilution and substitution.[15] Pre-war, the introduction of the labour exchange, unemployment insurance and sickness benefit had begun to establish state-supported definitions of what employment was, recognised in law, which drew upon but developed further the customary understandings which employers and trade unionists used as a basis for negotiation.

Angela Woollacott, in writing her history of women munition workers in the First World War, *On Her Their Lives Depend*,[16] has used the archives of the Imperial War Museum to argue that women introduced in this way were all engaged upon a process of 'doing their bit' which the state recognised. She argues strongly and persuasively that earlier writers on the same theme – Braybon, Marion Kozak (in her excellent survey of munition workers which, sadly, remains unpublished), Antonia Ineson and I – have been too pessimistic about the changes of wartime. She is right to see the centrality of the contribution that they made to women workers' sense of their own value and the historians' sense of their economic contribution. However, her book does not altogether demonstrate the complexity of the relationship between existing definitions of wartime labour and the novelties introduced to expand wartime production. Male labour was centrally controlled as a result of the changing pattern of military conscription, but the definitions of male labour were very much taken for granted. It was discussion of women that elaborated a whole discourse of the healthy worker, supported by state power engaged in national service, but it did so in the last year of war when already the labour opportunities for women were diminishing. By not explaining fully the impact of demobilisation or change-over time during the war, she also leaves out of the account the stunning sense of ingratitude that is so evident in looking at the post-war history of munition workers.

Zygmunt Baumann has written that the twentieth century can no longer be studied as if we expect the sums to come out even, in some accretion of improvement tending towards a modern and a better world.[17] Perhaps historians' belief that in social processes there is always a balance is also a byproduct of a kind of feminism that sees the major historical tensions as being between men and women constituted as groups. Part of the problems of this history of working women has been this belief that the war brings progressive change. This has been much discussed in cultural history, when debate has raged about how far the war leads to modernism or modernity. The group of authors whose writing on gender in both world wars were collected as *Behind the Lines* used the metaphor of the double helix to explain the process of separate but intertwined and developmental theories of gender. War, wrote Sandra Gilbert, gave women an opportunity 'to use their abilities and to be of use'[18] in a debate which also argued for the eroticisation of gendered relationships. Women writers' work was changed by war, sometimes by the addition of both a new excitement and a new bitterness, as in May Sinclair's *The Tree of Heaven*, sometimes by becoming timely commentators on the history of their own times, like the writer Vera Brittain, who made her name through the process of bearing witness in her *Testament of Youth* and *Testament of Experience*. Clare Tylee has discovered many writers on the war, as had Catherine Reilly, in her earlier anthology *Scars Upon My Heart*. The writers Gilbert and Gubar have seen the war as a major period of women's cultural redefinition. I argue in this book that the cultural significance of the war was very different for women of the working class. They assess the war, reflect upon it and comment upon its place in their lives and in social change. They do not, though, see it as such as opportunity, or as improvement. Many worker-writers have also produced their autobiographical accounts, letters and diaries of the war. What is striking about the vast majority of these accounts is their conventionality of form and language. Women, in other words, have been as likely to find comforting certainty in using established forms of writing and representation as they have in rupturing them for novel effects. Sexual difference cannot be perceived inscribed in prose in any simple way.

Thus it is rarely the style of representation that is new. What *is* modern is the content of representation. It may be newly perceived rather than newly present, but certainly novelty there is. Photographs were as important a part of the history of women in war as they were for the experience of the soldier. But the photograph, with its approximation to the naked eye and its connotations of realism, although a modern technique is not here an example of modernism itself. Reading photographs as texts is much more extensive a process than their use as visual representations of women's work can demonstrate here. The newsreel and the travelling exhibition were both deployed by a Government desperate to persuade rather than enforce a speedy expansion of the workforce to make munitions using the only resource available at the time, which was women who were not yet working in factories. As a result, light was thrown strongly on labouring women. But the spotlight of public attention on women doing new work, replacing men, obscured the continuing contribution of women doing much what they had done before to such an extent that it hid as much as it revealed.

The exposure of working women had its antecedents in pre-war agitation by social reformers, and thus the new visibility brought with it two images, the sweated worker of the past and the new wartime replacement. Purely contingent practices were often described as if they were integral to women's nature. The area made darker, around the bright wartime spotlight, was the existing nature of women's working lives, its diversity and specificity, both occupational and regional. There are many thoughtful histories of women of the Edwardian period, some of them written from the same sources that theorists and protagonists of women's labour used during the war itself, especially the publications of the Fabian Women's Group. The war came at the end of a period of sustained social enquiry and investigation. *Wage Earning Women and their Dependants* was published in 1913 to show that women were often breadwinners, and certainly never worked for pin-money; *Maternity Letters from Working Women* was initiated and published by the members of the Women's Co-operative Guild in support of their campaign for a maternity benefit, payable to the mother, as part of the new National Insurance scheme. The Women's Industrial Council published *Women's Industrial News*, which regularly surveyed groups as diverse as barmaids (whom some temperance groups wished to exclude from pubs), brush-makers and office workers. B.L. Hutchins and Clementina Black wrote *Women's Work in Industry* and *Married Women's Work* respectively to address the question of how far women's paid employment was of value to themselves, their families, the economy and society. These philanthropic women were reformers, and many of them were feminists, but their socialism distinguished them from the women-centred politics of the Women's Social and Political Union; and their refusal to prioritise demands of the working class separated them from the tiny socialist group organised by Sylvia Pankhurst in the East End, the East London Federation of Suffragettes. One of the leading members of the Fabian Women's group, Barbara Drake, wrote two books about women war-workers: the first of these, *Women in the Engineering Trades*, provided in 1917 a scholarly, thorough and detailed exposition of women's industrial situation at the workplace, and the second, *Women and Trade Unions*, in 1920, a history of their trade-union membership and activism which remains unsurpassed.

Imagery of the working woman was thus presented by many people before the war, and was very prominent in public debate when war broke out. Although the war itself, and its length, had been totally unexpected, and not prepared for, the issue of women's labour was not the novelty sometimes described since. The women who were photographed doing the new tasks in 'diluted' factories were newly employed there, and much gratified by public attention and recognition. The images presented in this book show the way in which imagery was presented and used, and place the extended wartime photographic record in the context of the existing record of women's labour.[19] When the propagandist photographer Horace Nicholls and his colleague Gilbert Lewis were employed by the Women's War Work Committee, they were instructed to take a series of photographs, 'for record purposes which shall show the most important processes in which women have acted as a substitute for men in the factories since the war'.[20]

Each of the essays reproduced in this book has focussed in the main on a different sort of source. The pre-war influences on wartime negotiation of women's entry to war work is based here mainly on the visual images which accompanied both the pre-war discussion and the wartime experience. I argue that imagery does more than create and replicate cultural assumptions, it actually informs policy and practices in the workplace. Part of the historians' debates about this period has been about numbers. Modernity, with all its bureaucratic complexity, is supposed to provide us with rational systems of counting. The science of social statistics was itself being elaborated in this period by Karl Pearson, following on from his mentor, Francis Galton, in a post and a laboratory funded by Galton's earlier travel writings and anthropometric surveys.[21] Social facts were increasingly seen as numbers. Social causes were increasingly described through the use of the correlation coefficient. It is very odd, then, that we still do not know for certain how many women worked in some occupations during the war. There are quite extensive quantitative records monitoring and describing women's labour during the war. The *Labour Gazette* itself was produced by the government's main monitoring agency, the Board of Trade, precisely to count and analyse workers' destinations and innovations in their organisation. The statistics became more sophisticated in time of war, but they also became more contentious.

War, with its massive shifts of personnel and material around the globe, should lead to better knowledge and clarity about how many people did what and where they did it. Yet the simple question of how many women worked in jobs where they replaced men, and how many supplemented the existing numbers of workers, is itself fraught with difficulty. We do not know for certain how many women were dilutees and how many substitutes. By 1917, when workers were first discharged because the demand for armaments appeared to have slackened, Government clearly wished to minimise the numbers who had done men's work because of the commitment to provide equal pay for women on men's work. Hence their figures, reproduced in the great survey of women's wartime work by the committee sitting under Mr Justice Atkin, the War Cabinet Committee on Women in Industry, tend to reduce the number of dilutees; whereas earlier accounting by the Ministry of Munitions, just after it was set up in 1915, tend to exaggerate the process of dilution to demonstrate to employers the desirability of this process and the benefits of dilution in terms of productivity and output. The reliability of Government numbers, then, requires careful placing in time. The third chapter on women's wartime work calls into question the use of some records of numbers by asking the simple question 'Who benefits from the definitions used?'. In the first years of wartime expansion, women's rates of work and the volume they produced were the subject of marvelling comments; after 1917 they were seen more as a potentially embarrassing encumbrance in the process of reconstitution of the labour market to come after the war was over. In a simple sense, there is not one war for war workers: they start the war celebrated for their dexterity, capacity to endure monotony and provide a sacrifice; they end it criticised for extravagance and greed.

The numbers are not just a question of quantity, they are also a question of definition. Inexperience in the workplace is offered as a desirable temporary attribute to sceptical employers in 1915, because it is thought women will be more malleable; by 1918 it is being used to explain women's innate incapacity to replace a man on some tasks. The evidence offered in the First World War was not scientific, nor was it based on measured comparisons. The minutes of evidence to the War Cabinet Committee on Women in Industry have been preserved in the Women's Work collection in the documents of the Imperial War Museum; some of them were abstracted and printed in the published record of evidence which appeared at the same time as the final report in 1919. This summary of contemporary opinions about women's labour is an interesting document, but it is a set of opinions rather than observations. There *is* a scientific investigation into workers' production rates preserved in the historical record, but it is not to be found in the sort of comments of witnesses to Mr Justice Atkin's committee, but rather in the findings of the Health of Munition Workers Committee, together with Dr Janet Campbell's medical investigation, which is appended to the committee's work. This too offers some extremely interesting insights into an experience peculiar to the First World War in Britain, namely poisoning from close work with TNT. However, both look to the effects of work on women's bodies, particularly the reproductive effects. They do not look at the effects of the women upon the work, except obliquely and in passing.

Physical health among women workers did generate some concern in the First World War. TNT poisoning itself was treated as a problem of labour management, but the health of the woman worker was taken seriously enough to generate the separate medical report to the War Cabinet Committee. It was also addressed because representatives of women exploited the political advantage given them by wartime labour shortage to make demands for improvements. However, the records show an interest in women's bodies which occurs in other contexts also. Labour management of women had a peculiar fascination for fine details of bodily management. Munition workers were instructed to change their underwear and wash regularly in direct language that contrasts oddly with the delicacy of euphemisms used to boy scouts in urging them to wash, change their clothes; odder still is the way in which soldiers were left to find out for themselves how best to cope with the bodily discomfort of trench life.

In educating women to be workers, their whole bodies were to be supervised, cleansed and monitored. Much of the motivation for this was primarily economic. Although most female work was technically 'unskilled', in practice it required expertise and dexterity which took time to learn. Women workers did, as they had done before the war, have more time away from work on sickness benefit and higher rates of absenteeism than the boy workers they worked beside. Much higher rates of supervision and the provision of welfare meant that their lives in the factory were monitored more closely, and therefore provided more of a historical record than any comparable group of workers before. Medical records, as published in the Health of Munition Workers Committee investigations, and the medical press provide the source for the argument and analysis of the history of TNT poisoning, but they are seen, as such records often are not, juxtaposed with records provided from the group of people who are the clients of medicine, the subjects of research: the women workers themselves. The historical discussion of the body as a text, upon which we can see much inscribed, has recently become much more prominent. Joanna Bourke in *Dismembering the Male: Men's Bodies, Britain and the Great War* has looked at the experience of soldiering, maiming, sex and death through the central image of the male body.[22] Women's gendered bodies have been seen as central to wartime commentary, but this is usually perceived through ideas of reproduction and sexuality, not in relation to labour or social class. The illness suffered by some munition workers, TNT poisoning, was one way in which the war's experience was 'written upon the body' in new ways. Skin colour changed, hair and teeth were dyed. But a worker's clothing, when she slept and ate, and how much eating and sleeping she could do, meant that war work was as manifest on the worker's body as it was on her social attitudes. Our account of the history of TNT poisoning shows how limited concern for reproduction was when the needs of war overcame it. It thus calls into account the enthusiastic representation of pro-natalist rhetoric put forward by Deborah Dwork, in *War is Good for Babies and Other Young*

Children,[23] and rather returns to ideas of the contingency with which pronatalism moved in and out of the foreground of British politics. Jane Lewis has been pessimistic about the extent of change brought about by the war in reconstituting the sexual division of labour or the political power of motherhood.[24] The experience of the TNT workers described in chapter 6 seems to support her argument.

Women in war were predominantly urban. Factory workers were widely perceived and numerically evident in the censuses in the Northern conurbations of Britain. The other stereotype of the manual worker was the 'sweated worker', whose conditions of work had aroused pity and anxiety in equal measure in the first years of the twentieth century.[25] The other sort of woman worker was the domestic servant, but usually she was distinguished from the factory worker on many grounds, loosely grouped around some notion of respectability. The history of women in the First World War is only recently coming to terms with the nature of this as an urban experience. My example in this study is of the workers in the largest munitions factory of all, the Woolwich Arsenal, as the Royal Ordnance Factory at Woolwich was known. The factory was like a town itself, with a theatre, an infirmary, numerous canteens, changing rooms, streets, railways and lights. Its workforce was huge, and came in to work each day through four large gates, travelling on trams, trains which unloaded at three different stations, buses and on foot, across the river through the Greenwich foot tunnel, or on the free ferry which crossed the Thames every fifteen minutes. The scale of it meant that people could, and did, get lost inside its gates. It was more like a town than a factory. It was, however, on the edge of a local borough with an independent Labour organisation of some significance, its own Labour paper, the *Woolwich Pioneer* and the Royal Arsenal Co-operative Society, the biggest co-operative stores organisation in the world. These institutions were not only for men, but women were by-and-large only centrally involved in the local Women's Co-operative Guild, which had been set up by the wife of a Woolwich vicar in 1894. Part of the story of transformation and continuity has to include the organisations of the working class itself. The claim this book will make is that women's experience of urban life was as changed for the young, unmarried women who worked in factories as it was for the urban housewives described so movingly by Ellen Ross in her account of London life, *Love and Toil*. As urban workers, they experienced factory life rather differently from their nineteenth-century predecessors.

Women war-workers were constantly addressed, interpreted to themselves and portrayed in print. The histories of their lives have kept the theme alive. There are some examples of their experience in the official representation of the institutions of public memory.[26] There are women in war memorials like the ones depicted in the windows of the memorial chapel of Edinburgh Castle; although this sort of representation is rare, it is probably, apart from the nurse, the single most noticeable example of the persistence of the image of the war for women to have become concrete. However, the collection of private, personal documents by the Imperial War Museum and by other archives, television programmes and the provision of opportunities for recall have tended to provide an opportunity for the women who went through this experience to be given a chance to record their views of it later.

The category of experience has gone through several shifts in the twentieth century, shifts which have been particularly pertinent to women. The provision of private documents and the tape recording of personal memories can provide a real problem of representativeness and veracity. Taking oral interviews in the 1970s, for example, often meant that 'the war' could, imperceptibly, become the war of 1939-1945 to aged witnesses who confused a Zeppelin raid with a V2 attack. The truth this revealed was that the war of 1914-1918 had registered just as much fear of bombardment as had the much more serious raids of the later war, so the evidence provided something of value. However, to accept that one interview cannot make a history is not to accept that many cannot. Paul Thompson has offered a description of the value of oral history in assessing the grand processes of structural change, and in so doing has pointed out the value of people's own perception of the past, which is, after all, in some respects better informed than the historian's, and in others much less well. The enterprise he outlined in *The Edwardians* was one in which many individual interviews were collated to create social facts, in which majorities mattered.[27] The information I gathered was much more limited because my witnesses were few in number, and the group consisted of those I could contact through local newspapers and radio and connections between people, which meant that one witness did sometimes lead to another, the procedure which sociologists call the 'snowball technique'. I cannot be certain that those who survived into their eighties, and had stayed in the same area since the war (as nearly all the people I interviewed had) did not share certain qualities which the others, now dead, had lacked. It is possible to hypothesise, for example, that the people who were unlikely to talk to me had they still been alive would have been those with powerful reasons for discretion which kept them silent. Guilt, rage or grief might well encourage any disinclination to discuss the past with a stranger. Recent accounts of the problems of silence in narrative and the difficulty of speaking about the unspeakable have been evoked in discussing the testimony of Holocaust survivors.[28] My use of oral interviews might well then raise the question of representativeness and validity, in that they may under-record the painful or embarrassing incidents or descriptions which people wish to forget. However, there was certainly no disinclination in my witnesses to discuss some matters of this sort, so I suspect nothing can be assumed about those who do not speak.[29] It might be said, though, to emphasise the positive, the 'speakable', in ways that other more contemporary sources do not. That is in itself useful, but a matter of emphasis that needs considering in relation to the changes in perception of the war over time, which I address in chapter 9.

The single overwhelmingly common impression of taped interviews with women who worked on munitions in the war is of bereavement. Next most common is the way in which they relate the world of the workplace and the chronology of the war to the troops fighting over the Channel in France. This was especially noticeable in interviews with women from Woolwich, which historically had a connection to the army, not the navy or airforce, and for whom therefore the war meant the Western Front in their imagination. This was true of Britain as a whole, as Nicholas Hiley and others have shown in looking at the impact of the film, 'The Battle of the Somme', in cinemas all over the country in the summer of 1916.[30] What it meant to a munitions worker was that the product of her labour was directly bound up with the progress of the war. But it also meant that her personal fortunes were seen by her as an integrated whole, when she might have suffered extensive bereavement, losing most of the adult male members of her family; or she might come from a family of skilled engineering workers who passed the war earning well and immune from conscription, although likely to lose some members among those who volunteered. The factory did seem very separate from domestic life, but the experience did not totally overwhelm all other aspects of everyday life, even though the hours of work were very long and domestic life was difficult. Much of the difficulty of getting at the meaning of the war for the woman worker lies in the way in which the evidence was first elicited.

There is a legitimate criticism of interviews of the sort I did and those gathered by the Imperial War Museum. They start from the presupposition of significance about certain aspects of the war experience. I was interviewing people who had worked at the Woolwich Arsenal, and thus put that singular aspect of the war in the foreground. During the interviews, I found again and again that the work was less significant to some than the general impact of 1914-1918 on their homes and families in general, but not to all. Some of the impact of war was the impact of certain stages of life in early adulthood. Transitions marked these stages. Women left home, entered paid work, married, had their first children and entered widowhood in four years. Many clearly felt the contradictions of a period of life when one element of life, earning a living, was pleasurable, even fun, despite the stress, while another part of existence could be distressing. Others found the generally-cheerful reaction of their contemporaries hard to take. They had hated the work, hated the war and had been delighted to see it end. Memory is both constituted by and constitutive of emotional responses. These women too could feel resentment at the way the post-war world ignored the war, the guilt of having survived when others had not, the irritation of reading inaccurate journalism about their activities just like male combatants. However, they had not suffered the same proportionate level of bereavement from among those they worked beside as the combatant soldier, nor had they had to deal with the complexity of feelings aroused not just by risking death but by participating in killing with their own hands. Making the weapons which killed people was removed from the sense of responsibility which some have recorded among front-line soldiers. In that respect, the experiences of men and women cannot be balanced in some scale as if they are comparable. There is a great difference between the poetic evocation of a dead German soldier – 'I am the enemy you killed my friend' – and the munitions worker who responded to the sight of a Zeppelin pilot going down in flames to certain death with the comment, 'All I could think was that that's some mother's son'.

Nor, however, can women be put together as if their war was the same. Despite all the efforts of government and orchestrated public opinion, women maintained the distinctions with which they had entered war work. Lilian Barker, in saying of the Woolwich munition workers, for whom she was welfare superintendent, that some were nice and some were rude, was emphasising the difference of repute, or of respectability. Some women were nice. They minded their manners, they did not swear, they were chaste. Some were rude. They swore, they jeered and they were likely to be, if not promiscuous, certainly sexually active. This distinction has been much discussed for the married Victorian artisan, for the 'new woman' of the middle class and the Victorian and Edwardian prostitute and suffrage agitator. What happens in wartime is very much an extension of these debates to all working women, in which women's public demeanour is scrutinised in ways which seem to see the ideological work of gender being carried beyond the previous domains of literature, medicine and feminist politics into all discussions about the state of the nation. Surveillance has been seen as characteristic of the observation by women police patrols, welfare supervisors and male trade unionists on women in and out of the factory.[31] The relationship between factory labour and sexual behaviour is unfortunately one of the most difficult things to elucidate either from documentary sources or oral history. Women's independence is commented on frequently in the press and elsewhere, but women's sexual activity tends to be assumed, not analysed. One group of women workers rejected the moral panic over war babies when they criticised the formation of the League of Decency and Honour, which had been set up by the National Union of Women Workers 'to raise and maintain the high standard of morals and manners among women at home as our soldiers are upholding the national honour and good name in the front line'.[32] They wrote as 'Three Respectable Maids'.

> It is a poor do if we men and women cannot look after ourselves, we might all be little tiny babies... these so-called ladies of Southport ought to mind their own business, and instead of joining the 'League of Honour' ought to join the 'League of Hard Work', and then they would not have so much time to bother about other people's affairs. We think it is one of the most wicked insults to us girls and also to the soldiers... If we join anything we shall all join the soldiers.[33]

This letter conveys very strongly the moral ethos of hard work as the indication of moral adequacy, and 'ladies' are here stigmatised for their lack of contribution to production, rather as the feminist Olive Schreiner did in *Women and Labour* for parasitism, or Cicely Hamilton did in her 1911 pamphlet *Marriage as a Trade*. Dependency was increasingly seen as the cause of moral inadequacy for women by those who advocated improvement in working conditions and wages, while others retained the belief that sexual incontinence was simply a result of moral disposition. Mary Macarthur, the trade unionist, was arguing against similar contemporary descriptions when she saw women's work as generating new standards of public behaviour in general. 'The working girl has good habits and is thrifty,' she said.

But these claims for the working woman as standing in for the moral status of society itself did not outlast the war. In many ways my concluding section demonstrates that the history of this experience does stand in for a wider history of attitudes to women's labour. The history of women's war work has reflected the changing fortunes of a feminist politics which means that there will certainly be more versions of the story.

Notes on Chapter 1

Full details of all publications mentioned here are in the bibliography on page 209.

1 Churchill, Lady R. (ed.), *Women's War Work*, 1916, p 2.
2 Fawcett, Mrs, *The Women's Victory and After*, 1920, p 106.
3 In Phillips, M. (ed.), *Women and the Labour Party*, 1918, p 18.
4 Strathern, M., *The Gender of the Gift*, 1985, p 35.
5 Lown, J., 'Not so Much a Factory, More a Form of Patriarchy: Gender and Class During Industrialisation' in Gamarnikow, E., Morgan, D., Purvis, J. and Taylorson, D. (eds), *Gender, Class and Work*, 1985.
6 Caine, H., *Our Girls*, 1916; Churchill, Lady R. (ed.), *Women's War Work*, 1916; Delafield, E.M., *The War Workers*, 1918; McLaren, B., *Women of the War*, 1917; Stone, G., *Women War Workers*, 1917. An example of a novel is Marchant, B., *A Girl Munition Worker*, 1918.
7 Pedersen, S., 'Gender, Welfare and Citizenship in Britain During the Great War,' *American Historical Review*, vol. 95/4, October 1990, pp 383-1006.
8 De Groot, G., *Blighty: British Society in the Era of the Great War*, 1996, p 130.
9 Scott, J., *Gender and History* and Riley, D., *Am I That Name?* are two very powerful statements of this position, which has continued to inspire discussion in *Gender and History*, *Women's History* and other periodicals. As I hope becomes clear, the project of critical interrogation of texts is an essential historians' task, as is identifying the

nature of interests involved in any discursive formulation required activity. What I do not share is the assumption that these discourses are all one process in the construction of one identity, woman, since most of those interpreted or described have their own discourses and historical formations as well, often remarkably independent of professional or governmental structures of thought.

10 Kingsley Kent, S., 'Gender Reconstruction after the First World War' in Smith, H.L. (ed.), *British Feminism in the Twentieth Century*, 1990, and later in her two books, has argued that the war's end sees the reestablishing of heterosexual domesticity; Pedersen, S., 'The Failure of Feminism in the Making of the British Welfare State', *Radical History Review* 43, 1989; Shorter, E., *A History of Women's Bodies* places the change more loosely in the relationship between men and women, as mediated through doctors since in his, peculiar, view feminism is a result of women's fear of heterosexual sex and the consequence of childbirth before birth control.

11 Hartmann, H., 'Capitalism, Patriarchy and Job Segregation by Sex' in Eisenstein, Z. (ed.), *Capitalist Patriarchy and the Case for Socialist Feminism*, 1979.

12 See Woollacott, A. and Cooke, M (eds), *Gendering War Talk*, 1993.

13 Brown, M., *The Imperial War Museum Book of the First World War*, 1991; Condell, D. and Liddiard, J., *Working for Victory: Images of Women in the First World War 1914-1918*, 1987.

14 Pugh, M., 'Politicians and the Women's Vote', *History* 1974, and his book.

15 De Groot, G., *Blighty: British Society in the Era of the Great War*, 1996 gets this wrong in what is otherwise an extremely good succinct account of the introduction of women's labour onto wartime work processes. He describes substitutes as those women who replaced a man on skilled work, whereas they were dilutees. Substitutes replaced an unskilled or semi-skilled man, and were therefore recipients of time rates, which were lower, rather than rates of pay based on the rate for the job: see chapter.

16 Woollacott, A., *On Her Their Lives Depend*, 1994.

17 Bauman, Zygmunt, *Modernity and the Holocaust*, 1989.

18 Gilbert, S., 'Soldier's Heart: Literary Men, Literary Women and the Great War', in Higonnet, M.R., Jenson, J., Michel, S. and Collins Weitz, M. (eds), *Behind the Lines, Gender and the Two World Wars*, 1987, p 216.

19 Condell, D. and Liddiard, J., *Working for Victory: Images of Women in the First World War 1914-1918*, 1987; Griffiths, G., *Women's Factory Work in World War One*, 1991, based on the archive of the

Women's War Work Committee at the Home Office Industrial Museum. Both have used the considerable archive of photographs to great effect to show the variety of tasks women performed.

20 Griffiths, G., *Women's Factory Work in World War One*, 1991, p 4.

21 Mackenzie, D., *Statistics in Britain: The Social Construction of Scientific Knowledge, 1865-1930*, 1981.

22 Bourke, J., *Dismembering the Male: Men's Bodies, Britain and the Great War*, 1996.

23 Dwork, D., *War is Good for Babies and Other Young Children*, 1987.

24 Lewis, J., 'The Working-class Wife and Mother and State Intervention' in Lewis, J. (ed.), *Labour and Love*, 1986; *The Politics of Motherhood*, 1980; 'Models of Equality for Women' in Bock, G. and Thane, P. (eds), *Maternity and Gender Policies*, 1991.

25 Schmiechen, J.A., *Sweated Industries and Sweated Labor: The London Clothing Trades, 1860-1914*, 1984.

26 Ideas of public memory have been little explored by historians of gender, but would benefit from such exploration. Connerton, P., *How Societies Remember*, 1990 and Gregory, A., *The Silence of Memory*, 1994 both provide valuable introductions to ideas of public memory, and in the latter case explicitly looks at the First World War.

27 Thompson, P., *The Edwardians*, second edn, 1977.

28 Luisa Passerini sums up these issues in her introduction to *Memories of Totalitarianism: International Yearbook of Oral History and Life Narrative*. Catherine Merridale also discusses how we can deal with suppression and the question of trauma in her discussion in

29 Slaughter, *Women's History Review* vol. 3/1, 1994

30 Hiley, N.P., 'The British Army Films "You!" and "For the Empire"', *Historical Journal*, 1985

31 Woollacott, A, 'Khaki Fever' and Bland, L., 'In the Name of Protection: The Policing of Women in World War One' in Brophy, J. and Smart, C., *Women in Law: Explorations in Law, Family and Sexuality*, 1985, pp 23-49; Levine, P., 'Walking the Streets in a Way no Decent Woman Should: Women Police in World War One', *Journal of Modern History*, 1994.

32 *Bristol Times*; *Carlisle Journal*, 17 November 1914, GTC at the TUC.

33 *Southport Visitor*, 24 November 1914, GTC at the TUC.

Chapter 2
Women and Work in
Wartime Britain

This chapter summarises the themes developed in the succeeding chapters by taking an overview of the 'experience of war'.[1] In particular it calls into question contemporary statistical evidence of the number of women working in different industries at different times during the war by asking how far the figures being sought represent not an absolute measure but an argument about women's work that varied over time. It was not a single common experience. Government defined women's labour differently at the beginning of the war, when they emphasised women's adaptability and ignorance, and at the end, when they emphasised lower productivity. The argument which has most commonly recurred in debating women's wartime contribution has been the one which contemporaries debated at different stages of the war. As I argued in my introduction, the war was discussed as an historically significant event, with an eye to posterity, almost from its outbreak. As I will argue in chapter 3, the Ministry of Munitions thought that it was presiding over revolutionary change in the organisation of production, especially where women's labour was being used. Statistics and pictorial data added to this sense of history being made. Contemporaries believed that this change existed not only in material practices and evidence but in the hearts and minds of women workers. Angela Woollacott has repeated this emphasis in her title *On Her Their Lives Depend*, which places women besides the front-line soldier as waging a war directly, but also as defenders alongside the men they supplied with armaments.[2] She believes that women shared this perception of their value to the war effort. Arthur Marwick, in particular, in *Women at War* propounded the view that women's consciousness was irrevocably changed by war.[3] Roger Fulford's earlier *Women on the Warpath* had seen women's war labour as new, direct replacement of men and leading to profound social and political change.[4] The question of change and continuity has thus been integral to the debate. It has also demanded a valorisation of different sorts of sources. The question this chapter directly addresses is the one of numbers, and how far we can take them as neutral, unaffected by political considerations. It is also about the significance of government views, of how far repeated description of women as new workers doing men's work affected their perceptions of themselves. This theme will be discussed more fully in both chapter 4, on the question of the photograph, and chapter 5, on the question of women's representation of themselves.

Some historians have argued that there was change, but that it was short-term because of the dominance of ideology or male hostility, expressed through men's trade unions.[5] There is some explanatory force in this argument, but it does not sufficiently explain the nature of the change that took place in employment or the ease of eviction from war occupations once the war was over and, in particular, women's own agreement with this process, which will be more fully described in chapter 5 on women's trade unionism. Women's attitudes are one factor, another is the shaping of the introduction of women into war work by pre-war attitudes, and a third is the added emphasis given by war to the political image of women as mothers.[6]

Women were not the serfs of Mrs Fawcett's description of post-war emancipation, though their work was the subject of concern and debate before the war. The 1911 census recorded about one third of all women as doing some paid work. These figures are inadequate in many ways. Much domestic work would not be recorded in the census for a variety of reasons. For example, the taking in of washing, charring or child-minding might not be relayed to the census-taker by the head of household. It is also difficult to know how many women would have wanted to work in peacetime because women were grossly under-recorded in the data on unemployment. The largest single category of women's work was domestic service, and this was not covered by the

National Insurance scheme. As most labour exchanges did not do much placement in service, which tended to be dealt with by private agencies, women were disinclined to register as unemployed.[7] The second-largest category of women's employment was work in the textile trades, and here the trade was 'half-recumbent' by 1914.[8] Women were involved in demands to extend the use of women's labour. They participated in the 'Right to Work' campaign of 1908. They argued that women had claimed more sickness benefit than men because their working conditions were bad, not because of any inherent female incapacity. Feminists campaigned for access to professions and education, and, for manual workers, that there should be protective legislation. In some trades they wanted to exclude women from work altogether, as in some work involving toxic chemicals for example, particularly lead. In other trades, associated with low-paid women's work, they wanted minimum wage levels fixed by trade boards or 'fair wages' agreements. This work was often concentrated in particular regions and restricted to a few occupations where the majority of the workforce, as in the textile and clothing trades, were women. Campaigns on the issue of women's employment were important in informing attitudes to it. They tended to have a dual focus, in that they either demanded admission to all jobs on the grounds of egalitarianism or, alternatively, insisted that society's need for fit mothers and children should be a primary factor in legislating or regulating employment or wage demands: these were in conflict with one another, but the effort was made to emphasise the social determinants of women's work.

The ideological component in descriptions of women working was evident in the views of organisations of, or for, working women: the women's trade unions. The image of women's work was based on their concentration in the 'sweated trades'. The paradigm, particularly as represented in graphics or photographs, was the women chain-makers who had fought and won a strike for minimum trade board wages in 1911. They had paraded through Britain's largest cities, notably London, carrying the chains they made: a disturbing double image of strength and skill allied to industrial slavery.[9] The pressure groups which agitated on behalf of working women were not only central to the formation of the image of the working woman: they were to be centrally concerned with the introduction of women into 'new' areas of work in the war economy. A small group met under a variety of different labels, wrote the commentaries on women's labour, and discussed and campaigned for maternity benefits, factory inspection, and against low wages for women and sweating as a part of the larger phenomenon of 'women's work'. The reference to 'women's work' was deliberately ambiguous, including as it did women's domestic labour.[10] Women trade unionists were closely linked with the network of anti-sweating campaigners, the infant welfare movement and the constitutional suffragists, in the National Union of Women's Suffrage Societies (NUWSS) and the Adult Suffrage Association (ASA). They shared the belief of Anna Martin of the NUWSS.

> The rearing of the child crop is, confessedly, the most vital to the nation of all its industries, being that which alone gives to other industry any meaning or importance; but although its quality is occasioning grave concern, no attempt has been made to apply... principles to those on whose care and devotion it necessarily depends.[11]

Married women workers provided the particular focus for this philanthropic concern; they were also most subject to the limiting factors on women's 'emancipation' through employment. They predominated in women's trades where, almost by definition, low wages were earned, and, as the chief woman factory inspector noted, they were mostly tied to one area by their families, and employed:

> in poor or underpaid industries and in towns and districts where women are largely employed without a sufficient balance of men's staple industries to enable the husband or father to be the main breadwinner of the family.[12]

Their work was not extra to the family budget, the 'pin-money' of popular journalism. In areas like those described above, and in cities of high unemployment, they were often the main wage-earners. A Fabian Women's Group (FWG) survey concluded that one third of all women workers were supporting dependants. It was not a scientifically-collected sample, and probably overestimated the number of women breadwinners, but it certainly reflected reality in the areas of high female participation in the labour force, Lancashire, Belfast and Dundee.[13] Such results showed the commitment of married women to paid employment, but they also demonstrated the connection between women's work and low wages, which was one of the reasons for male trade-union hostility to women in the workplace. At the same time as the FWG, the Women's Industrial

Council (WIC), the NUWSS and the Women's Trade Union League (WTUL) were investigating the living conditions of working women and the social reasons for low wages, working women were themselves beginning to agitate over conditions of work. The years before the war were marked by a steady increase in women's organisations of all types, but particularly in women's trade unions. This growth was partly the result of increased organising work by a few female members of the Independent Labour Party (ILP); for example, Julia Varley for textile workers and the metal-workers in the Midlands, Ellen Wilkinson among co-operative employees, Margaret Bondfield among shop assistants and above all Mary Macarthur and Gertrude Tuckwell through the National Federation of Women Workers (NFWW) and the WTUL.[14] It also reflected increased demand from women workers themselves, politicised by feminism and labour unrest. Women leaders used the arguments that trade unionism was socially productive of good as education, as preparation for marriage and for citizenship. Their trade unionism was, if the word can be used, maternalist. Trade-union demands were put into the context of the family, or domestic life, rather than the life of the workplace. Margaret Bondfield, for example, enjoined a meeting of Labour women, 'Every mother should get her girl a union card'.[15] Much of the organisation was achieved as a result of initiating strike action and only then calling in a union official. Union leaders pointed out to employers that union membership was as likely to prevent strikes as cause them.[16] Here the image of the defenceless woman worker was tempered by the recognition that women's inexperience meant they could be more subversive of the established order, which might mean either industrial militancy or passivity.

This agitation allied to the raising of the 'woman question' in the parliamentary sphere had a cumulative effect. Gender came to the forefront of public discussion. Trade-union organisations, those most closely concerned with women's employment, added their voice to those of others campaigning for support of motherhood, the vote and divorce-law reform. Trade unions concentrated on national welfare issues (including low pay), and thereby diminished the amount of public attention that could be devoted to the specific occupational problems of women workers. The effect was also to reinforce the notion that women were inherently deficient as workers. They were deficient because they were inhibited by family responsibilities, and because they were physically weaker and lacked a tradition of work expertise, except in certain forms of employment where they had not competed on equal terms with men.

Trade unionism protected women from their own inadequacies, it was argued, and thereby benefited the male majority by ensuring that they would not be undercut by low wages and undermined by worsening conditions.[17] Equal pay was demanded by some women on the grounds that their work was of equal worth; but the supplementary argument that it would eradicate the social evils of low wages for women, high infant mortality and prostitution remained. All these social evils were threats to a good family life, and originated in the existing conditions of women's work. As a result, working women were discussed in 1914 as potential or actual mothers rather than as workers, let alone specific kinds of workers.

The effect of the war was to accentuate the trends of social thought current in the pre-war period. This happened in two phases: the first covered the five-month period of unemployment at the beginning of the war; the second lasted about a year, the period of negotiation of the replacement of men by women. The textile trade contracted by 43 per cent in the first five months of the war, clothing manufacture by 21 per cent, women being particularly badly affected by lay-offs and short-time working. Large numbers of domestic servants and needleworkers were sacked as consumption fell.[18] The 'sacrifice' expected of households where servants were employed was often interpreted as the release of servants for war work but there was, as yet, no war work for women. The question of women's employment became the problem of women's unemployment. The belief that women were likely to accept inadequate conditions of work at low wages through a combination of ignorance, docility and patriotism was thoroughly reinforced by high unemployment among women, accentuated by the mobilisation of the volunteer army, the British Expeditionary Force, when many women were to be seen on the streets and at the railway stations, saying goodbye. The League of Decency and Honour and several other organisations counselled prudence and self-restraint[19] but others realised that social order could be better provided by removing unemployed women from the temptation of prostitution and the opportunity for promiscuity on the streets, particularly in transit and billeting areas. Working women's organisations were particularly worried by the threat that wartime unemployment posed to good relations with the wider trade-union movement. Feminist organisations were divided about the war itself, and the most militant unconstitutional suffragettes, the Women's Social and Political Union (WSPU), became active proponents of the wartime recruitment of men as soldiers and women as their replacements in the workplace.[20] However, the women who were already unemployed played no part in this, and many were in an impoverished situation from which there was no apparent escape. In a piece of notable class collaboration Mary Macarthur was recruited by Queen Mary to run the Queen's Work for Women Fund. Its motto was 'Women's help for women'. The fund amassed substantial funds and ran workrooms which were forbidden to compete with commercial manufacture, but could make good the loss of some German goods, such as toys and artificial flowers, retrain factory workers in domestic skills for their own homes, which in one instance involved making cradles from orange boxes, and 're-moralise' the unemployed by running herb gardens. The women in them were explicitly neither trained nor made self-supporting. They were removed from the labour market for 15 weeks and thereby, it was hoped, from the 'abyss of destitution'.[21]

In fact as early as November 1914 there were signs of some expansion in employment opportunities for women. The greatest expansion was in clerical and shop-assistant work. In these sections the process of 'feminisation' had already been under way before the war, but the numbers of clerical staff were to increase further during the war due to the increased volume of paper work in all spheres of administration. This development was contested by some male workers but, for a variety of reasons, their protest aroused little public interest or concern. In the first place, clerical unions were weak at the beginning of the war, and had very little control over job definition or hiring practices. Secondly, most of the women taken on were not replacements but extra workers. Finally, and most importantly, the 'feminisation' of clerical and shop work aroused no social concerns. Office and shop work was clean, respectable and presented no obvious threat to gynaecological health. They drew on women's innate qualities. As one NUWSS writer said, there were some jobs for which women are 'naturally suited,' and she adduced civil service clerk, teacher or salesman as examples.[22] Such work was also generally undertaken by single women, since marriage bars (dismissal on marriage) had operated before, and was seen as appealing particularly to women's interest in 'meantime' work to fill in the years between school and marriage. Women's work had been described as 'meantime' before the war, and even, as Mary Macarthur had argued, as good preparation for housewifery. 'The working girl has good habits, she is industrious and thrifty.'[23]

What was contentious to both the general public and representatives of women workers alike was the employment of women on new forms of arduous manual labour. One journalist wrote:

> The extremist feminist in her wildest moments would not advocate dock-labouring, mining or road-digging as suitable employment for women.[24]

Some feminists had, in fact, drawn attention to the rigours of domestic work, for example the lifting of heavy weights of water and the prolonged stooping involved in the scrubbing of stairs, but this was ignored. The TUC discussed the issue of women's employment very fully in 1915 and approved a motion which expressed the basis of the objection to manual work for women as well as the attempt to define processes as suitable for men or women. All their conditions were broken on occasion, but the consensus on 'proper' work for women was not a cynical bow to prevailing ideology.[25] Rather the TUC in this list was expressing genuine fears as to how far the needs of the state might override the needs of society. Trade unionists, particularly women, believed that their knowledge of industrial processes was greater than that of government, and that their duty was to present such information, thereby preserving the nation's health. They became reconciled to women working in industry – even on these processes – because it was temporary, because welfare services were provided and because tasks were, to some extent, reorganised to reduce the adverse effects on women's health. They also saw this concession as a necessary price for the greater consultation involved in the wartime negotiation between management, government and trade-union representatives over when, where and if dilution and substitution should take place. Dilution meant the replacement of skilled men by semi-skilled or unskilled workers; substitution meant the replacement of one semi-skilled or unskilled worker by another, usually in both cases thereby increasing the number of women in the workplace. Last of all, very few women did in fact do very much new 'unsuitable' work. The majority were to work throughout the war on work defined as 'women's' processes. Those who did undertake heavy outdoor work were explicitly there for the duration only.

The Government had started the war without a labour policy. The dual problem arising from its need of both men and munitions resulted in the creation of one, but it was little dignified by theoretical notions. Women were accepted reluctantly as a source of labour after other groups were shown to provide an inadequate resource to fill the factories. Belgian refugees were used, but there were not enough. Imperial subjects were too expensive to transport.[26] Women were demanding the right to contribute and Lloyd George used their demands to sponsor a 'Right to Serve' march organised by Mrs Pankhurst. Under the caption 'British Lion is awake, so is the Lioness' the newsreels of this march were shown in 3,000 cinemas. Some criticised the complete disregard of the march organisers for the rights of displaced men or replacement women as employees, but it was the marchers' rhetoric of service by all women that dominated government propaganda and journalists' descriptions as well as administrative arrangements. Women were to volunteer as women, rather than on the basis of particular qualifications, whether of labour experience, age, marital status or education. In the summer of 1915 the Women's War Register was set up, primarily to provide a workforce in munitions factories.[27] Unions had agreed to the process of dilution to make good the shortage of skilled engineers and to protect the existing workforce from attempts to lower wages, speed up rates of production or alter working procedures. The Government began to monitor the movement of labour in order to control the processes of production, particularly dilution, rather than to investigate the labour market *per se*. As a result the labour force figures were designed to demonstrate the success of dilution and substitution in the years 1915-17. They were figures for trends rather than absolute totals, since they were submitted only by those employers in large firms. The *Labour Gazette* published monthly dilution totals based on these returns, which were the source for most published surveys of the extent and effects of dilution on women (cf appendices 2.1 and 2.2).

All new female employees were inclined to be subsumed under the title of substitute, if not dilutee, although they were in many industries not replacements at all but extra workers. Such women were also likely to be described as though all came straight from the home, without history or knowledge of employment. Any figures of employment require careful scrutiny, but those provided by the British Government in the First World War need it more than most. There was the sustained growth in the numbers of women in the workforce (as the totals reproduced in appendix 2.2 confirm), but since the base year for comparison, July 1914, was a period of high unemployment for women (particularly in the textile industry), the amount of growth seems larger than would be shown by a longer view. Wartime is given the credit for many changes that were already underway, so that dilution and substitution should take their place among other trends which influenced the level of women's employment, as opposed to being considered as its sole determinants. Some of the changes are only indirectly attributable to the war because it was a time of full employment, while others were distorted by the war but fundamentally unaffected by it, for example the deskilling of work on the typewriter. Trade unions had assented to dilution in exchange for a commitment to restore the pre-war situation immediately the war ended. Women's representatives and most general unions had not participated in either the initial discussions or the final agreements over dilution since the agreements were not for them but for the men they 'replaced'. All such workers were defined as replacements, and increasingly the word 'dilution' became a synonym for the introduction of women. Pay for dilutees was regulated by the Treasury agreement of May 1915.

> The agreement stated shall not adversely affect the rates customarily paid for the job, and the rates paid shall be the usual rate of the district for this class of work.[28]

This agreement did not cover all cases because of the difficulty of defining 'district', 'customarily' and 'usual', above all at a time when the number of jobs had suddenly multiplied, thereby changing the essential character of the task. By 1916 pay was being decided by the sex of the worker. Women on men's work were given a minimum time-rate of £1 for a 48-hour week, which protected learners and those on inadequate old machines, since they could not fix the machinery themselves. This commitment to 'equal pay' was entirely expedient. It was not designed to attract women into war work or as a recognition of 'worth', but was solely intended to win over men's unions to the process of dilution; nor in practice was it paid. Employers were, in the event, much more resistant to Circular 447 of 1917 – which was designed to fix a minimum rate for women on women's work – since it cost them much more.[29]

Any assessment of the impact on women of their waged work in wartime needs to begin with an assessment of their reasons for seeking work. The official histories of the Ministry of Munitions tend to assume that munitions factories were successful in attracting and keeping women workers because of the availability of welfare services and stricter regulation of the work environment, when the potential workforce, as the population in general, was in fact enthused with patriotic fervour.[30] However, state intervention in employment, equal pay and welfare provision were not mentioned by any of some 60 former munitions workers in their recollections. Nor does the chronology of changes in employment in general bear this out. A leading civil servant, Humbert Wolfe, who wrote later on labour policy of the time, said that more women entered the workforce before their wages were protected than did so afterwards. July 1916 did see the largest number of additional women entering the workforce, according to the government statistics published in the *Labour Gazette*. However, there is no evidence that these were all new workers, since severe shortages of labour in 'traditional' women's trades indicate that much of this movement was from one form of employment to another. What was new, and took some time to bring about, was the eviction of men from their occupations. In fact, it was only during the course of the year July 1916-June 1917 that women came to contribute nearly half of the workforce (see table 2.1).[31]

Table 2.1   Trends in female employment, 1914-18

Period, measured from July	Women entering the workforce (000s)	Females in workforce (%)
1914-15	382	–
1915-16	563	26.5
1916-17	511	46.9
1917-18	203	46.7

Source: IWM.EMP 4.282, Standing Joint Committee of Women's Industrial Organisations, *The Position of Women After the War*, p 4

In any event, women's wages were protected by law only in those industries defined as munitions industries: trade-union power alone provided a protection in those trades where dilution had been agreed between unions and management, like the boot and shoe trade or co-operative employees.[32] And in the munitions industries the government did not begin to be a producer in its own right, in the national factories, until 1916.

As pointed out above, the first phase of the move of women into the workforce was not principally into industry at all, nor into male jobs, but into clerical and commercial occupations. By 1915, the textile trades had begun to pick up the trade lost at the onset of war and take on more workers as they diversified into serge and khaki, the new workers being all women, as had mainly been the case before. By July 1916, the privately-owned industries and the arsenals were in full production and had expanded considerably, so that in that summer the largest number of new entrants to industry were to be found in textile factories (see appendix 2.1) while the largest proportion of growth was in the Government's own armaments factories (cf table 2.2).[33]

These additional women had entered the workforce following a variety of individual decisions. Government posters had characterised the work as 'Do your bit: replace a man for the front', so that the life of the factory worker was not portrayed as such, but as war service. Government had attempted to see all women as a vast 'reserve army of labour', but women's own experience of work, locality and family role ensured that there was no easy match between labour needs and supply. Male unemployment encouraged many men to enlist (although more probably chose to do so from what historians of troop recruitment have called 'the culture of necessity'). The women, conscious of low pay and harsh physical conditions at work, not unnaturally found mobility and munitions work that much more attractive. On the other hand, engineering areas like outer London, Birmingham, Leeds and Clydeside had a large number of men in reserved occupations as skilled engineers or shipbuilders whose wives had a laborious domestic life – rendered more laborious by wartime shortages – but a higher household income which kept them out of the labour market. Their daughters meanwhile simply replaced domestic service with war service in their local factory, a familiar environment in that when younger they had often taken their fathers, uncles or brothers their lunch. The mobility of war service mimicked the pre-war mobility of domestic service for the group of young women aged between sixteen and twenty. Government encouragement made the workplace accessible, gave respectability to the industrial environment and encouraged a choice of industrial employment, but it did not create the underlying need for work which had been so evident in the pre-war agitation. Of some 60 interviewees, 'My country needed me' was mentioned only once directly, and just twice was the patriotic form, 'I wanted to do my bit,' used, in all three cases by domestic servants. Within factories and offices there were greater differences in attitude between women in the same workplace than had been the case before the war, differences that were not submerged but emphasised by the different ways in which they dealt with the experience. Management at the outset of the war was inexperienced in the organisation of socially mixed groups of women, but soon learnt to sort them by social class as well as industrial experience and so on. In some factories, for example, explosives work went to married women because they were considered sensible and 'steady'; in others it went to girls because of the suspected gynaecological hazards of work with chemicals. The best-paid jobs in engineering tended to go to those with family connections in the workshop; sewing jobs to those from the needle-working trades; bullet-making, inspection and gauging to the blue-eyed, because they were supposed to be more myopic and thus able to cope with close work. A survey of one munitions factory showed that about one third had found work through the help of friends or relations, another third had simply turned up at the factory gates to be taken on, leaving only the final third to be supplied directly from government labour exchanges.[34] In Scotland, Ireland and Wales there was more travel far from home, analogous to male military recruitment, but such young women were often described as causing massive problems for management. The diary of one woman police officer, Gabriella West, on deposit in the Imperial War Museum, mentions one outstanding example. She left the Woolwich Arsenal partly because she could not stand the 'dirty, stinking, swearing people,' but found her North Wales factory as difficult. Women from the Rhondda were always 'getting up strikes' and full of 'socialistic speeches'; girls from Ireland started a riot by singing Fenian songs and casting aspersions on the Tommies. They had to be sent back to Ireland covered in mud after a pitched battle between Irish and Welsh.[35] Such experience seems to have been rare, but it demonstrates, as the statistics on labour mobilisation do not, the many forms of 'mobilisation' and the variety of experiences behind the term 'war work'. It is questionable how many of these women workers who entered new jobs during the war were replacing a man. The machinery of dilution gave a misleading impression of wholesale replacement of skilled men by women in the factories. Dilution officers toured the country to demonstrate the efficiency of women workers and the ease with which skilled work could be reorganised for the unskilled. They mounted exhibitions of photographs both of machines and of women actually at work. The Imperial War Museum's photographs, the nucleus of a large collection after the war, were a product of the new detailed attention to work processes that dilution encouraged.[36] The War Office produced a pair of handbooks on dilution and sent 40,000 out to employers.[37] The result was a developing iconography

have been very popular in areas where such facilities would have been unfamiliar, though in areas where it was customary for married women to be employed, they were well supported, and women argued that they should be kept on after the war. Janet Campbell, who surveyed nursery provision for the Ministry of Reconstruction, asked Medical Officers of Health to report on nurseries. Most disliked them on the grounds that they encouraged mothers to work, but some pointed out that they were better than child-minders, to whom mothers who needed to work would turn in their absence.[45]

Women's reaction to the issue of welfare depended critically on the nature of the welfare on offer. Canteens were popular. For many women, particularly married women, it was the first time they had been able to sit down for a full meal on a regular basis. Uniforms, washrooms, lighting and seating were only noticed if deficient. Since welfare workers were employed primarily 'To ensure good time-keeping',[46] they could be seen either as helpful, humanising the factory or, alternatively, as disciplinary, reflecting another face of management. Trade Unions were suspicious of welfare. As Mary Macarthur said, 'There is no word more hated among women workers of today than welfare'.[47] However, the way in which many women reacted to the new environment of the factory was often crucially determined by the particular characteristics of the welfare system. Until 1917 nearly all agitation among women was over issues of supervision and welfare, most commonly combined in demands to keep or sack welfare supervisors. In Armstrong-Whitworths in Newcastle there was a major strike which began as 'the tea-break strike' and spread to become a strike of women for workshop representation. The result was a ten-minute tea break, a welfare system, some new lavatories and union recognition and organisation. Yet one of the leaders of that agitation could not recall ever having met one of the welfare workers.[48]

Male militants have been much analysed and described in the industries of wartime Britain. Women's militancy has gone unrecognised, apart from the equal pay agitation of 1918.[49] Yet although employers lauded female docility, eagerness and dexterity during the introduction of dilutees in 1915-16, they were as enthusiastic in deploring their poor time-keeping, lack of commitment to work and low productivity when called upon to assess women's employment in 1918 for the Hills Committee (of the Ministry of Reconstruction) and the War Cabinet Committee on Women in Industry. A part of the explanation for this change of heart lay in the way in which working women did in some respects behave no differently from men. They learned to use the same industrial weapons as men, whether organised in trade unions or not, and they began to organise in trade unions in larger numbers. Mrs Blanco White in a very interesting piece of evidence to the War Cabinet Committee saw the process in two ways. One was class mingling. 'The old hands,' she said, discouraged eager workers from staying, corrupting those that did. The other, she believed, was the women's union, the NFWW, which made them discontented with their lot, with which otherwise they were perfectly happy.[50] Women's trade-union membership grew from 437,000 in 1914 to 1,209,000 in 1918, a much faster rate of growth than their proportionate membership of the workforce (see appendix 2.1). Certainly the confidence to organise, the money to pay the subscription and the need to prevent exploitation were all accentuated by war conditions, but these abilities and aspirations were not new, and partly continued trends which had been set in motion before the war.[51] However, much of the wartime organisation could not continue after the war because it was in the hands of the NFWW which turned itself into what amounted to a union of women war workers, and was committed to the removal of all dilutees after the war. In so doing, the Federation paid a high price for acceptance into the wider world of trade unions, in that it helped to perpetuate the secondary status of the working woman.

The end of the war came before 1918 for some women workers. The first demobilisations for them followed on the closure of the Russian Front. As Churchill, then Minister of Munitions, said to his staff,

> The War Office are blamed like Pharaoh of old, because they will not let the people go. Our difficulty is we cannot let the people stay. We have actually succeeded in discharging nearly a million persons, the bulk of whom did not want to go.[52]

Just as the beginning of the war had turned nearly all women into potential war workers, now nearly all women were assumed to have been war workers. Married women, it was assumed, should revert to their previous occupation 'in the home'. The TUC supported the demand for 'mothers' pensions', as a speaker argued in 1919 using military terms and biological description.

If we have got to have an A1 nation we must protect the mothers... I honestly think that the institution of pensions for mothers would go a long way towards checking the race suicide that is going on.[53]

She used the pre-war language of social degeneration to argue for a concept of motherhood that, it was argued, war had supported, not undermined. The Hills Committee also argued on similar lines. Although the Committee acknowledged that married women would continue to work and that they should not be prevented from doing so, they added a telling rider that women should be discouraged from doing work that was itself injurious to health, like fur-pulling, rag-picking and gut-scraping on the grounds that:

> The primary function of women in the state must be regarded, it is not enough to interfere with her service in bearing children, and the care of infant life and health, but she must be safeguarded as home-maker for the nation.[54]

To this end the report recommended exclusion from unhealthy trades and the award of mothers' pensions and equal pay. Equality of pay was assumed to exclude women effectively from manual work because employers would prefer to employ men. The policy of the Ministry of Labour also effectively excluded married women from employment. They were not allowed onto the few occupational training schemes set up after the war. They were denied 'out-of-work donation' as 'not genuinely seeking work' if they turned down employment because of domestic obligations. No woman could refuse domestic service work on the grounds that she had had another trade as a war worker. Even the limited opportunities offered by 'alternative work', the production of peacetime goods in the war factories, were available only to the widowed mothers of large families. After some pressure from Lilian Barker, the former woman welfare superintendent at the Woolwich Arsenal, the Ministry did provide some domestic training, either to turn factory girls into domestic servants or into housewives and mothers. A leaflet for the scheme stated:

> A call comes again to the women of Britain, a call happily not to make shells or fill them so that a ruthless enemy can be destroyed but a call to help renew the homes of England, to sew and to mend, to cook and to clean and to rear babies in health and happiness, who shall in their turn grow into men and women worthy of the Empire.[55]

As far as the 'working woman' was concerned, the 'experience of war' was ambiguous. Women had demonstrated that they could do work requiring physical strength. They had heaved coal and driven trams. One group of women navvies had built a shipyard. They had demonstrated dexterity and skill. Women had used the new technique of arc-welding, and built aeroplanes and airships, and were employed on the sub-divided tasks of engineering. Dilution had not been achieved in the bastions of male trade unionism, the shipyards and the workshops where men made heavy artillery. Women formed the majority of the workforce in fuses and cartridges, which had been women's work before the war, but they remained dependent on male tool-setters in work on shells. Some had considerable experience of the supervision of a large number of workers in war factories, but it was supervision of women on temporary war work. Despite frequent demands from workers themselves and their organisations, very few women had been trained in general skills. When 'blind alley' jobs were perceived as a problem, the problem was only for boys, not for women. Individual women managed to 'beat the system' and learn skills, make their own tools and set their own machines, but it seems to have been more common among boys who missed the normal apprenticeship scheme because of the war but could pass as time-served men after the war when no woman could.[56] Many women were ambivalent about war work, because it produced death-dealing objects. The prize-winning essay in a projectile factory magazine expressed this:

> Only the fact that I am using my life's energy to destroy human souls gets on my nerves. Yet on the other hand, I'm doing what I can to bring this horrible affair to an end. But once the War is over, never in creation will I do the same thing again.[57]

They were not ambivalent about work in factories. Most of the 60 women interviewed recalled the work of wartime as a happy time because of the friendships they had formed, the wages, the amusements in the factory, such as hair competitions, football matches, concerts and running jokes. They would have welcomed a chance to have continued to work in a factory, but on another product. In the event, most of the interviewees out of 50 women war-workers were reluctantly forced back into domestic service, but there were several women who, through their war work, had lost the chance to train as servants, and found later that this option was no longer available because they were too old, too work-roughened or viewed with suspicion as an ex-factory worker. Some employers learnt a different lesson from the war. Food production, light engineering and clothing expanded in the inter-war years using female labour, often organised on the same principles by the same managerial group who had organised the war. At a higher level the same phenomenon could be observed. Mary Macarthur, Margaret Bondfield and Julia Varley continued to be active in labour or trade-union politics; Clara Collet, Adelaide Anderson and Dr Janet Campbell pursued careers in the civil service; the Fabian women, Beatrice Webb, Barbara Drake and Mrs Hutchins, continued campaigning. The influence of all these on the quality of public debate on topics concerning women and the family was increased by the war, but they did not, as Philip Abrams has argued, severely distort the politics of the Reconstruction against the interests of organised labour, because they shared the same concerns for the re-establishment of family life.[58] The activities of these prominent women suggest increased self-confidence and a new perception of work, but in no sense a total emancipation from pre-war assumptions about women's nature or potential.

The same is true of the question of equal pay. War wages are one of the issues on which published sources are least reliable. The major source is the War Cabinet Committee on Women in Industry, set up to propitiate striking transport workers who demanded equal pay in the summer of 1918. The importance the Government attached to the report's verdict that government had kept its promise to preserve wage levels is evident from the attempt that was made to prevent Beatrice Webb issuing her minority report.[59] The committee's report concluded that most women had not in fact done men's work, but that when they had taken over a particular job from a man they had achieved about two-thirds of his level of output. Beatrice Webb, however, argued in her minority report that although they had been doing the men's work, women had not received the men's pay. The evidence given by employers and managers was contradictory, often vitiated by their desire to report on the general principles of the employment of women rather than to record actual wage levels. Such comparisons as were made were of doubtful value. The availability of labour, the number of hours worked and work organisation were all different in wartime. Inexperience was frequently confused with gender. Few witnesses compared women with the boys beside whom they worked, and if they did, it was only to contrast their respective levels of ambition in munitions factories where most boys were deployed. Clearly women on average earned less than men. They received cost-of-living bonuses later, and these were lower than those offered to their male counterparts. Even the women working at exactly the same tasks as men did not in general receive equal pay. Just a few achieved equal pay rates by negotiation through a special arbitration tribunal for women's pay and conditions. For example, in the Woolwich Arsenal, the biggest factory, only three small groups had equal pay, two after strike action: crane drivers, inspectors and wages clerks. Most women on engineering processes had to pass on some of their wages to the skilled engineer who set their tools. Their earnings, though, much higher than they had been before the war, averaging about 30s a week against 11/6 a week, pre-war, were still only approximately half of comparable male earnings. Wages rose in industries other than war production too, though it took longer than in munitions factories. Agitation by women for increased wages accompanied the first lay-offs of women workers in the autumn of 1917. Men lent support to these demands because, as the Ministry of Munitions's secret report on labour noted cynically, they thought it would ensure fewer women would be employed after the war.[60] The women I interviewed considered that their wages had been sufficient for their needs. Although a few complained of differentials between groups of women, in general it was felt that the inequality of sacrifice between workers and soldiers renderèd such complaints immoral.

Women's war work did not affect women evenly. Their experiences of work differed according to occupation, family responsibilities, previous work experience, education and where they lived. Munitions work dominated the records and obscured both the continuities and long-term change elsewhere. The rhetoric of war gives a seductive completeness to a period in which demand for labour fluctuated and the relative power of women and women's organisations changed. War experience was not simply an anticipation of later developments, either in general or for individuals. The absence of training, of permanent alterations in the organisation of production, of any change in the relationships of power within the workforce or in relation to the employers ensured that women did not keep jobs specifically designated as war work. The Restoration of Pre-War Practices Bill took jobs away from working-class women while middle-class women benefited from the Sex Disqualification Removals Act (which applied to the professions). Skilled occupations performed by women in wartime

Appendix 2.2   continued

40	Precious metals	125	0.3
41	Hotels, public houses, cinemas and theatres, etc.	123	2.5
42	Clothing trades: boots, shoes, slippers	121	0.7
43ª	Other trades	119	0.2
	Agriculture	119	0.9
45	Paper and wallpaper	117	0.2
46	Hosiery	113	0.5
47	China and earthenware	109	0.2
48	Teachers (local authority)	108	0.7
49	Woollen and worsted	103	0.3
50	Sugar, confectionery, jam, bread and biscuits	102	0.1
51ª	Tinplate	100	0.0
	Silk	100	0.0
53	All other food trades	98	-0.1
54	Linen, jute and hemp	97	-0.2
55	Printing, bookbinding, newspaper printing and publishing	93	-0.4
56ª	Tailoring, shirtmaking, dressmaking and millinery	90	-2.2
	Stationery, cardboard boxes, pencils, gum, ink	90	-0.2
58	Cotton	84	-4.0
59	Other clothing trades (except boots and shoes)	82	-1.9
60	Lace	81	-0.2
61	Wood trades: basket and wicker work	70	0.0
62	Docks and wharves	–	0.0
	All sectors	151	100.0
	No. of women employed November 1918	4,940,000	
	No. of women entering employment July 1914-November 1918		1,663,000

Notes

a Tied ranks

b Minus values indicate movement out of sector

Source: as Appendix 2.1

Notes on Chapter 2

Full details of all publications mentioned here are in the bibliography on page 209.

1   A version of this chapter first appeared in Wall, R. and Winter, J. (eds), *The Upheaval of War*, 1988. I am grateful to the Syndics of the Press for permission to reproduce it.

2   Woollacott, A., *On Her Their Lives Depend*, 1994.

3   Marwick, A., *Women at War*, 1977, states the case most strongly.

4   Fulford, R., *Women on the Warpath*, p 19.

5   Hartmann, H., 'Capitalism, Patriarchy and Job Segregation by Sex' in Eisenstein, Z (ed.), *Capitalist Patriarchy and the Case for Socialist Feminism*, 1978; Braybon, G., *Women Workers in the First World War*, 1981.

6   Thom, D., 'The Ideology of Women's Work in Britain 1914-24, with specific reference to the NFWW and other trade unions', unpublished PhD for the CNAA at Thames Polytechnic, 1982, has a fuller version of this thesis.

7   'Report on Occupations', census report, PP 1913, lxxxviii, Cmd 7018; Brown, K., *Labour and Unemployment, 1900-1914*, 1971, notes women's involvement in the right to work agitation. Buxton, N.K. and Mackay, D., *British Employment Statistics, a Guide to Sources and Methods*, 1977, points out the general inadequacy of the relation between statistics for unemployment and employment and exclusions under the National Insurance scheme but ignores the question of women. Under-recording is suggested by the different findings of oral historians and the regional variation in numbers registered as unemployed according to industry as well as close qualitative studies as in Hutchins, B.L., *Women in Modern Industry*, 1915, and Black, C., *Married Women's Work*, 1915.

8   Chapman, S.D., *War and the Cotton Trade*, 1915, p 9.

9   Annual Report, National Federation of Women Workers, 1911, pp 186-8; Boston, S., 'The Chainmakers of Cradley Heath' TV programme, 1977, mostly based on materials in the GTC at the TUC.

10 These groups included the Fabian Women's Group, the Women's Labour League, the Women's Industrial Council and the Women's Trade Union League.

11 Martin, A., *The Mother and Social Reform*, 1913, p 7.

12 Anderson, A., *Women in the Factory*, 1922, p 161.

13 Smith, E., *Wage-earning Women and Their Dependants*, 1911.

14 Olcott, T., 'The Women's Trade Union Movement', *London Journal* 2, 1976; Lewenhak, S., *Women in Trade Unions*, 1977; Boston, S., *Women Workers and the Trade Union Movement*, 1980. All are based to some extent on Drake, B., *Women in Trade Unions*, 1920.

15 *Woolwich Pioneer*, 5 May 1916.

16 Drake, B., *Women in Trade Unions*, 1920, p 46.

17 See chapter 5.

18 Fabian Women's Group, *The War, Women and Unemployment*, 1915).

19 This organisation was set up by the National Union of Women Workers, which demonstrates in itself one major shift of wartime as it was an organisation of unwaged social workers to promote the 'social, civil, moral and religious welfare of women', 17 November 1914, GTC at the TUC.

20 Fulford, R., *Votes for Women*, 1958; Pankhurst, E.S., *The Suffragette Movement*, 1931.
21 Hamilton, M.A., *Mary Macarthur*, 1925, p 138; Woodward, K., *Queen Mary*, 1927, p 190; 'Interim Report of the Women's Employment Commission', PP 1914, 1916, xxxviii, Cd 7848, pp 4, 11; Pankhurst Collection, Institute for the Study of Social History, Amsterdam, minute books of East London Federation of Suffragettes, 1915 (exact date unclear), report of a delegation to Mary Macarthur.
22 *Spectator*, 19 September 1914.
23 *Lancashire Post*, 17 May 1915, GTC at the TUC.
24 *New Age*, 19 August 1914, the start of a correspondence lasting into 1915.
25 Reports of the 1915 TUC, *Evening Times and Echo*, 11 September 1915, GTC at the TUC.
26 Macassey, L., *Labour Policy: False or True*, 1922; Hammond, M., *British Labor Conditions and Legislation During the War*, 1919; Wolfe, H., *Labour Supply and Regulation*,, 1923, p 77.
27 Lloyd George, D., *War Memoirs*, 1933; Addison, C., *Politics from Within*, 1924); PRO.MUN 5.70.26, 11 August 1915.
28 Cole, G.D.H, *Trade Unionism and Munitions*, 1923; Hinton, J., *The First Shop Stewards' Movement*, 1973.
29 Drake, B., 'Historical Introduction to the Report of the War Cabinet on Women in Industry', PP 1919, xxl, Cmd 135, p 108.
30 *Official History of the Ministry of Munitions, A History of State Manufacture* vol. 6, PRO.
31 Wolfe, H., *Labour Supply and Regulation*, 1923, p 169.
32 File of dilution agreements lodged with the Board of Trade, 1916-17, IWM.EMP 19.
33 IWM.EMP 4.282.
34 *Labour Gazette*, produced monthly by the Board of Trade for Labour Supply. See Thom, D., 'The Ideology of Women's Work', interviews, for allocation procedure; see chapter 7 in this volume.
35 Diary of Gabrielle West, IWM, documentary section. I am grateful to Jean Liddiard for this reference.
36 Many of the photographs exhibited were taken by Horace Nicholls, who produced much telling wartime imagery on women's work.
37 See *Women's Work in Munitions* and *Women's Work in Non-munitions Industries*, 1916.
38 John, A., *By the Sweat of Their Brow*, 1984.
39 Memo from F.H. Durham to Miss Conway in 1919, IWM.EMP I; insisted that the exhibits should stress achievements in wartime.
40 PRO.MUN 2.27, 5 February 1916.
41 Pankhurst, E.S., *The Home Front*, 1932, pp 78-82.
42 See chapter 6.
43 Reports of the Health of Munition Workers Committee, PP 1916, xxiii, Cd 1185; 'Memorandum on the Employment of Women', PP

1917-18, xiii, d 8511, interim report; PP 1918, xii, Cd 9065, final report.

44 'Report of the War Cabinet Committee on Women in Industry', medical memorandum, PP 1919, xxxi, Cmd 135.

45 Ministry of Reconstruction papers at BLPES, box 4, doc. 90.

46 Ineson, A., interviews.

47 She added, 'They don't like being done good to,' IWM.TE, evidence to the War Cabinet on Women in Industry, 4 October 1918.

48 Thom, D., interviews, Grace Robson.

49 The full literature on this subject was first evoked by Hinton, *Shop Stewards' Movement,* and is summarised in Alastair Reid's contribution to the volume, in which this first appeared, chapter 7.

50 Evidence of Mrs Blanco White, 12 October 1918, IWM.TE.

51 See chapter 4.

52 PRO.MUN 5.55, 24 February 1918.

53 1919 TUC report cited by Braybon, G., *Women Workers in the First World War,* 1981, p 199.

54 Report of the Women's Employment Committee for the Ministry of Reconstruction, PP 1918, xiv, Cd 9239, p 60.

55 Ministry of Labour leaflet, IWM.Emp 80, as cited by Kozak, M., 'Women Munition Workers During the First World War with Special Reference to Engineering', unpublished PhD, University of Hull, 1977, p 379.

56 See chapter 7.

57 IWM.MUN 28.

58 Thom, D. 'Women Workers in the Woolwich Arsenal in the First World War', *Oral History,* 8 (Autumn 1978); see chapter 7 in this volume.

59 Abrams, P., 'The Failure of Social Reform, 1918-1920', *Past and Present* 24 (1963).

60 Webb, B., Diary, entries for 21 November 1918 and 8 September 1919, LSE.

61 PRO.MUN 2.16, 31 August 1918; the report of the War Cabinet Committee on Women in Industry shows this very clearly.

62 Health of Munition Workers Committee, memo 4, 1916; Taylor, P., 'Daughters and Mothers – Maids and Mistresses: Domestic Service Between the Wars' in Clarke, N., Critcher, C.C. and Johnson, R. (eds), *Working Class Culture,* 1979.

Chapter 3

'A Revolution in the Workplace'? Women's Work in Munitions Factories and Technological Change 1914-1918

The history of wartime employment is often seen as typical of the process of the social inscription of work in the lives of women. It is certainly influentially mythical in creating a story of women's work which has emphasised women's secondary wage-earning, vulnerability to male hostility and reliance upon government rather than their own organisations for improvement. Work is a cultural formation in the lives of women as much as for men, despite the history of over-emphasis on gender of most accounts of wartime innovation.[1]

The account of the turning of young women into women war-workers is one, then, that looks at the experience of learning to be a factory worker. It also raises the questions of the contribution of the women workers of the day to social change. Paul Thompson argues for the profound effect of the experience of war on people's understanding of their world in his study *The Edwardians*, so the experience of war work for the woman worker should also demonstrate such change.[2] Motherhood has famously been described in this period as 'women's highest service to the state', which women had, it was argued, set aside to perform war service.[3] One of the problems of histories of work is the layer of understanding imposed on the worker's experience by her subsequent labour history. In this instance, this presents a substantial methodological problem precisely because war work was so unlike much of the industrial employment, not of all women, but of the women who were war-workers. The rhythms of work, the nature of the training on the job, the social relations of the workplace were all altered by the fact that the work was undertaken by women who were addressed in a threefold description as women war-workers. The evidence is also more than usually opaque, though it looks so much better than most evidence about women because it is voluminous and thorough, where usually it is sparse and subject to the random accidents of survival. However, the abundance of evidence reflects the political needs that record-keeping served at the time. The best collections about working women are those of the Imperial War Museum in London, which were explicitly gathered to demonstrate the novelty and success of war work for women; and, in a more restricted way, the collection called the Tuckwell Collection at the Trades Union Congress (TUC) which is focussed around the Women's Trade Union League (WTUL), and its daughter organisation, the National Federation of Women Workers (NFWW), which became in wartime, as its leader Mary Macarthur said, 'virtually a union of women war-workers, especially munitions workers'.[4] Government demonstrated an unusually keen interest in these women, and produced a massive survey of their activities, reported as the War Cabinet Committee on Women in Industry in 1919.[5] This committee was set up to exonerate government from the claim made by striking transport workers and munitions factory workers that they had not honoured their promises to award the women doing men's work equal pay. At the time it was not clear to women themselves whether they were doing a man's or a woman's job, whether it was skilled or not, even, or perhaps especially, whether they were paid on the basis agreed by their trade union. Hence, in order to understand how much innovation there was, it is necessary to investigate the perceptions of government, employers and the workers themselves, while remaining aware that the history of women's work itself was a political counter in debates about the responsibility of government, making any final conclusions difficult.

The state was the innovator in the field of women's employment, and this too makes this a history which is both better-recorded and more polemical than most accounts of women's contribution to technological change. Winston Churchill, as we have seen, was briefly Minister of Munitions, and he called it, ironically enthusiastic, a 'great argument for state socialism'.[6] The process by which women were turned into new sorts of workers was one that was overlaid with a specific and contingent kind of paternalism. This paternalism had limits, as when many workers began to show signs of the toxic effects of TNT (tri-nitro-toluene), and the solution was to ensure that processes of management would be used to ensure that no single worker would be exposed for very long to the poison.[7] However, this paternalism shaped and defined the debates about women's labour, and therefore the historical record. The theory of dilution and substitution was based on a discourse about the woman worker which presumed that she was weaker, undisciplined and uninterested in technical knowledge because women were not usually factory workers in engineering. Government both reflected and encouraged this view, and produced propaganda based on this assumption, much of it pictorially vivid. Women's own industrial organisation tended to work on some of the same sets of assumptions, exploiting them in the interests of their members but thus reproducing an argument which has been attributed only to their male peers. In examining this theory, the placing of technological change in a discourse of innovation peculiar to wartime creates a misleading impression of innovation and novelty. The change is not in the area of technology, nor in the capacities or skills of women, but in the management of large groups of women that dilution and substitution brought. The machinery on which they worked and the organisation of production was either imported from the United States or borrowed from factories where it was already in use, copied and reproduced in much greater volume.[8] The organisation of production was different only in that larger numbers of semi-skilled workers were engaged in workshops where previously skilled workers had been producing the same goods more slowly.

The labour theorist and historian G.D.H. Cole was one of the most interesting theoreticians to write about the wartime processes of dilution and substitution. In his book on workers' control in the workplace he defined dilution thus:

> the introduction of less skilled workers to undertake the whole, or a part of the work previously done by workers of greater skill or experience, often, but not always, accompanied by simplification of machinery, or the breaking up of a job into a number of simpler operations.[9]

This book was written in 1923, and the clarity of the definition was in part the result of the debates over what had been dilution in wartime when, as Ministry of Munitions officials pointed out in 1917, dilution became 'synonymous with the introduction of women'.[10] The record has remained muddled as to who was a substitute and who a dilutee. For government and employers as well as men's trade union officials the problem of dilution was the spreading of scarce skills; for workers it was the relationship between labour and conscription. Labour management was integrally related to the management of soldier supply. When dilution could be achieved in the context of mass conscription, male workers mostly became replaceable. Paradoxically, those men whose skill was essential to maintain semi-skilled or unskilled workers' machines became more in demand than ever before. Engineers, in particular, resisted the introduction of dilution as they had done since American practices of innovation in engineering had been mooted in Britain in the years before the war. Those engineers eligible for membership of the Amalgamated Society of Engineers (ASE) were to remain central in the process of job definition because they were essential to the smooth expansion of wartime production as, since they had all served apprenticeships, they both made and set machine tools which made the armaments which were used so prodigally in France, Belgium and the Dardanelles.[11] Agreements about dilution then were primarily about skill, not gender, and they do not mention women as such at all. Much dilution did involve men without completed apprenticeships, so that dilution cannot be limited to the introduction of women, any more than all women should be assumed to be replacing skilled men on diluted tasks: many of the dilutees were men who had not undertaken (or in some cases not completed) apprenticeships.

In 1915, after a major scandal about the production of shells, a new Government investigated the possibility of re-organising production and conscription. The two were integrally related. The Cabinet rejected all alternatives in favour of women they were already being urged to employ by women's organisations of the left, worried about unemployment, and of the right, worried about prostitution. In March the Women's War Register was set up to enrol women, whatever their labour history, for war-work.[12] The Ministry of Munitions was set up in May as soon as the trade unions, led by the Amalgamated Society of Engineers, had signed the Treasury agreement that, in exchange for an industrial truce and accepting dilution, they would have a guarantee of equal pay for dilutees doing men's work. Government did not thereby get the kind of direct control over the labour market which some had advocated, since enlisting women was not the same as training them, and agreeing equal pay for some women was not the same as ensuring that they got equal earnings.

Trade unions and employers were essential for the smooth acceptance of the scheme and for running it in practice. Women's organisations participated in the celebrations of the new war register, the equal pay agreement and the labour exchanges with mixed feelings. Many women were opposed to the war, which they regarded as man-made. The biggest suffrage organisation, the National Union of Women's Suffrage Societies (NUWSS), split on the subject. The Women's Social and Political Union (WSPU), the leading non-constitutional suffrage organisation, on the other hand had been largely responsible for organising the march of women demanding the 'right to serve'. Emmeline Pankhurst had negotiated from Lloyd George a substantial sum to pay for costumes and publicity. They had originally called the march a 'right to work' march but that presumably had too many connotations of the demands of male marches in 1908 against unemployment.[13]

The existing skills of industrial women were hidden by this process. Willingness to work had really never been in doubt, but the capacity to replace skilled engineers in munitions factories was, and incapacity was emphasised by the description of all women as being in the same position. In war all their other characteristics became submerged in a general, and generalised relationship to the labour market of wartime. Mary Macarthur had described women workers as 'meantime' workers, in the labour force between school and marriage; they now became 'meantime' for the period of war. Differences of labour history, social class or racial or regional origin were submerged in descriptions of them as gendered labour power. The discourse of the day and the shaping of experience that four years of war gave to their lives meant that their temporary status was always included in the description which linked their gender to their role as workers in wartime. All working women tend to be referred to as women war-workers, and many used the compound phrase themselves.

Trade unions anticipated exploitation as a consequence of the mass enrolment of inexperienced women factory workers. The anonymous official historian of the Ministry of Munitions described it thus:

> Women were badly organised, prone to manipulation by employers, ignorant of workshop practices, in particular defensive, restrictive practices; and content to work in lowly positions for low pay. Women did not enjoy the protection of custom, they were not organised in strong Trade Unions nor could such organisations be built up in an emergency.[14]

This account represents the view of male trade unionists as represented in the War Emergency Workers' National Committee as well as Government and employers. Most importantly for the impact of change on women themselves, it represented the views to some extent of trade unions organising women, but for them it was an opportunity to improve organisation among women and thus demonstrate these were not innate characteristics of the woman worker but contingent upon a history when women had had much less opportunity to exploit labour shortage in their own interests. The education and propaganda of women trade-union leaders similarly emphasised inexperience in women, their lack of training and need for organisation. High unemployment in the first years of war gave support to this position, which meant women were seen as recipients of change rather than innovators in their own right.[15] When the process of dilution was being discussed by employers and trade unions in engineering and shipbuilding 'No representative of the women was consulted: and this was not unreasonable in itself as the women at the time had no *locus standi* in the matter,' wrote Mary Macarthur in 1918.[16]

Yet the introduction of dilution in 1915 through the Defence of the Realm Act (DORA) and the Munitions of War Act of March 1915 had removed several important rights for organised labour. No employee could leave a job on munitions without an employer's 'leaving certificate', strike action was outlawed, and pay was detached from the workplace and subject to government scrutiny in tribunals.[17] Dilution was introduced after agreement in May 1915, and the discussion about what it meant in practice continued throughout the war, but most nearly affected women's experience of the wartime workplace in the year after the Treasury agreement.[18] Once conscription was introduced in 1916 the issue shifted from skilled men's work being done by women to that of substitution, a woman replacing an unskilled or semi-skilled man for the front. The views of women's organisations have to be interpreted through a recognition that war work was not the same in legal status or public discourse throughout the war; and that much of the discussion of work and work process is actually about more general issues than whether women are or are not engaged in technological change.

The first agreement on dilution was signed in November 1914 between Vickers, a major armaments firm, and the Amalgamated Society of Engineers, at Crayford. Dilution was to be limited for women to work on automatic machines.[19] It therefore meant more shells could be produced, but any expansion would increase or maintain the need for skilled engineers who set and mended the machines these women used. Women already worked in engineering on mass-production tasks making fuses, cartridges and bullets, so their representatives would have been seen as irrelevant to the discussion; women were lined up in this way with unskilled men, and both groups of the unskilled seen as having no identity of interest with skilled men. The Treasury agreement of 1915 formalised this by giving the TUC formal control over its own members 'that the existing supply of labour be more economically used'[20] and ensuring that dilutees should be the first to leave their jobs, used only for the duration of war, subject to arbitration to make up for the loss of collective bargaining by strike and superintended by a National Labour Advisory Committee.

In March 1916, the Government moved into manufacture in its own right as well as taking more extensive control over existing armaments manufacturers. The hated leaving-certificate system was to be replaced by conscription, with a system of reserved occupations for men and voluntary registration for war-work. Government had moved into control of the labour supply, which effectively was to mean the new resource the mass mobilisation of women provided.[21] The basic assumption of the negotiations was that women (and all diluted labour) would never equal skilled men in quantity or quality of output, so that if the skilled man's level of pay was protected employers would return to their pre-war workers with great relief when war was over. Only Sylvia Pankhurst, organiser of a tiny socialist organisation aimed at the East End of London, noticed initially that the agreement of 1915 could cause major problems in holding rates at pre-war levels.[22]

The Treasury agreement read:

> The Agreement stated shall not adversely affect the rates customarily paid for the job and the rates paid shall be the usual rate of the district for this class of work.[23]

The problem was how to define 'customarily' and 'district'. In South London and nearby there were two customs side-by-side; in Woolwich and neighbouring Erith and Abbey Wood, all munitions processes were done by men and boys at the Royal Arsenal, while at Vickers, which was privately owned, women worked on fuses and cartridges, particularly in paper- and chemical-filling, rather than engineering.[24] It was engineering that posed the most difficult problems of definition. Engineers went through frequent changes in the rate at which a job was paid and the speed expected of each job. Custom could be of no longer duration than two weeks.[25] The agreement anticipated the regularity of mass production that war was to create. In effect it left the fixing of wages, especially for dilutees, for negotiation. Hence the enormous importance attached to unionisation of war workers by existing union members.

Nationally this debate was temporarily subdued by the introduction of circular L2. This fixed a guaranteed time-rate to women on men's work of £1 for a 48-hour week, with overtime rates on a proportionate basis.[26] Government thus now took steps to enforce this wage in all munitions industries, a new step in Britain. The debate over dilution has often been characterised as a debate over equal pay. It was widely believed at the time that women war workers had been promised equal pay on men's work, and this belief has been reproduced by some historians.[27] In fact it was not until Government orders on pay were consolidated as Statutory Order 885 in 1917 that even dilutees were guaranteed the minimum rate of L2, and in many factories – especially ones with new wartime production, and therefore neither custom nor a usual rate for the job – L2 created a minimum that speedily became a maximum. Both in theory and practice, women were seen as needing a safety net to prevent them becoming what contemporaries called 'sweated labour' rather than equal pay. For women trade unionists these negotiations did not deal with the issues that were to be central to their members: actual, rather than minimum, rates of pay; working conditions; the future of their jobs. They also entirely ignored the much greater number of women doing war work who were not replacing men as dilutees but as substitutes, or in entirely new wartime occupations. This was not seen as a problem until large proportions of these women were organised in trade unions and pressed their claims. In July 1916, they got the same sort of safety net as dilutees; women on women's work were to get a basic hourly rate, four-and-half pence on time work and four pence on piecework or the 'premium bonus system', which was much used in wartime to encourage rising production rates by relating rates of pay to comparisons between work-teams. In 1919 it was said that this order, 447, 'aroused more antagonism among employers than circular L2'.[28] This resentment was because there was no shortage of unskilled women workers, except briefly over the winter of 1915-16, and they cost as much in extra expenditure on canteens, lavatories and changing-rooms as women replacing skilled men.

The benefits of these proceedings for women were not in the rates, which were very low compared to men's rates, but in the principle of government protection. In looking at discussion of women workers on munitions, the question of whether innovation took place always has to be seen in the context of the discussions about pay, because the status of the worker, and therefore her bargaining power, was vitally affected by her relation to a male worker rather than any independent assessment of her skills. This is underlined by the question of when women entered the workforce, since many more did so before they had firm agreements, and therefore government protection, than did afterwards.

The workforce altered less than contemporary accounts might seem to indicate. 382,000 entered between July 1914 and July 1915 while the next year saw 563,000. The change seemed larger than it was because they became a much larger proportion of the workforce; by July 1916 they were already 26.5%, while by July 1917 they were 45.9%. How many of these workers were doing work that was new to women? The Standing Joint Committee of Women's Industrial Organisations (SJCWIO) argued in its 1916 report on the substitution of women that it was irrelevant.[29] It thought there was no real distinction between an increase caused by women replacing men, and a general expansion in the workforce. The report asked if women were replacing men what the category of work on which they were doing so really was. They claimed that the Board of Trade's *Labour Gazette* exaggerated the inexperience of women war-workers because so much of women's occupational experience was not previously in their sights, being in small, unrecorded workplaces or domestic work; while, they wrote, they overestimated 'the middle-class women who would not normally become wage earners' and 'the return of married and widowed women for patriotic reasons'. The SJCWIO argued that the effect of this distortion was to maximise the impression of industrial inexperience and encourage employers to exploit women workers.

There were large numbers of women who moved within industry. Employers in traditionally female industries complained that they were losing their workers to the lure of munitions. As the Ministry of Munitions, monitoring the labour supply, noted in December 1915:

> They do not find the supplies of labour at existing rates of wages adequate to meet their demands and... in fact there is at present a shortage of women.[30]

And in February 1916:

> Although the women who would normally be engaged in industrial
> work are now all fully occupied, there are large reserves of women,
> principally married, who have had previous industrial experience, and
> who could be utilised in special circumstances.[31]

The impression that Government did not know what it was doing
is borne out by these quotations, since it simply did not know what
would move women back into production. Women were recruited
from rural areas, particularly Ireland, and housed in some munitions areas by building hostels.[32] The major influence on women's
recruitment, though, was their relation to the family economy. The
Board of Trade reported in 1915 that women were not being forced
to work in munitions areas because of the high wages earned by
men, and, they noted a month later, women were keeping more at
home, 'a fact due to the large number of soldiers billeted in the
division'.[33] Servicemen earned low wages, and dependants'
allowances were low too: 11/6 for a woman with two children, 6d
extra for each child under ten. Areas of high male unemployment
were often areas of high enlistment, though not necessarily, and
also often areas of high female unemployment.

The debate over dilution focussed on women workers as
replacement for men at work. But it took place in a fluctuating
labour market and the context of debate over all women's domestic
activity and social roles as well as their paid labour. By the time
government regulated women's employment, most women had
made a choice already about how to deal with wartime demands.
They had already decided to enter factory work or to move to an
area of labour shortage because they had to do so. Trade unionists
were quick to perceive some of the implications of this change but
slow to recognise that some change was in the attitudes, aspirations and mobility of women themselves. Mary Macarthur, for
example, addressing a trade-union audience, agreed with some of
the old attitudes:

> Women could not do the work of men and in some industries that was
> true. There were occupations that she would be sorry to see women
> undertake (Hear, Hear) and they were objected to on the ground that
> they were cheap, and it was a natural objection to be met in only one
> way, namely where they did men's work they should have men's pay.
> The newspaper reporting this speech interpreted her speech as arguing

from heavy work women must be barred, while less arduous work must be made easier if they are to do it; but where they do work equally with men they ought to have equal pay for it.[34]

The elision between *some* unsuitable jobs and *all* heavy work was common at the time, and shows the inflexibility of thinking about women's labour that was still common in 1915. Later in her speech Macarthur pointed out how war had demonstrated society's need for the manual worker: 'They now saw how important the common people were'. Throughout the war women were to be discussed as Macarthur did here, either in relation to the male workers they replaced or as heroines for the meantime doing an unnatural job for patriotic reasons.

At the 1915 TUC, women's work was unusually high on the agenda. A resolution on unsuitable trades was passed unanimously:

That, in order to sustain the physique of Britain and to prevent physical degeneration, no relaxation of Trade Union rules shall lead to the employment of women on work of a character unsuited by
1   carrying or turning over weights or operated by heavy foot pressure;
2   employment on hot or dusty trades in which lime, oil, grease, fire-sand or emery are used;
3   or on heavy machinery producing fatigue, or such machines where often male employment produces a large number of accidents.[35]

This was a pious hope. All these conditions occurred in at least one of the trades on which women were engaged. Lloyd George pamphlets on women's work, and the dilution photographs at the Imperial War Museum, show that they were broken in turn by women who were coal-heavers, navvies, lathe operators, chemical workers, vehicle maintenance workers, pottery-makers, clock-makers and munition workers. The TUC was not very bothered by the practice of wartime because of all the agreements which suspended these protections for the duration. When TNT turned out to be toxic, and therefore more dangerous than the explosive, lyddite, it replaced, the TUC had little to say. They were in this context fairly reluctant to speak for the national 'racial stock' or other abstractions; the physique of Britain was therefore a highly negotiable concept in wartime because of the advances for labour possible amidst extreme labour shortage. When they discussed dilution, this centrality of union organisation and its dominance over other conditions became clear. The motion they passed – which was not unanimous, as on women – at 111 to 43 votes, was:

> This Congress recognises the dangers that are likely to arise from the wholesale introduction of women emergency war workers in the engineering trades and is of the opinion that to facilitate the replacement at the close of the war of women by more suitable male labour and the returning of women to industrial pursuits more fitting generally, local committees should be established for each suitable area which should include representatives from the employers' and workers' organisations in the trade together with representatives of the women's labour organisations.

This resolution clearly separated women from workers, and left unstated either the dangers of war work or the more fitting post-war occupations that were to succeed it. Those who voted against the motion were from the general unions, while the craft and industrial unions supported it. On the same day, two resolutions on equal pay and the need for more trade-union organisation among women were carried with no dissenting voices.[36] But the crucial question for trade unions was who should organise the women? The Amalgamated Society of Engineers (ASE) concluded an agreement with the NFWW that they should organise women war-workers in engineering, and they would assist with recruitment in exchange for the federation's commitment to hand back all diluted jobs done in wartime by their members.[37]

The General Federation of Trade Unions (GFTU), on the other hand, argued for unionisation on the grounds of both women and men. First they argued for a war 'ticket' in April 1915:

> For women as war-workers on the grounds that unorganised women workers are dangerous, and might be used to reduce the wages of the men.

Appleton, GFTU general secretary, went on to say:

> There is a danger, when you have a lot of women in an occupation in which they have not been employed previously, and have no commercial knowledge of the value of their work, that they may be exploited, and not only their conditions but the general conditions made very much worse.[38]

Addressed as a danger, and always characterised as affecting men rather than themselves, it is perhaps not surprising that women learned not to be 'workers', new to factory life with all the problems of any novice group of workers but 'women war-workers', inherently temporary and dealt with as agents in deteriorating the working conditions of their male colleagues in the factory.

There were those who argued against these preconceptions of dilution and women workers implicit in dilution. The *Daily Herald* attacked male intransigence:

> Loyalty to any one nation, class or sex is noble only so long as it is a weapon against the oppressor: it becomes a vice as soon as it closes the door of equality against the oppressed.[39]

Alice Smith defended women:

> The average woman worker is an instinctive rather than a conscious trade unionist. Her inexperience leads to a mistrust of officials and she distrusts her own capacity to organise others in her trade union. In my trade union of 22 thousand, 19 thousand are women, all the officers are men.[40]

This defence simply displaced the idea of a problem of the women's innate qualities from work to trade-union organisation. Women had to create forces for their own protection and simultaneously carry the organisation of women in order to protect men's jobs. Inexperience was a transitory phase in an individual's working life, but seen therefore as describing all war workers, however experienced they might be in other forms of industry, and therefore all women.

Dilution was carried out almost without careful monitoring or discussion of principle at all. Lord George Askwith wrote in Industrial Problems:

> My view is that in labour matters the Government had no policy, never gave any sign of having a policy, could not be induced to have a policy. The departments never followed any policy in labour matters except of disintegration.[41]

The Left feared a policy aimed at attacking union organisation and saw the new woman worker as a main weapon in the attack. They were particularly fearful of the extension of Government control involved in the entry of Government into manufacture through the creation of a Ministry of Munitions. Mary Macarthur, a left-wing member of the Independent Labour Party (ILP), described its introduction as coming 'like a thief in the night'. The introduction of female labour onto new forms of work thus became inextricably entwined with debates about state power and the militarism of Britain.

> Dilution of labour was only supposed to increase production. But undoubtedly it has been used to regiment the workers and cheapen labour.[42]

Employers were encouraged to take advantage of the new supply of female workers by seeing descriptions of every single task newly performed by dilutees, increasingly female in fact, entirely female in propaganda because only a woman doing the task sufficiently dramatised the change. Each dilution officer had a looseleaf handbook through which the daily novelty of women's industrial innovation could be portrayed. Exhibitions, photographs and a group of women actually performing tasks toured the country. Two pamphlets, *The Employment of Women on Munition Work*, and a companion on non-munitions work, were produced to make the same point. 40,000 copies were sold or given away. Women's work became visible in a new way.[43] Even posters made women seem central to production in war-work: 'Do your bit', 'Replace a man for the front'. Popular fiction moved from the staple mill-worker or domestic servant to depicting war-work.[44]

Employers were actually quite resistant to this process. They were happy to dilute but not necessarily to introduce women into the workshops. 'Dilution is for the purpose of increasing output and not of reducing labour costs.'[45] Women were increasingly contrasted not with men but with boys, the other group potentially able to make good the shortfall in skilled labour. The comment of a Vickers works manager was widely reproduced to convince employers that women were better dilutees because they had the merits of not being serious workers:

> Girls are much more diligent on work within their capacity than boys... the boys are naturally expecting to become fully-fledged mechanics and are not content to stay on one job indefinitely; moreover they have great curiosity, and it is impossible to prevent them continually looking around, whilst the girls, as a rule, do not enter the factory with

the idea of staying for more than a few years, and concentrate their attention on attaining dexterity at the particular job they are set to.[46]

Trade unionists were given support for their belief about how highly a worker was gendered in her attitudes to work by these plaudits which emphasised docility and acquiescence. More and more women were classified as dilutees as the definition of work susceptible to regulation as munitions increased. Skilled workers found it tolerable because of trade-union agreement about their withdrawal after war and the commitment to equal pay. In the short term they also benefited directly from increases in output:

> The male operator is responsible for both machines, and the total price paid for the product of the two lathes is the same as was originally paid when two men worked these two machines. The man gives the woman every possible assistance and when the total earnings of the two machines are distributed, the division is such as to considerably increase the earnings of the male workers.[47]

Despite this, not all women found it easy to enter a male workplace, and met physical abuse sometimes, verbal abuse often, on their introduction. Some men argued that women simply could not do the work, although production soared as mass production entered munitions manufacture:

> In many workshops it can safely be said that the women are not a success. As a matter of fact, in some places there has been no attempt to make them a success. They are consequently treated with amused contempt as passengers for the war.[48]

Women union representatives were in the forefront of defining what women were as workers, but they had different tactics for dealing with that sort of contempt. The NFWW dominated the journals, newspapers, government bodies and the TUC, but its policy was more clearly defined by other trade unions than by its members. They revived their paper, the *Woman Worker*, in 1916, and enrolled a large number of wartime organisers. The ASE helped in this drive for members. One slogan was 'Join the great industrial army. Don't blackleg your man in Flanders.'[49] There was an implicit maternalism about the assumption that the woman worker was an inexperienced child; Margaret Bondfield, now working for the NFWW, told a meeting, 'Every mother must get her daughter a union card.'[50] This was successful in terms of membership levels, and a common union interest between men and women. 'Some of our branches have been literally made by the ASE men.'[51] Mary Macarthur, its leader, accepted these constraints as she accepted the need to exclude war workers after the war. Her philosophy was much like other women's organisations at the time, pro-natalist, feminist and pragmatic.

> Women are at heart conservative, but conservative in the best sense of the word. They desire above all else to conserve the race. Big questions of domestic policy will appeal to women insofar as they affect the welfare of children.[52]

Other organisations for working women shared some of these principles but rejected the implications about the essential difference between men and women as workers. The Workers' Union (WU) had organised women making armaments before the war, and they too saw war as an opportunity to turn previously unorganised low-paid women into workers. They organised men and women together in some cases in mixed branches, others separately. Julia Varley, their leading women's organiser, argued, 'Both sexes should pay in the same book and both meet in the same room'. The WU saw war as a 'lever for progress'.[53] The editor of the union journal argued in July 1915:

> Then the women's question. The woman is going to stay after the war. Why not? If she has undercut the man in the past it is the man's fault. His conceit of his craft has led him to take up an attitude of contempt and both have suffered in consequence. If the women have been poor trade unionists it is due to the indifference of the men. Generally speaking, the men have not, until the last few years taken the slightest interest in teaching the women Trade Union principles.[54]

As a leading member argued:

> Woman is bringing revolution into the industrial world, she is going to be responsible for an amazing increase in the powers of production, one to which that of the 18th century will be clean lost by comparison and she is going to be on our side.[55]

He thus demonstrated yet again that even for the most sympathetic and enthusiastic supporter of women's industrial labour and wartime innovation in their placing in the workforce, women were not part of the us of the workers, only a group who would be on the same side. Dilution was seen by such socialists as an exposing and educational process revealing the complexities and inequalities of industrial life. It would also tend to lead to unionisation, and hence also to be welcomed.

Precisely because war work was novel and could not be measured against tradition, women workers could exploit the situation to improve trade-union strength, or could be exploited by war to weaken trade unionism. The 'experience of war' was then profoundly ambiguous. Women's own experience of war was always mediated by how they entered it, who they worked beside and how far the skills they acquired were transferable. Women entered work, as before, through family and neighbours. Previous work operated in two ways. For married women, it excluded. Housework coarsened the hands and motherhood affected the frame so that sedentary delicate work was ruled out by the welfare officers who processed new workers and allocated them to workshops. Married women cleaned railways and trams, built a shipyard, mended roads, made rope, were porters. Many of them directly replaced a family member. Some skills were transferred into war work. Cooks went into canteens for soldiers or munitions-makers; sempstresses and nursery maids did these tasks in 'the wider worlds of the factory'. Organising or clerical work fitted women for workshop labour as foreman or supervisor; typist or filing clerk. Most women workers in wartime were not new workers at all, and even factory workers had often worked before, though very few had made munitions. Of the 110,628 women working in metal trades excluding engineering and subject to the munitions acts, 53,249 had worked in the same trade before; 18,927 were previously unoccupied or in the household, and about 12,000 each came from other industries or domestic service.[56] In other words, the assumption of novelty was an ideological filter through which war work was viewed, which affected the record in ways which make the experience difficult to recapture.

The industries which usually employed women complained of shortages of labour attracted away to munitions by patriotism and the high wages.[57] Dilution continued on munitions-related tasks. Many of these women popularly described as dilutees were in fact substitutes, and they met both verbal and physical abuse. In Liverpool, women were marched into the docks under armed guard but still suffered stone-throwing. This experience only lasted for ten days but must have been frightening.[58] Women involved in this process were beginning to redefine what it meant to be a worker, and ignore the banalities of arguments about sexual difference that had caused problems in the past. When women were accused of accepting low pay at the railway clerks' conference a delegate demanded male clerks' help: 'They should work together as workers, not exactly as men and women, to raise the standard of life together'.[59] Tram drivers' unions organised women on trams despite their initial reluctance to believe that women would be safe if they drove as fast as men.[60] The tendency of all this debate was to accept the principle of sexual difference enshrined in the wages system, to assume inexperience and prescribe unionisation as the solution.

Protectionism allied with feminist arguments about equal pay and pro-natalism to create a remarkable consensus. Once dilution was well underway, the Ministry of Munitions began to address the practices of women workers rather than the theory of their introduction to work. The Health of Munition Workers Committee charted the activities of women workers in their regular reports. In a pamphlet, the 'Employment of Women', they recorded:

> The report reveals many instances of the devotion and enthusiasm of women workers. It is notable that this is the characteristic of no-one class in a movement which knows no class distinction. These women have accepted conditions of work which if continued must ultimately be disastrous to health.[61]

Women in engineering were actually part of a pre-war move towards the introduction of machine tools and the increase in semi-skilled workers to use them. The Historian of the ASE sees the 'minor revolution in workshop practice'[62] happening before 1914; W.F. Watson wrote a book called, quite deliberately, *Machines and Men*, about his life as an engineer in which the war features as a background to strike action but not as a period of women's labour.[63] The growth in the workforce in engineering is from skilled to semi-skilled, while unskilled remain at 20%, semi-skilled grow from 20% to 30% at the expense of skilled men who fall from 60% to 50%.[64] Insofar as women were part of the semi-skilled workforce briefly they were part of this change. However G.D.H. Cole, in his account, indicates neatly that the need to make munitions quickly did not encourage certain kinds of innovation at work.

Even when new factories were built, or new plant installed, specifically for women, the form, design and methods of operation were mainly influenced by traditions made by men for men.[65]

Cole was, unlike most observers of the period, not tied to any particular interests in this debate, except insofar as his guild socialism led to his favouring some general notion of the workers, which included women but did not privilege them. The question of how far women did enter certain skilled occupations was to cause controversy later in 1918 when a committee of the War Cabinet assessed women in industry in order to let the Government off the hook, as it had broken its promise to give such women equal pay. More than most, such questions as the question of how far women did innovate in industrial production need to be asked very carefully, dependent upon the interests of the witness. The ASE continued to argue that most of what women were doing was women's work anyway, and had been before the war, but even they felt that increased welfare provision, greater public scrutiny and the growing confidence of women workers meant that this assumption that not much had changed was untenable. In 1915 the union journal of the ASE argued:

the innovations (of the shells and fuses agreement) are not so real as they appear, as female labour has been engaged in the manufacture of these products in many parts of the country for some time.[66]

The 'problem' of women's labour was thus demonstrably seen by the ASE as its trespass upon the work done by ASE members, when it left areas previously designated as women's work. Hence what was actually going on in those areas where women had been working before received very little attention, and rarely reached into the deliberations of officials or thence into the historical record. The 'women's work' so much reported in wartime was the work that was likely to lead to strikes, that dilution officers described minutely with photographs to convince employers that women could do it, that was the subject of trade-union agreement and discussion. This work was war work and it was so described and regulated because it was seen as temporary for the duration only, and discussed in the interests of the men they had nominally replaced. Much of it indeed was temporary because it was war production and redundant in time of peace. The mass production of shells, bullets and armour plating ended with the armistice in November. New types of production that women had done in wartime like arc-welding and large-gun-making did continue after the war as did the development of less flimsy aircraft late in the war. These tasks, with all the technical innovation they had created, were taken – by male trade unionists, with the consent of women members of trade unions also, especially the Women's Trade Union League – to be men's work, and therefore due to return to men. This price the unionists felt worth paying for the recognition of women as full members of the trade-union movement in peacetime. It was more important to these union leaders to prove that women would not undercut male wages and conditions by staying in these areas of work than it was to protect the interests of a handful of their members doing these new trades.

The innovation, then, and the technological change were implicit in the practices of Government and employers, and the changes in trade-union practice and behaviour, not in the work process itself, which – despite the development of mass production in industries where the tasks had previously been undertaken by craftsmen with semi-skilled assistants – was little affected by the war. Machinery for war use was not new. Whence comes the impression of novelty, of technological excitement evident in so many accounts? It derives from many factors. First is probably the novel attention payed to technology, particularly that created by dilution. These women were measured as workers, photographed, displayed, praised and held up as heroines, not as conventional workers, but as dilutees. Their own awareness of their work in oral testimony is all of themselves as replacements for men, doing the men's work as dilutees, although the jobs they were doing – for example making bullets – were actually described as women's work because women had mostly performed the same task, although more slowly, before the war. Even when the task was new, it was reduced to male or female work by analogy as in arc-welding, which was completely new and almost entirely in wartime done by women. Most women interviewed from the Woolwich Arsenal and the few from Vickers works at Erith or Crayford nearby had enjoyed their work, and could reproduce its patterns after 60 years; most thought they had done a man's job, but only two had wanted to go on working in the same sort of work once peace was declared. Those who were trade unionists had acquired that knowledge in wartime mostly through disputes about welfare supervisors, canteen arrangements or tea-breaks. A few had struck for equal pay in 1917, but not one spoke of wanting to use or learn new technological skills. The work was their war work and it was described only negatively as bearing any relation to a future career, in that it ruined some women's chances of domestic or needlework because of the effects on respectability of war work in a factory or its direct physical effects on the hands.

Women had learnt to be workers as part of a vast, undifferentiated cohort of women war-workers. They were in uniform, or specialised work clothing, often making the transition between work and outside through an institutional cleansing and transformation of great rigour, involving the move from clean to dirty sides of the workplace. They had to leave all hair ornaments, jewellery, purses, cigarettes and lighters behind. One woman even got six months hard labour for taking matches into her work in the danger buildings. The work was organised for safety to keep it as far away from the normalities of factory life as possible. It was dangerous, and its boundaries were very strictly maintained. Women were set apart still further if they worked with TNT, which dyed the skin yellow and made them instantly visible as munitions workers. The culture of the workplace, although it was often highly organised in trade unions, and of war-factory mass-production work itself emphasised the separateness of the workers from everyday concerns, and was peculiar to wartime. Although contemporaries worried about militarisation of the workplace, they had no need to fear the transfer of these modes of operation into peace, because they had been so specific to the war. Although individual women had learnt to think of themselves as workers, most thought of the experience as one that they had enjoyed, valued and never wished to repeat. It had been an experience of war rather than of work that they remembered.

> Our place in industry in the future depends upon our determination not to undersell the men or to undermine the family standard of life.

So argued Mary Macarthur in 1918 at a march for unemployment benefit on equal terms with men called 'The Right to Work, the Right to Life, the Right to Leisure'.[67] This discourse of the social, rather than the particularities of differing workplaces, explains how far the experience of war shaped the experience of war work, and means that women of very diverse experiences at work did legitimately prioritise their gender as the basis for political claims rather than their work. The change was in the technology of people-management, and the real beneficiaries of it were the managers, the welfare supervisors and the technicians of health in the Health of Munition Workers Committee.[68] Women munition workers had contributed to that change, but they did not have enough time, for which they were indeed grateful, to do more to affect technology than that. The women's own contribution was in the formation and support, for a few years more, of female industrial unionism, but this too owed little to technology and much to pre-war factors. Until the significance of political and social factors affecting the employment of dilutees on munitions work is recognised, the experience of that work cannot be measured.

Women's work in wartime is the subject of intense ideological negotiation, not least among the representatives of those women, and it cannot be depoliticised as if the workplace and civil society remain forever separated. To introduce women to areas of work new to them is inevitably to change the women and the workplace, but the effects are greater outside the workplace if the introduction is for a period of war, making war materials, because they are no longer necessary once peace is declared. Women's own memories of this period are overlaid with the memories important to them, which are those of home, family and friends, and then of a brief period in a working life that is also, for them, the war. Even though they can reproduce bodily the activities they did 60 years ago, they cannot usually describe them verbally. The pictures we have of the woman worker on munitions were all gathered for a temporary, pragmatic purpose and the infant science of work-study directed towards the imperatives of war production. Concerns for women's social role were suspended during 1915-1917 because of labour shortage, but they were not removed, and they were concerns through which these women too formulate their own reactions to the experience. Although there were very few who wanted more training, more work and preferred factory work on adjusted machines to later experience of paid employment, they were a tiny minority, and met with virtually no supportive response. The patterns of dilution had been laid down to ensure that there should be no specific work to be taken from war to peace; hence technological change in time of war, anyway limited by the short-term nature of war planning, did not endure into the peace. It is only by assessing technological change in its wider context that we can ensure that employer or Government propaganda does not mislead later generations into ignoring the essential differences that arise by including the women's own viewpoint and recollections, if only to argue that some of the discourse of work is as difficult to understand as other discourses of gender. Labour history has been as limited by its own boundaries and a misleading and disempowering acceptance of separate spheres for too long. One of the most valuable things the study of women can do is refuse to allow such historic separations to mislead.

Notes on Chapter 3

Full details of all publications mentioned here are in the bibliography on page 209.

1   See chapter 2.
2   Thompson, P., *The Edwardians*, 1974.
3   Braybon, G., *Women Workers in the First World War*, 1981.
4   *Womens Trade Union League Journal*, Oct 1916, p 5-6.
5   Report of the War Cabinet Committee on Women in Industry, PP 1919, xiii, Cmd 135; summaries of evidence to the above, Cmd 167.
6   Winston Churchill, Minister of Munitions, MUN.5.52.78 and MUN 2.21, cited in *Official History of the Ministry of Munitions, A History of State Manufacture* vol. VIII, PRO.
7   See chapter 5.
8   Watson, W.F., *Machines and Men*, 1935, pp 12-15, 60, 74-75.
9   Cole, G.D.H., *Workshop Organisation*, 1923, p 48.
10 *Labour Gazette*, monthly digest of information from the Board of Trade.
11 See Hinton, J., *The First Shop Stewards' Movement*, 1973, for a clear account of the relationship.
12 See Thom, D., 'The Ideology of Women's Work in Britain 1914-24, with specific reference to the NFWW and other trade unions', unpublished PhD for the CNAA at Thames Polytechnic, 1982.
13 Pankhurst, E.S., *The Suffragette Movement*, 1931, pp 593, 597; records of meetings between Loyd George and Emmeline Pankhurst, 11 and 28 August 1915, PRO.MUN 5.70.26.
14 *Official History of the Ministry of Munitions, A History of State Manufacture* vol. IV, pt 1, p 57.
15 See chapter 5.
16 In Phillips, M. (ed.), *Women and the Labour Party*, 1918, p 22.
17 Lloyd, E.H.M., *Experiments in State Control*, 1924, p 22.
18 Wolfe, H., *Labour Supply and Regulation*, 1923, p 20.
19 Drake, B., *Women in the Engineering Trades*, 1918, p 17; Cole, G.D.H., *Trade Unionism and Munitions*, 1923, pp 53-54.
20 ASE Monthly Journal and Report, July 1915, cit Hinton, J., *The First Shop Stewards' Movement*, 1973, p 196.

21 Twelfth Report on Conciliation and Arbitration, PP 1919, XXIII, Cmd 185, pp 8-9.

22 Pankhurst, E.S., *The Home Front*, 1932, p 232.

23 *Ibid.*, p 10.

24 Scott, J.D., *Vickers – a History*, 1963.

25 Report of a visit of Woolwich Shop Stewards to the Ministry of Munitions, 18 July 1917, PRO.MUN 5.53.91.

26 Circular L2 from Beveridge papers, BLPES; Drake, B., *Women in the Engineering Trades*, 1918, p 18; Andrews, I. and Hobbs, M., *The Economic Effects of the War on Women and Children*, 1921, pp 140-6.

27 Marwick, A., *Women at War*, 1977, p 57; Milward, A.S., *The Economic Effects of Two World Wars on Britain*, 1970.

28 Drake, B., Historical Memorandum to the War Cabinet Committee on Women in Industry, PP 1919, xxiii, Cmd 135, pp 108-12.

29 Standing Joint Committee of Women's Industrial Organisations, 'The Position of Women After the War', IWM.EMP 4.28/2, p 4; *Labour Gazette*, July 1916.

30 PRO.MUN 2, 27, 11 December, 1915, p 9.

31 *Ibid.*, 5 February, 1916, p 3.

32 Hammond, M.B., *British Labor Conditions and Legislation During the War*, 1919, pp 114-5.

33 *Labour Gazette*, February 1915, p 27; *ibid.*, March 1915, p 79.

34 *Leicester Mercury*, 22 November 1915, GTC at the TUC.

35 Bristol TUC, *Evening Times and Echo*, 11 September 1915, GTC at the TUC 531.

36 TUC Report 1915, pp 370-375.

37 ASE Monthly Journal and Report, June 1916, ASE Executive Committee minutes, cit Hinton, J., *The First Shop Stewards' Movement*, 1973, p 72.

38 *Daily Call*, 9 April 1915, GTC at the TUC.

39 *Daily Herald*, 28 September, 1915.

40 *Cotton Factory Times*, no date, 1915, GTC at the TUC, 501.

41 Askwith, G., *Industrial Problems and Disputes*, 1920, p 443.

42 *Solidarity*, April 1917.

43 See chapter 4.

44 Marchant, B., *A Girl Munition Worker*, undated (1918?), IWM.EMP.

45 Macassey, I., memo in BLPES, Bev., vol. 1, 15 December 1916.

46 *Dilution Bulletin*, August 1916, PRO.MUN 2.27.

47 War Office, The Employment of Women on Munitions Work, section 2, p 18.

48 Murphy, J.T., *The Workers Committee*, 1917, pp 17-18.

49 Women's Trade Union League Annual Report, 1916, pp 5-6.

50 *Woman Worker*, January 1916.

51 *Ibid.*, p 13.

52 Macarthur, M. in Phillips, M. (ed.), *Women and the Labour Party*, 1918, pp 18, 28.

53 *Workers' Union Record*, July 1915, p 15.
54 *Ibid.*, p 2.
55 *Workers' Union Record*, July 1916, p 7.
56 *Labour Gazette*, December 1917, p 438: see chapter 2 on the question of numbers employed in different trades and the historical circumstances which meant that expansion was emphasised in the first year of war, the short-term nature of the contribution after 1917.
57 Central Advisory Committee on Women's Employment, 1916 Report, IWM.EMP 20, pp 6-8.
58 *Liverpool Post*, 17 March, 1916, GTC at the TUC.
59 *Birmingham Post*, 1915, GTC at the TUC, 504.
60 GTC at the TUC, 504 (no date).
61 ORO.MUN 2.27, 12 February, cit the Health of Munition Workers Committee pamphlet, 'On the Employment of Women', the same sentiment is expressed in BLPES, Bev., vol. V, p 161.
62 Jeffreys, J.B., *The Story of the Engineers*, 1946, p 122.
63 Watson, W.F., *Men and Machines*, 1935.
64 Balfour Committee on Industry and Trade, Survey of Industries, vol. II, 1928, p 152.
65 Cole, G.D.H, *Trade Unionism and Munitions*, 1923, p 217.
66 ASE Monthly Journal and Report, April 1915.
67 *Woman Worker*, September 1918, p 8.
68 Woollacott, A., 'Professionalisation and Industrial Welfare Supervisors in World War I Britain', *Women's History Review*, 1994.

Chapter 4

Free From Chains?

The Image of Women's Labour

in London, 1900-20

The development of photography brought new visual imagery to the depiction of women's work. Historians tend to use this to ask questions about photography ('Who took this picture and why?'), but much less has been said about the effects of pictorial representations. The existing genre of photographs of working women had already helped to sustain an image of the working woman. Women had already been objectified, and their work turned into both exotica and a species of social problem in the last 20 years of the nineteenth century.[1] Photographs dramatised the sense of discovery characteristic of late-Victorian social investigation. This chapter is an attempt to assess the impact of representations of working women created before and during the First World War, representations partly created by photographs of record. It also examines the contribution of London to this image. London dominated social commentary in the early twentieth century. It was the period in which mass national newspapers began to exploit photography in the interests of campaigns for social reform, and in which technical change made portable cameras usable in all sorts of lighting conditions.

Ideas about working women in this period shifted, and visual and verbal representations of the working woman changed. The image was no longer that *some* women worked because they were poor or unsupported. It was now one in which *all* women's labour was that of the weak and defenceless. The woman worker was, paradigmatically, the sweated worker. This became the frozen image of working women perpetuated through the changes of the First World War and beyond. The persistence of this image had profound consequences for social policy, trade-union organisation, and working women's own understanding. From it followed important assumptions about wages, collective organisation and family life, assumptions which were built into legislation and practice. But before examining the production and effects of these images, the context in which they were produced must be set out by looking at the social investigations and the organisations of working women from which they came. The essay will discuss the situation of woman workers, the groups who represented them, and the two campaigning issues on which they focused: sweating and motherhood. Then the actions and representations themselves will be described and the whole drawn together around the changes of the First World War.

In the years after 1900 there developed a new form of representation of working women. These women were no longer an interesting survival of quaint, old days. They were becoming a symbol of the unacceptable present, a new cause for concern; and the most photographed objects of such concern were to be found in the capital. It was the conditions of London working women that were increasingly used as a metonym for the condition of the female working class, ignoring all local variations and considerations of the labour market. Of course imagery of the working woman was not only photographic. Although some of the great governmental analyses of female labour lay some time in the past – when women's labour had been eliminated from underground, on lead and on some night work – the demand for women's exclusion from certain trades which had prompted them remained a live issue, as did the question of the economic value of the work done by the low-paid.[2] Women continued to work with dangerous chemicals, to suffer gynaecological problems seen as arising from their employment and to excite the concern of reformers as a result.[3] The new factor in the discussion in the 1900s was the growth of women's own organisations which had begun to base themselves in London. These organisations campaigned primarily on issues of general social need to do with women as social beings, mothers and daughters, rather than upon the specific interests of workers in certain trades who happened to be women. Even in the most powerful image most people have of London women organising at the end of the nineteenth century – the match-girls at Bryant and

May and their strike in 1888 – the pictorial theme that most caught the public imagination was their piteous poverty, meagre dress, physical frailty and sheer need.[4] Here was a damning indictment of an industrial system that left women physically unprotected against lethal industrial disease and exploitation. Working women represented forces which, if magnified or accelerated, would produce social damage. This strike remained a fairly isolated image of the potential power of working women until organisations representing the woman worker came together ten or 20 years later, but it set the agenda for later struggles to organise women in industry.

The Fabian Women's Group (FWG) was the best-organised of these groups. It was small, and primarily a forum for discussion and presentation of research findings. Its members appear to have seen themselves as a propaganda body, and were, almost to a woman, London-based. They were not among the Fabian Society's small working-class membership. They were supported either by family money, as wives or daughters, or by those few middle-class professions like journalism that enabled independence from family.[5] Other groups included the Women's Industrial Council, which had some members in common with the Fabians and produced as many reports as did the FWG, as well as a campaigning journal, the *Women's Industrial News*. The women's trade-union organisations – the Women's Trade Union League (WTUL) and the National Federation of Women Workers (NFWW) – both located themselves in London (in 1903 and 1906 respectively) in the same offices and with the same administrative staff. The WTUL had been in existence for many years, but had been revitalised by the appointment, as general secretary, of Mary Macarthur, a shop-owner's daughter who had gone into trade-union work for the Shop Assistants' Union in Scotland. She was lured south by Margaret Bondfield (of the shop assistants) and Gertrude Tuckwell (president of the WTUL) to help revive women's unionism. The WTUL was supposed to encourage unionism among women in general; the NFWW was set up in 1906 by the WTUL to provide a trade union where there was no suitable union in existence, or where the existing unions did not admit women, so this was to be a general union based on sex. They too ran journals: the *Women's Trades' Union Review* (from 1891 until 1919) and the *Woman Worker* (from 1907 to 1911 and 1915 to 1920).[7] The location in London and the concentration on London's workers were not accidental. Among legislators, an increased interest in social reform was noticeable, and women workers were seen as an essential focus of that reform. Among

A young woman in engineering. The image of the woman war worker: heroic, with an immense machine under her control, alone. (Women's Work Collection, Imperial War Museum. Reproduced by permission of the Trustees of the IWM.)

Young woman and old man in a rope works. This kind of photograph, which contrasted the contributions of the woman and the man, was not used in propaganda about women's capacities.

Chain-maker, in a widely-circulated photograph, 1912.
(Reproduced from the *Daily Record* by kind permission of the Gertrude Tuckwell Collection.)

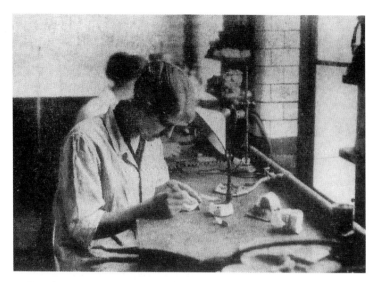

Dentists: not new work but described in those terms. (Women's Work on non-Munitions Industries, Ministry of Munitions, 1916. Reproduced by kind permission of the University Library, Cambridge.)

A group of silica workers, 1918–19. (Women's Work Collection, Imperial War Museum. Reproduced by permission of the Trustees of the IWM.)

Women workers on cranes working with large shells, one of the few groups who got equal pay because they were so visibly doing men's work – in trousers. (Reproduced by permission of the Trustees of the IWM.)

Gauging shells, 1915: a dilution picture. (Women's Work on Munitions, Ministry of Munitions, 1916. Reproduced by permission of the University Library, Cambridge.)

Women mechanics: another dilution photograph, 1915, before regulation. (Women's Work on Munitions, Ministry of Munitions, 1916. Reproduced by permission of the University Library, Cambridge.)

Shipyard – working on a propeller: the heroic woman dilutee, 1915.
(Women's Work on Munitions, Ministry of Munitions, 1916.
Reproduced by permission of the University Library, Cambridge.)

A woman stoker at the furnaces of a large South London factory: the
exotic image of women in trousers, 1915. (Women's Work in non-
Munitions Industries, Ministry of Munitions, 1916. Reproduced by
permission of the University Library, Cambridge.)

Women workers in the tailoring shops, doing work traditionally defined
as skilled men's work (although it involves sewing and is very like other
sorts of women's work) but paid at equal rates by trade union agreement.
(Women's Work Collection, Imperial War Museum. Reproduced by
permission of the Trustees of the IWM.)

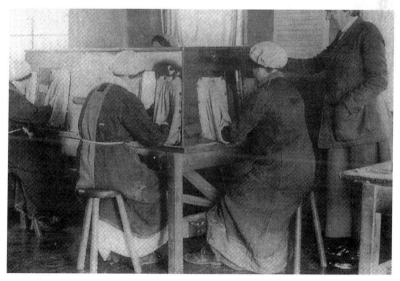

Women in the danger buildings with the welfare superintendent, Lilian
Barker. Although this was danger work, it was actually not men's work;
it had been done by women in the district before the war, so it was paid
at the women's rate. (Women's Work Collection, Imperial War Museum.
Reproduced by permission of the Trustees of the IWM.)

Left to right: Jessie Stephen, Mary Macarthur, the NFWW organizer Mrs Hewson (?), Julia Varley, at the NFWW headquarters, *c.* 1908.

women's organisations the move towards parliamentary lobbying was well under way. It was particularly aimed at sympathetic MPs capable of proposing and drafting reforms of interest to working women. These London-based organisations concentrated on legislative change more than organisation at the point of production.[8]

There were two preoccupations shared by all these organisations. The first was the campaign against sweating; the second the organisation of working women in their own defence. Sweating is best defined loosely as contemporaries defined it. It was work that did not take place in factories, that was not protected by government agencies or trade-union representation, that did not provide a living wage. It was done not only by women, nor was all women's work sweated.[9] Sweating had been identified as an evil by a variety of pressure groups in the 1880s, and the House of Lords Select Committee on Sweating had concluded that certain labour conditions usually associated with the term should be eradicated by registering outworkers and subjecting their workplaces to sanitary inspection.[10] This was ineffective because workers were not well enough organised to enforce supervision. It was thus the agitation of the industrial women's organisations that began the process of rescuing these occupations from the vicious circle of low wages and the absence of union organisation. The membership of these organisations was small, but their representatives allied with Liberal reformers and some male trade unionists to form the Anti-Sweating League (ASL). This was the major force agitating for a minimum wage, and would remove such trades from their marginal position. Its main effect was to bring the issue of low wages, especially women's low wages, before the general public.[11]

The ASL shared premises in Mecklenburgh Square with the WTUL and the NFWW, beneath the apartment of Mary Macarthur, its main organiser.[12] Macarthur had a valuable link with the editor of the Liberal *Daily News,* and it was this newspaper's sponsorship of the exhibition against sweating in 1906 that led to the forming of the league.[13] The exhibition was organised by George Shann, a paid organiser of the Workers' Union which was beginning to organise widely among sweated workers, mainly in the government sector.[14] The exhibition handbook, written by Richard Mudie-Smith, and the reprinting of photographs of exhibits in the *Daily News,* shocked polite society. Macarthur's most notable propaganda coup was a piece of detective work tracing the line of sweated workers who participated in the manufacture of baby clothes. She nearly lost her own life when one of the sweatshops turned out to be infested with diphtheria and the baby clothes by implication were thereby dangerous even to the privileged children who wore them. This piece of exposure carried ambiguous benefits for working women. It implied they were disease-ridden, carrying contagion, as well as a social problem to be deplored.[15] Other issues which were raised by the anti-sweaters tended the same way. Workers in luxury goods – tennis balls, artificial flowers, millinery, embroidery, toys – were all featured in issues of the *Women's Industrial News* as subject to sweating. Their work was attacked not only because it produced inessentials but because it damaged the women's health – and the health of society – because of the toll taken on both motherhood and on men by the lowering of male wages. Concerns over employment were often used to express wider anxieties about social health.[16] Barmaids presented one case where the state was urged to use powers or general regulatlon to deal with matters of sexuality arising from work, because barmaids were felt either to be in especial moral danger or to cause it because they were in regular contact with the temptations of both men and drink. The Women's Industrial Council devoted considerable space to a discussion on barmaids in 1910-11; it seems reasonable to surmise that some of the discussion reflected a particular concern about women whose work involved the entertainment of men. Finally, the state was called in to deal with danger to motherhood, both because of the effects of working conditions on physical health and because it affected these women's ability to look after children: women were at work, often in their own homes, when they should have been mothering.[17]

As a result of this emphasis on sweating by organisations representing women workers, sweating became a synonym for women's work. Such an equation is clear in the work of Edward Cadbury – one of his books about sweating was called *Women's Work and Wages* – but it was also implicit in the books by B.L. Hutchins and Clementina Black, *Women in Modern Industry* and *Married Women's Work*. Thus the type of investigation into women's employment that became prominent at this time implied that such employment was problematic, that it should, if possible, be altered in major structural ways, but that such changes were beyond the capacities of the sweated worker herself. Sweated workers were defenceless ones, and therefore could play little part in the eradication of the sweating system. One of the major structural changes envisaged by commentators and reformers was that the state should intervene to end sweating, by taking an active role in controlling women's work in general. This intervention was not seen as necessary for male workers, who were deemed capable of effective organisation. Gender was therefore being turned into the prime division distinguishing different groups of workers in agitation over working conditions, and to a lesser extent over maintenance of wages levels.

What part did photographs play in this emphasis upon the weakness of the sweated woman worker to resist exploitation? Arguably, their role was central because of their association with the growing power of the national press. Newspapers as well as social reform organisations were based in London. Fleet Street was taking over from the provincial press as moulders of opinion as the press proprietors began to extend centralisation. Even quite impoverished journals of the left began to use illustrative evidence. A new tie-up between journalism and the exhibition reinforced the power of photographs to underline social commentary. In a novel way, women's working lives became an exhibit, and an exhibit based almost exclusively on the experience of work in London. This was a marked feature of the catalogue of the 1906 exhibition. Novel shots of interiors dramatised a notion of revelation of the previously hidden.

The first trade boards were set up in 1909, mainly as a result of this agitation and the campaigning in Parliament of the two MPs, Sir Charles Dilke and J.J. Mallon. The trades they covered were not as exclusively London-based as the exhibition photographs and the 'sweating' literature had been; but those that were were mostly trades involving women: the paper-box trade, shirt and tailoring operations.[18] Government workers were also covered by the Fair Wages scheme of 1906, primarily those making uniforms in Pimlico (Westminster).[19] The other large groups affected by these new pieces of legislation were women chain-makers in Birmingham and others engaged in metalwork or pottery work around the Black Country.

Increasingly social reform organisations resorted to mass action to dramatise their campaign demands. Women were at the forefront of this process. One of the national demonstrations of 1908 was that for the first International Women's Day. The campaigners for the vote had learned from their Independent Labour Party (ILP) tradition to use the press, in particular by highlighting the drama of demonstrations. Women had added a touch of pageantry to many of their processions by wearing historic costume or massed 'colours', by carrying banners specially embroidered or painted for the occasion, or by singing special songs. The use of spectacle was not new, but the political emphasis on it was. Many political actions were designed solely to gain the attention of the press. The first event of this sort, the great suffrage demonstration of 1906, marked the relocation of suffrage organisations in London.[20] Industrial women participated in these events in tiny numbers, and were usually represented by Annie Kenney for the WSPU or by anonymous mill-girls in the National Union of Women's Suffrage Societies (NUWSS). In London, where they were a token presence, they were always represented by 'respectable' working girls, not the impoverished, married worker about whom the suffrage organisations were often ambiguous, frequently arguing that the vote would eradicate both married women's work and sweating.

On the other hand, trade unionists and anti-sweating organisations did parade sweated workers. The great impact of the chainmakers' agitation derived from a street demonstration of women, who forged chain by hand, carrying their chains draped about their persons. It was a profoundly disturbing image, and was backed up by photographs of their homes and workplaces; in one of these photographs was to be seen an infant's cradle, the only clue that the burly figures, lit from underneath by the light of their forges, were in fact female. The campaign struck at the heart of the ambiguity inherent in these depictions. Were these women heroines or victims? As far as trade unionists were concerned they were of course both, but the impact of their chains was one which could not lightly be overridden in trying to portray women workers as equal partners in the social and political order. The chain-makers' own arguments about their case rested upon the claim that their work needed both skill and strength, and that it was underpaid. But their representatives argued the case for a minimum rate of payment with appeals to the needs of society, the demands of social justice, and the deservingness of the women concerned. The most effective images were probably those of the sweated worker as victim.[21]

Such an emphasis continued in the period of industrial unrest and sex war, even though it was challenged by imagery of a more threatening character. In 1911-12 the East End of London was both the major area of union organisation and the major source of propaganda. The NFWW increased its membership and its public visibility in a series of strikes among jam-makers, clothing-workers, biscuit packers and other workers of the East End. Mary Macarthur used her considerable speaking powers to the limits of her strength in turning these strikers into union members.[22] By some definitions they were not, strictly speaking, sweated workers at all because they worked in factories. They were unrespectable by comparison with the previous group representations of organised women workers, because they were working-class, mothers, and militant. The imagery derived from this agitation was of the growth of the notion of female masses, women as members of a working class. It was helped along by the newsreel and brilliant manipulation of the public sphere by other women's organisations, the WSPU in particular. In the process, class tended to be emphasised. But this representation was at odds with the dominant one, and was soon to be dropped again, once war began.

Such imagery was, in any case, qualified by the renewed interest of reformers in the protection of motherhood. This interest in working mothers has been characterised as 'social imperialism', and has led to much debate among historians about, in particular, the interests.of reformers in improving the condition of the 'race'.[23] But it is clear that there was no necessary contradiction between the interests of the imperial nation and those of working women, and that women could often exploit official concern to get what they wanted. Woman's social role was increasingly defined by her potential or actual motherhood. This was especially the case for working women. The inspiration of empire was manifest in the notion of the working women of 'Darkest England',[24] a newly-explored set of social images derived from an analogy to the exploration of 'Darkest Africa'. They became an object of attention in a new way. The exhibition, photographs, and reportage were all used to render them visible, to bring the hidden to light. This sort of exploration was not new in London, but the concentration on women was. The women on whom this attention focused were those who were particularly defenceless, not only because of their work in sweated trades, but also because motherhood, rather than waged work, was seen as their vocation.

This preoccupation coincided with a ferment of self-organisation, in which women struggled to achieve representation in the state and within the trade-union movement. Trade unionists were particularly active in campaigns to protect gynaecological health: the campaign against lead was organised by the WTUL, and the interest extended to other potteries' poisons.[25] Again, the emphasis was placed upon the workers' need to rely on external protection by the extension of factory inspection and/or union organisation; both would be achieved from outside the workplace and outside the worker's social circle: indeed, for women workers, often outside their social range altogether, as the lightly fictionalised account of union organisation by Kathleen Woodward in *Jipping Street* makes clear. She believed that the social distance between workers and organisers was effectively too great to enable them to understand each other fully. (A fuller account follows in chapter 5.)[26]

The first months of war reinforced this picture of defenceless women and imperilled motherhood as a result of severe unemployment in women's trades, concern over war babies, and the sacking of domestic servants. Tiny numbers of women were aided by the Queen's Work for Women Fund set up by Queen Mary with the aid of Mary Macarthur. Macarthur railed against the extent of unpaid patriotic labour, which she called 'sister Susies sewing shirts for soldiers'.[27] Most of the women who helped here were London-based, as were many of the trades whose functions the workrooms took over. The far greater numbers of textile workers and domestic servants were unrecognised in the propaganda about female unemployment. The pictures of the unemployed typically show a small workroom environment, and this was replicated in the fund's centres. The work done in many of the workrooms was to replace previously imported goods based on luxury trades, for example, the German toy industry, artificial flowers and fur.[28] This was one way in which the war accentuated the prevailing imagery of women's employment; the other was even more influential, and more visual.

Mrs Pankhurst and Lloyd George were both shrewd users of the mass media, successful demagogues and stagers of events. Together they organised a demonstration that was part of his campaign for the leadership of the Liberal Party and thence of the Government itself, and hers for the vote. It was originally called the 'Women's Right to Work' march and became the 'Right to Serve' march. Records of discussions between the two of them in the Ministry of Munitions archive at the Public Record Office show that it was designed to attract public attention, and that it was extremely expensive to mount.[29] The aim of this unusual event was to publicise the Women's War Register, and it was extremely successful, with both major newsreels featuring it in their shows. The main impression was of an entire gender made militant, this time in pursuit of an acceptable patriotic end rather than of the interests of their sex alone. Joan of Arc and other historical figures were more prominent in the demonstration than existing women workers.[30] The intention was to emphasise the novelty and heroism of women's war service, not its continuity. The register itself was based on these notions. Women were not to be conscripted but they were to register as all men did briefly at the beginning of the war. They were to become one vast pool of labour power. They were all to sign on for war work, in order to make good labour shortages, particularly in engineering. They were not enrolled on the register according to their skill or experience, and no commitment was given on their rate of pay, hours, or conditions of work. In the eyes of trade unionists, as the 1915 TUC discussion shows, all these women were seen as potential sweated workers.[31] Either they were already sweated workers or, as domestic workers and housewives, they would know nothing about trade unionism or industrial life. The common factor of their gender was seen as inherently likely to allow them to be sweated. The demonstration accentuated this by emphasising women's detachment from industrial work as a positive qualification for such service rather than a barrier to it.

Dilution on display

The Government's pursuit of new workers to make armaments meant that the photograph came into its own as an adjunct in campaigns to convince both employers and workers that women were capable of filling the gaps in the economy. The organisation of dilution, the replacement of skilled men by semi-skilled or unskilled workers, was particularly dependent upon photographs. The War Office commissioned photographers to survey new work done by women, and published two booklets using selections of these photographs over Christmas 1915.[32] These photographs were deposited in the Imperial War Museum, in the Women's Work Collection. Some categories were not represented in the booklets. Chosen images included a larger proportion of single figures than might be expected from the overall total. Two aspects seem to be stressed in the selection: the novelty of the task (mending or making false teeth, gauging instruments, working lathes, making howitzers); or the socially unusual (getting dirty or wearing trousers). The capacity of women to undertake such work in wartime was described as though it was novel or unnatural. Although Horace Nicholls (the best of these photographers) took some striking group photographs, formal and informal, they were not reproduced in these booklets. Nor have large group scenes been much used by historians to illustrate arguments about women's work in wartime. Historians have tended to prefer the greater drama and visual effect of individuals or small groups. It was not in the Government's interest to remind employers that women were already workers, with workers' inconvenient attitudes and divisions. Women were thus pictorially characterised as novices, heroic workers motivated solely by patriotism. (Mixed in with this simple propaganda aim was also the general drama and sex appeal of young women engaged in vigorous physical activity, bound to appeal to professional image-makers at the time and particularly appealing to historians since.)[33] The 'Replace a man for the front' poster campaign similarly reduced women to units of labour, and emphasised the novelty of war work by portraying all workers as directly concerned in war production, wearing uniform. It also assumed that all workers would be doing men's work and thus replace a newly mobilised conscript or volunteer, although many women workers were in fact part of an expanded workforce, doing women's work.[34] All these images of working women tended to assume that work, like gender, was homogeneous. The only category noticeably excluded from the booklets were those shots in which the women looked regional or disorderly. London brewery workers, for example, were represented by three young, comely barrel-cleaners in trousers rather than the much larger number of skirted cockneys, arms akimbo, whom Nicholls photographed in the brewery yard.

In fact, war work was not like that at all. Not all war work was munitions work, but the effect of the organisation of dilution was to make it seem that way. Each dilution officer carried a handbook with photographs of women doing new tasks; exhibitions in each major town showed women doing these new tasks.[35] The impression conveyed to contemporaries was of a much larger amount of replacement of men than took place, and a much larger number of women new to the workforce. The focus on London added to this distortion. The paraphernalia of royal visits and of officially-sanctioned journalism all focused on London munition workers. For example, Gilbert Stone's book *Women War Workers* includes only one large group of manual workers, Arsenal girls; Hall Caine's *Our Girls* had several pages of text on the same group, and was published complete with a special page for a message, 'From one of our girls to one of our boys,' to enable Arsenal workers to use it to make direct personal contact with the front; in the Topical Budget newsreel films on women's war work it was munitions work that represented working-class women, but statistics show otherwise.[36] Women war-workers were as likely to be doing women's work as men's, and women workers were more likely to be doing work that women in general had done before. The biggest expansion was in commercial work, or in industries which had already employed women. Women did go into larger workplaces in larger numbers than before, but the photographs did not show the larger workplaces, they showed individual workers within them. (The exception here was in munitions, but this was necessarily seen as 'for the duration of war' only, and therefore emphasised the differences, rather than the continuity, of factory labour for women.) The image of women workers in wartime, then and now, is of a frail girl wrestling alone with a machine, working heroically and against her nature for the duration of war only. This added to the impression of novelty and difference that Government and employers wished to emphasise in the reports on women's labour at the end of the war, designed as they were to vindicate the effectual failure of equal pay in wartime. Working women were seen as unable to organise in their own defence and likely to accept unequal pay. This was partly implicit in the response of their own organisations, which was to increase the number of unpaid organisers on the same assumption. All women were treated like the sweated workers of the great unrest of 1910 and 1911 in the East End.

What were the effects of this potent image of the working woman on women themselves? They did not imagine their own work that way. They do not keep the heroic war pictures at all: they keep the group portraits, the souvenir programmes from the workshop canteen concerts, the war worker's badge. They stayed in London as workers and retained the distinctions with which they went into the factories.[37] But legislation and regulation had absorbed these images. The two major official documents discussing women's work, the War Cabinet Committee on Women in Industry and the Hills Committee of the Ministry of Reconstruction,[38] retained the presumption of deficiency in experience and priority of motherhood from the pre-war period. It was these assumptions that they read into the war experience rather than more specific points, for example the formidable physical strength of women railroad navvies, the technical skill of women arc-welders, or the engineering capacities of lathe workers. The London labour market had been placed on the social map of women's work, with extremely important social implications. The continuation of the older paradigm of women's organisation – outside organiser appealing on social grounds to a wider public interest – resulted in an ignorance about important changes that had taken place. Thus the 'new trades' of outer London which were increasing at the expense of the sweated work of the old female labour market went unnoticed.[39] In this process, photographs had been extremely influential because they had determined the visual image of the 'working woman' in public discourse. Far from the novelty of wartime superseding the old picture, photographs implied either that the novelty was due to war and therefore reversible, or else that there was no novelty. War workers were doing what came naturally to women; they were more women than workers, workers only during wartime.

Images influence people. The coincidence of the exploration of women's work by social investigators using the pictorial to accentuate their points with the development of concern, particularly for the welfare of Londoners, was to distort legislation by Government and organisation by labour. Women were turned into objects of public concern in ways that had profound consequences for the organisation of production. A new concentration on the needs and problems of London arising in part from the centralisation of women's own organisations, added to this distortion and increased the power of the image. It has also greatly affected the view of historians. The concentration on London for suffrage has been much criticised, and quite rightly; it overemphasises certain groups and certain strategies. A similar concentration on the woman worker in London also needs criticism. For she is as much an ideological construct as the suffragette. Large numbers of women did work in sweatshops; they did find it hard to be mothers and workers in a society which gave them little support in the process; but the emphasis of the photographs distorts historical interpretation by implying that changes in the lives of working women came solely from outside. What they erase are all those changes for the better achieved by working women at the beginning of the Welfare State as the result of their own activities – the unheroic, undepicted struggles over tea-breaks, premium bonus systems, excessive discipline at work, milk depots and health visitors' clinics – dependent on Government and social reformers, but not created by them alone.

Notes on Chapter 4

This chapter was first published as 'Free From Chains? The Image of Women's Labour in London' in Feldman, D. and Stedman Jones, G. (eds), *Metropolis London: Histories and Representations Since 1800* (1989, Routledge). I am grateful to the publishers for permission to reproduce it here.

Full details of all publications mentioned here are in the bibliography on page 209.

I Changes within photography have been very thoroughly analysed by, among others, Dyos and Wolff (eds), *The Victorian City,* 1973; Hiley, M., *Seeing Through Photographs,* 1983; Braden, S., *Committing Photography,* 1983. I am very grateful too to Angela John, whose work on pit-brow women first helped me to see photographs in a new light *(By the Sweat of Their Brow,* 1980), and whose conversation has been of great benefit. I would also like to thank Nigel Wheale, who discussed the issues. Since writing this essay the book based on the photographic collections of the Imperial War Museum and elsewhere by D. Condell and J. Liddiard, *Working for Victory? Images of Women in the First World War,* 1987, has been published, some of which bears out my arguments, and some of which I find myself arguing against.

2 Lewis, J., *Women in England,* 1984; the bibliography of contemporary sources in Vicinus, M. (ed.), *Suffer and Be Still,* 1973, pp 193-4.

3 Mess, H.A., *Factory Legislation,* 1923; Hutchins, B.L., *Women's Work in Modern Industry,* 1915; Anderson, A., *Women in the Factory,* 1922: all describe the need for Government intervention; Lewenhak, S.,*Women in Trade Unions,* 1977.

4 Stafford, A., *A Match to Fire the Thames,* 1961: it was partly publicised so well because the match-workers brought their case to Fleet Street itself to enlist the support of Annie Besant, and were taken up by campaigning newspapers.

5 The introduction by S. Alexander to a reprint of one of their pamphlets provides a good brief guide to the group: Pember Reeves, M., *Round About a Pound a Week,* 1979, first published 1911.

6 Mappen, E., *Helping Women at Work,* 1985.

7 Hamilton, M.A., *Mary Macarthur: A Biographical Sketch,* 1925; Bondfield, M., *A Life's Work,* 1951.

8 Although Mary Macarthur described herself as a Tolstoyan (Woodward, K., *Queen Mary,* 1927, p 190) she did not share any of

the syndicalist politics that the description might imply, and her 'left' politics were far more concerned with welfare than with industrial militancy. See chapter 5 in this volume; see also Webb, C., *The Woman with a Basket*, 1927. The only national organisation for working-class women not based in London was the Women's Co-operative Guild. But the Guild's main interest was in the organisation of the working-class housewife.

9   There is an extensive discussion of sweating in Schmiechen, J., *Sweated Industries and Sweated Labor*, 1984; Morris, J., 'The Characteristics of Sweating: Late-nineteenth-century London and the Tailoring Trade'; Mappen, E., 'Strategists for Change: Social Feminist Approaches to Women's Work', in John (ed.), op. cit.

10   Schmiechen, J., *Sweated Industries and Sweated Labor*, 1984, op. cit., p 140.

11   Sells, D.M., *The British Trade Board System* (1923).

12   See note 5.

13   Schmiechen, J.A., *Sweated Industries and Sweated Labor: The London Clothing Trades, 1860-1914*, 1984, p 180.

14   Hyman, R., *The Workers' Union*, 1971.

15   Cole, M., *Women of Today*, 1938, pp 109-10; Hamilton, M.A., *Mary Macarthur: A Biographical Sketch*, 1925, p 66; 'The Cry of the Woman Worker', *Penny Pictorial*, cited in *ibid*. pp 109-10.

16   Stearns, P.N., 'Victorian Working Women' in Vicinus (ed.), op. cit. Lewis, J., *Women in England*, 1984; for example, the Board of Trade inquiry into wages of 1906 and the Royal Commission on Outwork of 1907 both looked far more at women than similar inquiries of the past.

17   Lewis, J., 'The Working-class Mother and State Intervention' in Lewis, J. (ed.), *Labour and Love*, 1986, pp 99-120.

18   Sells, D.M., *The British Trade Board System*, 1923, ch. 1.

19   Colston Shepherd, E., *The Fixing of Wages on Government Employment*, 1923, pp 1-2.

20   Liddington, J. and Norris, J., *One Hand Tied behind Us*, 1978, has a good short account of differences between suffrage campaigners in the introduction; Garner, L., *Stepping Stones to Liberty*, 1984, also out-lines the differences; Mackenzie, M., *Shoulder to Shoulder*, 1975, contains examples of the demonstration and other representations of the political cause.

21   Boston, S., BBC television, 1977: programme about the chain-makers of Cradley Heath first alerted me to the powerful imagery of this strike, and her book added to this; Hamilton, M.A., *Mary Macarthur: A Biographical Sketch*, 1925, p 87.

22 Hamilton, M.A., *Mary Macarthur: A Biographical Sketch*, 1925, pp 101-7; Rowbotham, S., *Hidden from History*, 1968, cites this and first opened the question of centrality of women's unionism and Mary Macarthur to the 'new' working women of the post-war period.

23 The debate is summarised and criticised by Dwork, D., *War Is Good for Babies and Other Children*, 1986, in which she attacks Anna Davin, Jane Lewis, and Carol Dyhouse for not seeing the benevolence of reformers, and the worthwhile effects of their endeavours; it does not seem to me, as I state in the text, that there is any necessary contradiction here.

24 Stedman Jones, G., *Outcast London*, 1971; Keating, P., *Into Unknown England*, 1976.

25 See chapter 5.

26 Woodward, K., *Jipping Street*, 1928, pp 120-1.

27 *Daily Sketch*, 8 November 1915, in GTC at the TUC.

28 Interim Report of the Central Committee for Women's Employment, PP 1914-16, xxxvi, IWM Cmd 7848; Pankhurst, E.S., *The Home Front*, 1932, p 202, has descriptions of her dispute with Macarthur over the workrooms.

29 Ministry of Munitions records at the PRO.MUN 5.70.26, 11 August, 28 August 1915.

30 Topical Budget newsreel, BFI 2140A.

31 See chapter 1 and Braybon, G., *Women Workers in the First World War*, 1981, ch. 6, deals with the public image of women workers.

32 War Office, *Women's Work on Munitions and Women's Work in Non-munitions Industries*, 1916.

33 Marwick, A., *Women at War*, 1976.

34 Poster, IWM.

35 Dilution officer's handbook in my possession.

36 Thom, D., 'The Ideology of Women's Work in Britain 1914-24, with specific reference to the NFWW and other trade unions', unpublished PhD for the CNAA at Thames Polytechnic, 1982, app. 1.

37 This assertion is based on interviews with women war-workers carried out 1976-81.

38 Report of the War Cabinet Committee on Women in Industry, PP 1919, xxxi, Cmd 135; Report of the Hills Committee, 1919, xiv (the central committee on women's employment).

39 Glucksman, M., 'In a class of their own, women workers in inter-war Britain', *Feminist Review* 24, Autumn 1986.

Chapter 5
'The Bundle of Sticks': Women Trade Unionists and Collective Organisation Before 1918

It came to me that the women in the factory were too tired for the revolt urged upon them, too deeply inured to acceptance. I had no doubt as to the utter desirableness of an increase in our wages; I believed that this we could achieve by the organisation advocated by the speech-makers who came to us – if only we could have effected the necessary organisation, unity, and flank attacks. Forlorn Hope. For the women in the factory continued stonily to eye the preachers of revolt, the liberators who descended on us from unknown worlds of competence and comfort, too palpably unblemished by the experience that was ours. Yet I do not think their insufficiency proved so great an obstacle as the subscription fees to the Trade Union from women to whom even two pennies a week represented a loaf of bread that, for a time at least, would quiet a family of hungry children.[1]

Kathleen Woodward's account of women workers in Bermondsey reflects the basic facts of women's lives at work in early-twentieth-century England. Trade-union organisers who tried to improve those lives were often too distant from such women, who were too poor to pay their dues and too bowed down with family cares. The question should thus be, not why did so few organise themselves into trade unions, but why did so many, against such considerable odds? Working women's organisations of the late nineteenth century were shaped more by the interests of social reformers than by the demands of working women themselves. Trade unions would, it was hoped, prevent both exploitation and degradation, and thus improve the condition of the nation as a whole. The process of organisation did not follow in any simple way from this founding impulse. The national leaders of women in trade unions were either middle-class women or men, but that did not mean that when women first planned to join a union or keep one going they were passive recipients of the ideas and principles of others.[2] It has often been argued that the first 'take-off' for women's organisation in trade unions was the result of an unusually strong organising impulse led by one outstanding woman, Mary Macarthur.[3] In the years between the foundation of the National Federation of Women Workers (NFWW) in 1906 and the end of the First World War in 1918, women's organisation did increase both absolutely and relatively.[4] However, this increase arose from a muliplicity of factors against which the individual contribution of leaders needs to be measured. I am going to look at the organising practices, and principles, of two trade-union leaders in order to assess the contri-bution made by individuals to this union growth. In doing so I shall argue that in some respects their ideology of organising women put a brake on the women who applied to join unions, ran strikes and entered the labour market, as well as being a shaping force for women's trade unionism. The two individuals are Mary Macarthur and Julia Varley. Macarthur is well known. She was the heroine of books by Mary Agnes Hamilton, Kathleen Woodward and Barbara Drake written in the 1920s. She was middle-class by origin, and was only economically active as a union organiser, initially of shopworkers and then for the Women's Trade Union League (WTUL) and the NFWW. Varley, on the other hand, was active as a suffragette, mill worker and Poor Law Guardian, as well as a trade-union organiser for the Birmingham Trades Council, the NFWW and the Workers' Union (WU). The specific details of the growth in women's trade unionism during this period demonstrate a far more complex picture than most labour history has allowed of the woman worker and the trade union. The balance between the interests of a specific union's members and that of trade unionism as a whole was not a dilemma peculiar to women, but it was often discussed as though it was.

In looking at the nature and theories of women's collective organisation, the historians of women's trade unionism have adopted two stances. One feminist account of unionism, that by Heidi Hartman, has argued that women were both oppressed and excluded from the benefits of new occupations in time of war by male workers, particularly male workers organised in trade unions. The First World War has been seen as the period when this was most true, since women were welcomed into war work when needed and then later excluded when the Government honoured its commitment to male craft unions to 'restore pre-war practices'. This view is valid in the case of a few small specialist trade unions in wartime, particularly the Society of Women Welders, but it is not a true description of the fate of the majority of women in general unions, whether those unions were for women only, such as the NFWW, or mixed, such as the WU. Gail Braybon, in *Women Workers in the First World War*, has shown how the wartime admission of women to men's jobs was constricted, or constructed, by the needs and attitudes of male workers. I want to argue that a part of that construction was made by women, as trade-union organisers, and that its roots are to be found in the late-nineteenth-century experience of women workers. Nor does the alternative conventional explanation for the changes in women's unionism quite work. In this socialist or labourist explanation, as in the books by Sheila Lewenhak and Sarah Boston, women represent a part of the 'forward march of labour'. They are organised late, and in specific forms, because of the force with which the tradition of the past weighed on the attitudes of the present. These historians attribute success to good leadership.[5] The careers of two outstanding leaders show the processes and ideology of the organisation of women. Growth was as much to do with social change as heroic individual action. The argument is that the organisation of women was highly structured by ideological notions of the weakness of women at work and in society at large, and that in looking at such a formation, notions of patriarchy are inadequate and ignore the activities and ideas of women themselves. Women of whatever class did differ in their strategy and tactics of organisation, and this difference mattered and cannot be explained in class terms. In 1918 the historian of the Ministry of Munitions described women workers as they were seen in 1914 when their use in wartime factories was being discussed in government circles.

> Women were badly organised, prone to manipulation by employers ignorant of workshop practices, in particular defensive, restrictive practices, and content to work in lowly positions for low pay. Women did not enjoy the protection of custom, they were not organised in strong Trade Unions, nor could such organisations be built up in an emergency.[6]

Histories of Women in Trade Unions

This viewpoint could have been stated at any time in the preceding 30 years: indeed was still being stated in variant forms until the Second World War. It strikingly reveals the vicious circle that women unionists tried to break. The history of women workers was used to argue a case based on notions of what was natural and inherent in labouring wonen. Notions of trade-union organisation reflected this bifurcated vision. Discussion about trade-union organisation among women reflects, in the same way as did all general discussions about women current at that time, the belief that women are more strongly affected than men by their gender, and that this is a problem. The sources for the history of women's trade-union organisation add to the historian's problem. Biographies and autobiographies emphasise the individual contributions. Mary Macarthur was very much loved, and her biography by Mary Agnes Hamilton reflects this love; as does the shorter account by Margaret Cole. Both accounts obscure the sharper, astringent, even autocratic, woman portrayed by the oral evidence of Dorothy Elliott and Grace Robson.[7] Margaret Bondfield's biography reflects a long career in public service, in which trade unionism was an unproblematic part, compared to her unhappy experience of government. On the other hand, official or government sources have the immediacy of being recorded during or near the events they describe, so they are less able to use hindsight to construct a palatable narrative. If they record trade-union views at all they tend to be those of the leaders. They emphasise trade unions as a problem. We know far more about women's lives in factories in wartime than we do in peacetime because they were so closely scrutinised by Government agents. In the 1900s women were widely discussed because of concern for 'the race', feminist agitation and welfare politics, and a great deal is known about their public activities. The fact that the Government had not been that concerned does not mean that women had not previously been as active in the workplace as were the war workers of 1917. The records of women's organisations themselves provide a valuable contrast to official records and memoirs. Unfortunately the most important organisation – the NFWW – lost its own records on amalgamation into the General and Municipal Workers' Union (GMWU) in 1922. The Trades Union Congress houses such records of the WTUL, together with the large collection of press-cuttings, leaflets, handbills and pamphlets that are known as the

Gertrude Tuckwell Collection after the secretary of the League, built up in the course of her life's work for women's trade unionism. This source has been used for a large number of secondary works on women's trade unionism, but it too should be used with caution. It represents the interests of one woman, or one organisation, and therefore includes a large amount about the NFWW (which the WTUL set up) and a great deal about league activities in London and nearby. Its coverage of the biggest single group of women workers, and women trade unionists – workers in wool and cotton – is limited and unrepresentative.

The writings of the Fabian Women's Group (FWG), particularly those of Barbara Drake, tend to suffer from the same geographical and political limitations. Drake's book, *Women in Trade Unions,* first published in 1921, remains the best account of women's unionism. It is thorough, detailed and lucid, and makes its viewpoint explicit. It is, however, very much a work of its time. It is partly based on Drake's wartime work on *Women in the Engineering Trades* and the historical memorandum for the War Cabinet Committee on Women in Industry which reported in 1919.[8] Women had been engaged to do war work. They had demonstrated what feminists had always argued, namely that most women could do what most men could do. War work was, however, seen primarily as temporary war-service based on patriotic impulse rather than any more enduring intention to compete on equal terms with men. She therefore emphasises the overwhelming force of history and the state as the main agency of change in the face of history. It was, after all, the state, she argued, that had convinced employers of women's capacity by using travelling shows depicting women at work, displaying excellent photographs (now in the Imperial War Museum), pamphlets and all the evidence gathered by dilution officers. The other main component in Drake's analysis was the assumption common to many in the Fabian tradition of familial feminism: women were inhibited by biology and the social order from certain activities, and potential or actual motherhood was their main function. As Drake said in her evidence to the Atkins committee, as a representative of the Fabian Women's Group, 'The residue of women would provide a margin of labour for periods of good trade. If either sex is to be short of employment it had better be the women.'[9]

Suffrage

There was an alternative to the tradition which placed a woman firmly in the family as her primary sphere of operations. In such an analysis, women were united by their sex and oppressed by men, who excluded them from political power by withholding the vote. Both suffragettes and suffragists organised independently from men, although both included men as supporters. Feminist historians have recently begun to rediscover the vitality and variety of suffrage organisation at the local level, as well as to look at men's share. The same vigour and difference is noticeable in looking at trade unionism in any women's trade. The two were not integrally related. Women were divided by class, region and occupation more than they were united by gender, except in a very few areas of suffrage movements. Julia Varley's early life campaigning for women's suffrage with her sister in Bradford was distinctly separate from her life as a union organiser in the Black Country. In an individual career the one might well lead to the other, but far fewer women went from suffrage to trade unionism than the other way round. The lessons of such an experience, whether direct and personal or not, were learned and expressed. Julia Varley's feminism was explicitly directed at working-class women, working women:

> 'We work shoulder to shoulder with the men in the mills and in the councils of the workers; why should they deny us the right to help to choose the men who make the laws that govern the workers... Our motto is "Rise up, Women" and the battle-cry, "Now!"'[10]

The first half of this statement is characteristic, while the second is conventional, echoing the Pankhursts, since Varley worked closely with Sylvia Pankhurst at this time.[11] She argued that working-class women particularly needed the rights of a citizen from which they were excluded by their lack of the vote, because they were especially in need of legal protection. Mary Macarthur, who supported the Adult Suffrage Association (as did Margaret Bondfield), thereby expressed her view that the vote was a class matter, since to demand the vote for all adults was to demand it for excluded men as well as women.[12]

The other strand in the theory and motive force of trade-union organisation among women was the Anti-Sweating Campaign. Macarthur was particularly closely associated with the London campaign, and was given frequent access to the Liberal *Daily News* at periods when she was not editing the *Women Worker* for the federation. In 1906 the *Daily News* had organised an exhibition of sweated industries in which women had worked at their sweated trades in order to educate the public in what it meant to sew shirts, make nails at paper-boxes and so on. It also produced some vividly expressive photographs, reproduced in the handbook to the exhibition, which sold widely. The Anti-Sweating League which resulted was a powerful force for change; Macarthur sat on its executive after 1906.[13]

Julia Varley

Julia Varley's return to trade unionism in adult life after her early experience as a textile workers' representative came through association with an anti-sweating organisation. She was invited to Birmingham by Edward Cadbury in 1909 after she had successfully organised the chain-makers of Cradley Heath into the NFWW in 1907. She was employed by the Birmingham Committee for the Organisation of Women as secretary, sat on the Trades Council, and was a member of its executive committee. She successfully organised card-box-makers, bakery workers and chain-makers, as a member and organiser for the NFWW. Cadbury wrote the book on sweating that exposed the working and living conditions of sweated workers and argued that the concept involved no moral description of the workers themselves but 'was a material condition caused by income inadequate for basic expenditure'.[14] Cadbury's argument about the need for organisation among women to compensate for the disadvantages of being a woman worker in Edwardian Britain smuggled back the notion of the inherent incapacity of women to defend themselves properly for social reasons:

> The competition between the inefficient, unmarried girls, the wife whose husband is out of work or drunken or dissolute, and whose children must have food, and the widow who also has many mouths to feed, plays into the hands of the unscrupulous employer.[15]

Varley was the most explicit exponent of a theory of organisation based on the defencelessness implicit in the description 'sweated' when she described democracy in the inspirational words of her Chartist great-grandfather:

When you grow up you'll know what the word means and then you will work for the people, think for the people and live for the people – for they don't know how to do it for themselves.[16]

Varley and Macarthur were both pragmatists.

Mary Macarthur

Macarthur's biographer pointed out that she was not an intellectual and did not claim to be one. Like Varley she had a facile pen and a powerful speaking presence. Mary Macarthur's use of the homely metaphor of the bundle of sticks illustrates the style which she adopted in *The Woman Worker* and in her leaflets. Macarthur's picture is explicitly defensive. One stick can be broken, a bundle cannot:

> A Trade Union is like a bundle of sticks. The workers are bound together and have the strength of unity. No employer can do as he likes with them. They have the power of resistance. They can ask for an advance without fear.[17]

Later she wrote of girls who do not join, 'They are not only selfish they are short-sighted'. It is a personal, direct approach, arguing that women have a duty to society to organise in unions. She described her power over meetings to Arthur Salter when she gave an account of an angry speech she made to the girls of a North London factory after their employer had refused their wage rise: 'I suddenly realised,' she told me, 'that if I didn't at once stop them they would tear him limb from limb'.[18]

Julia Varley did not have that power or – it would seem, reading the accounts – the charm of Macarthur, but she had force and wit, as well as a quick tongue. She often told an anecdote about marriage in which she explained that she had not seen many advertisements for the married state in the course of her career, and instanced the woman in the casual ward, where people stayed for up to three nights at a time, when she was 'on the tramp' – the term used for walking in search of work – who told her how to deal with a husband: 'Always go for his nose with something sharp, my dear'.[19]

Organisation

Neither woman wrote any systematic statement of beliefs and principles, but both expressed a consistent set of attitudes which can be used to understand the different trajectories they took. Julia Varley moved trade unions after 1912. She left the NFWW, and her work for the Birmingham Committee, and became women's organiser in Birmingham for the WU, that union's first women's organiser. She described her decision in the union's journal:

> Believing that where women work with men they should be organised in the same Union, she finds the Workers' Union more fully in accord with those ideas, and when her work under the voluntary committee came to a close she had little difficulty in accepting the position our Union had to offer.[20]

In some respects there was no major change in Varley's activities. She had been organising men and women together as a member of the Trades Council Executive and as a supporter of the anti-sweating movement. The NFWW had been founded because women had got in touch with the WTUL in order to join a union, but had found that either the union in their trade did not admit women or that there was in fact no union in that trade. It had not been founded on any feminist principle. When Macarthur negotiated the transfer of the federation into the General and Municipal Workers' Union (GMWU) – a mixed general union – in 1924, she said that she had always intended such a merger.[21] She did argue, however, together with her organisers, that it was both more successful, and right, to organise women as women in women's branches using women organisers. There had already been the occasional conflict of interest between the two unions, since they were attempting to organise in the same occupational and geographical areas at a time of labour unrest. There is no record of any quarrel, but the WU account of the transfer strongly implies that there was one, as does the hint of bitterness in relations between Varley and the federation thereafter. It is certain that the WU did begin to have a sizeable women's membership and that much of the growth in membership among women was in Varley's area.[22] The federation did suffer from a lack of internal democracy, as Dorothy Elliott agreed when looking back in 1975. In 1913 a Miss Hedges attempted to challenge the leadership on these grounds but failed. (By 1918 the membership carried a motion giving greater powers to shop stewards on the same grounds.) But in this case Varley remained sufficiently friendly with the Federation to take Miss Hedges's place at the TUC in 1913.[23] There was no simple division between the two organisers or their organisations based on a different conception of men and women. They shared the same view. The difference lay in their understanding of the processes of organisation. It did not even appear significant until 1913, but a year later, at the onset of war, the differences in organisational theory were to prove crucial to war workers. Since the experience of Macarthur and Varley and the other trade-union organisers of the war years had been gained from the principles and practice of the ten years preceding the war, it was this, added to the theory of nineteenth-century unionism, that was then most influential, rather than the war experience.

Sex War?

In July 1914, a month before war was declared, Mary Macarthur wrote (in a series of articles entitled 'Women's Discontent'):

> I am most concerned with the industrial unrest among women, and I don't think it is any sense a sex unrest; it is merely that the general industrial unrest is now being shared by women.[24]

The industrial unrest of the years 1907-14 has been described by historians as the 'great unrest'. In parts of the country it was in fact unrest among women, for example in London and the Black Country.[25] Women did join unions in greater numbers than before, they went on strike more frequently, they were more often to be seen on the public platforms of the labour movement. But it is not true to say that this was women catching up with men. There were specifically female characteristics to the unrest. Women were more likely to take strike action, they used suffrage tactics of propaganda and demonstration, and produced many leaflets, songs, postcards, ribbons and badges to publicise their struggles. Women were much more likely to attempt a public display of their conditions of work and their grievances, possibly because of the legitimation given to their demands by both feminism and the advocates of improvements for the nation's mothers. Contemporaries saw and wrote of a sex war; some women felt that that was what they were urging. Macarthur did not, but she was mistaken in denying its existence.

The 'sex war' in industry resulted in, as well as accompanying, a general expansion in union membership. Women's trade union membership expanded greatly in the years before the war. The problem of describing this growth is demonstrated by the table of trade-union membership (see Table 6.1, page 140).

Union membership

Women were under-recorded in two ways. The first is that women's employment was generally under-recorded in employment statistics. Their work did not count as 'occupied'; they did not choose to let officials know (as Ellen Smith noted in her survey for the FWG of 1915); their employers did not wish officials to know (in the case of women returning early after having children for example); it was likely to be seasonal, tennis-ball-making, for example.[26] Their union affiliations, for some of the same reasons, may have been limited by time and place. Of perhaps even greater importance, women's work fell into some categories in which union organisation, despite all attempts, was almost impossible, pre-eminently domestic service, in which one third of all occupied women were employed. If one excludes from the potential membership all domestic servants, the figures for union density might be a more accurate representation of the expectations of union organisers. There were also, of course, reasons for general labour unrest which, added to women's campaigns, gave powerful impetus to unionisation. The context for a general growth in trade unionism was an economy in which real wages fell, high unemployment in some trades and increased production in consumer trades. There was also widespread discussion of the rights and duties of the individual and of the state as both Labour and Liberals demanded old-age pensions, unemployment insurance and provision for infants and children in the interests of the state. Working women, particularly mothers, found or placed themselves in the middle of the political discussions of a highly political period.[27] One of the specific causes of the growth in women's unionism was the development of the trade boards system. The trade boards had been set up to prevent sweating as both a moral and an economic evil. The main effect of the imposition of a trade board was the development of a list of minimum wages organised by task but also by the age and sex of the worker. The trades of the first boards were mainly women's trades, but they also included occupations which were effectively organised on the family lines of early capitalist enterprise. They were nearly all to be found in major conurbations, as many of these trades had developed around the finishing processes so that the small employers who predominated could be near their outlets in both retail and wholesale trade. The shirt-making processes were in London while the chain-makers who supplied the engineering trade were to be found in the Midlands. These trades also depended on the existence of surplus labour. Margins of profit were slight and trade fluctuated. As a result, they tended not to be found in areas of steady, respectable, artisan employment for men where a part of male respectability was based on a non-working wife. An example of the contrast in local trade-union organisation could be found between Plumstead and Charlton in South-East London. In the latter, the work for men was seasonal casual labour, housing was poor and overcrowded, and large numbers of women were engaged in a variety of 'sweated' occupations: making tennis-balls for Slazenger, working in the Wood Street shirt factory, gut-scraping in Deptford, or doing other smelly, unpleasant, arduous work on 'food processing' elsewhere in South or East London. In Plumstead, with the rate of owner-occupation and artisan work amongst the highest in London, few women worked, very few at sweated occupations.[28] Any trade-union organisation had to recognise the specificity of the female labour market and the domestic surroundings of work described as sweated if it were to succeed in the difficult task of organising in any new trade. In women's trades there was the added problem of the social aspiration of any women's movement at a time of such intense activity. In 1909 the first Boards were set up for tailoring (ready-made and bespoke), paper-box-making, lace-making, and chain-making. In 1913 those for embroidery, hollow-ware, shirt- and tin-box-making, sugar confectionery and food processing were added. The definition which made a trade liable to the imposition of a board was that the wages were 'exceptionally low compared with those in other employments'.[29] The effect does appear to have been to raise women's wages from an extremely low average to a low one.[30]

Were the trade boards, as Gertrude Tuckwell argued, the basis for the growth in women's trade unionism, or were they a product of it? They were, of course, both, but it was as a component in the ideology of organisation that I wish to argue that they were important, representing as they did the culmination of a set of demands current in women's unionism since the 1890s, when Sir Charles and Lady Dilke first attempted to improve both the wages and conditions of work to stop the raising of 'our industrial structure above an abyss of inefficiency and misery'.[31] The campaign for the trade boards increased the emphasis in women's unionism on the need to make demands on the state. Although women did tend to a syndicalist style in agitation and organisation, they did not follow a syndicalist politics, that is organise to achieve socialism at the point of production rather than through political parties. The absence of women from the literature of British syndicalism is not an omission deriving from partriarchal attitudes, but the representation of their absence in fact. There was a real disjunction between the needs and demands of women from the working class at that time and those of syndicalist men. Syndicalism was most successful in heavy industry, single-occupation areas which were also areas of heavy domestic work for women and little paid work outside the home. Organisation at the point of production excluded women who did not work at the face in the mines or in the docks, where syndicalism was strongest. Women's agitation was directed at a state which they felt could provide the reforms they desired: infant welfare centres, family allowances, the reform of the poor law. Women in paid employment tended to want more intervention, not less, in the form of factory inspection, wages legislation and the limiting of hours of work.

There was a similar distance from the systematic rejection of legality by some suffragette groups. Trade unionists shared the demand for representation, but did not thereby reject the state as an agent of change. They were reformists, however much Macarthur chose to shock polite society by describing herself as a 'Tolstoyan'. As Julia Varley said at the end of her long life, 'God has enabled me to live to see the fruits of my labours – a joy denied to most reformists'.[32] The trade board route to improvement in the condition of women in industry was emphatically not one that challenged the social and political order; it was one which asked for women's participation in it. A second effect was to emphasise the mediating role of trade-union officials. Trade boards had an equal number of representatives of employers and employees. Worker representatives often sat on several trade boards as representatives of the workers in the trade in the same general union. There had to be a woman representative on a board for a trade in which the majority of the workers were women, so the small number of women officials sat on several boards at once. Mary Macarthur, Susan Lawrence, Margaret Bondfield and Gertrude Tuckwell all sat on boards. They met in London fairly frequently, and this excluded many other activists. Their role was to negotiate wage minima in the light of the state of the trade and general conditions of wages. The minima thereby established quickly became maxima. The women who sat on the trade boards, and in wartime on the arbitration tribunals and other negotiating bodies set up for war work for women, were those who had education and negotiating experience. They were the women who were least likely to have direct personal experience of work in the trades they represented. The class difference between men and women trade-union officials was noticeable in the case of Macarthur, Lawrence and Tuckwell; it did not exist in the case of Varley or Bondfield. It remained true that the most public representatives of working women were not, and had not been, working women themselves, and that representation on the boards accentuated this phenomenon. The final contribution of the trade boards to the nineteenth-century image of working women was the persistent belief that low wages were a permanent feature of women's work. The wage-scales established in protected trades were much higher than their previously shameful levels, since that was the justification for the existence of a board in the first place. But they remained relatively low within the trade, and in general when compared with men's wages. They remained at about half the male average, and the board perpetuated this relationship. Beatrice Webb tartly remarked in her minority report, 'Women in Industry' (1919), that there was nothing logical or rational about this ratio, but that the only way to abandon it would be to pay for the job done rather than to pay the worker who did it. As contemporary commentators pointed out, women's low wages were based on the assumption that the wage was secondary to a main breadwinner's contribution. They argued against this assumption that it was the least-well-paid women who were most likely to have no other support, because they were able only to take work that could fit in with family commitments. The solution advocated by Clementina Black in *Married Women's Work*, Mrs B.L. Hutchins in *Women in Modern Industry* and Edward Cadbury in *Women's Work and Wages* was double-pronged.[33] First it was for union organisation among working women, to prevent employers paying low wages; secondly it was for state support for motherhood and wages, to remove the weakest competitors from the industrial struggle. There was no challenge to this notion of motherhood as primary, even if these authors did argue that the 'good mother' could be the one who worked out of the home.

Women, family and workplace

The implications of this set of attitudes for trade-union organisation were direct. Women tended to be perceived by their familial role before any other description of them was made. Oral evidence shows how much family relationships did in fact influence union affiliation. Joanna Bornat has argued that women's work relationships can only be properly understood by relating them to family connections.[34] However, with so few women belonging to unions for any length of time, family tradition tended to go from fathers to daughters rather than mothers. Union members are often described as girls, as though they were young, and speeches of trade-union organisers to their members tend to be as from older to younger women. Julia Varley was quoted (a long time after she made the speech) as convincing factory workers thus:

> I can't understand you women. You used to walk around the fields of Bournville with the lads and they'd whisper sweet nothings in your ears and tell you if you'd only marry them they would make heaven for you. And what sort of heaven have you got? A seventeen-and-tenpenny one – eighteen bob a week and twopence off for the hospital.[35]

There were many other examples of such speeches, but rarely did they get made to male workers. Women were seen as particularly concerned with, and related to, their households. Their industrial demands were perceived in a domestic context; industrial organisation was often argued in general, almost sociological terms, as if women should take on the wider social burdens as well as their own immediate material needs. Trade-union organisation was also their way of meeting male objections to their being in the workforce at all. Lady Dilke argued this in a pamphlet for the WTUL in 1891 in a neat summation of the argument:

> Once women are brought within the rates of the callings that they seek to pursue, the just objection to and fear of their labour felt by men will disappear, and not only so but the whole social position of women themselves will be advanced.[36]

Women were also expected to improve the moral tone of industry. This could lead to exclusionary policies being argued in the name of the greater good of society. A delegate from the postmen's union argued for the 'wholesale prohibition of married women's labour' at the 1909 Labour Party conference on the grounds that 'the woman is the greatest humanising factor we possess'.[37] In arguing that women's work contributed to civilisation, trade-union organisers had to be careful not to allow their role as improvers of society to conflict with their role as representatives of the existing women workers. More immediately, practical problems added to the ideological loading of the concept of womanhood. Women were particularly difficult to organise, suffering from such major deficiencies as workers as to be secondary in organisational terms as well as in employment. To argue, as did the union organisers, that there was more urgency in dealing with the weakest was not to undercut the argument, merely to restate it. Women did have a dual burden of domestic work in the home and paid work outside it. Evening meetings were difficult to organise and often unsuccessful: any account of a working woman's day shows how the evening was often used for sewing, baking, pressing and cleaning, with little time for rest or reading, let alone two hours sitting listening to speakers. The best procedure was to organise on the job or at the factory gates, but although this was also true of men (except in the craft unions), it was generally attributed to women's lack of motivation rather than to lack of time.

Strikes

Many women participated in the 'great unrest' of 1910 and 1911. At its peak in London, in the summer of 1911, Mary Macarthur organised some 2,000 women in the course of 20 concurrent strikes. The process was generally that the women struck and the union then intervened to negotiate for them, and so won negotiation rights. Macarthur argued that this was a demonstration of the power of unions to control their members, a clear instance of unions as mediators rather than agents of struggle.

> A strike of unorganised workers should always be utilised to form a trade union amongst them. In such cases one is frequently able to point out that had an organisation existed, the strike in all probability would not have occurred, because the employer would not so confidently have ventured to assail the rights of Trade Union workers. It is quite a mistaken idea that strikes are caused by Trade Unions.[38]

Macarthur did, however, accept the reverse, although her officers denied it, not liking to associate with striking even as an agent of organisation. Mrs Hewson wrote, 'She did not believe in strikes which were very bad things, but when she talked to some of the girls the only thing they knew of trade unionism was strikes'.[39] Gertrude Tuckwell also argued that trade unions prevented strikes. She approved the result in a Christian Socialist pamphlet on the organisation of women: 'Again and again strikes have been averted by the power of bargaining that combination gives'.[40] Organisation was advocated to remove women's weakness and dependence but some argued that women needed to take on their own affairs on a permanent basis if that power was to be maintained. Margaret Bondfield saw this lack of persistence, or of experience, as the central difficulty among these new women members:

> The problem was a lack of continuity of membership, and it is a notable fact that a large part of the membership [of the NFWW] was built up as its organisers came to the help of unorganised groups of strikers.[41]

Barbara Drake wrote of this period ten years later, in her history of women in trade unions, as if it was characteristic of women as a sex to depend on outsiders, or figures of authority to do their bargaining for them. She did argue that the experience of striking should be seen as educational, so that the use of the strike weapon should not be regarded as evidence of inherent instability among women workers.

> Women learn very slowly the fact that their union is inside and does not consist of an organiser outside. They undertake no duties of shop-stewards and seldom interview the firm or manager but call in the organiser in every difficulty. To get women to take up these duties with any enthusiasm they must go through a strike and lose their fear.[42]

She was here quoting an unnamed organiser who was probably reporting on war workers who were mostly new to the type of work-place and associated organisation in which they found themselves. As was often the case, what was as much to do with inexperience was attributed to gender. It is almost impossible to detach the expectations of the organisers from the practices of the organisation they undertook. What we can do is see how far what people thought they were doing determined what they did do.

Chain-makers

Paradoxically, the greatest successes of the women's trade unions, the campaigns against sweating, were later to confine them most. In particular, the organisation of the chain-makers added such weight to a general picture of the waged work that women did, that in wartime, when their labour was in demand, they were organised as if it was still subject to the same constraints as the sweated labour of peacetime. The chain-maker's strike is a distillation of women's trade unionism at the period. It displays its magnificence and its deformation by the way it posited women's need for protection as the dominant force in the agitation. Women chain-makers at Cradley Heath struck in 1911 over the employers' attempt to evade the provision of the trade board. The strike was organised by Julia Varley with Charles Sitch. She appealed to them as women, and helped to orchestrate the public campaign that emphasised womanhood in chains.

> We went in and out of the forges, talking to the women as they hammered away, awakening their consciousness to their responsibilities; appealing to their pride and their motherhood.[43]

> At the end of the agitation I had about twenty women between the ages of sixty and ninety parading the streets with necklaces of the chains they had made, and the words, 'Britain's disgrace, 1d an hour!'[44]

Women in chains appeared at demonstrations, on public platforms, in dramatic woodcuts, on song-sheets and in some very effective, though less emotional, photographs which are still at the TUC. It was a powerful visual image of the servitude of the industrial woman, a servitude from which she was released by the benign intervention of the state, mediated by trade unions. Women were exhorted to organise, to act for the general good, for their own good only in their role as mothers.

Organising women

The ideology of woman as sweated worker, defenceless, in need of protection, was reinforced by the organisational practices of women's unions. They tended to rely more on organisers – paid or voluntary helpers from outside – than on elected officials. This was a circular argument often used against the organisation of women. It was seen as making them more expensive to organise but less 'worthwhile' because they contributed less from their low wages in union dues. Will Thorne told Mrs Hutchins that he did not think women should be organised because he said, 'They do not make good trade unionists'.[45] Despite the slightly contradictory association of women and insurrectionary behaviour in strikes, women were thought to be less capable of self-activity. Women did stay less time in jobs than men in some trades; they did remain in unions for a shorter period. Contemporaries described women as 'meantime workers', in work until marriage, and therefore interested only in the short-term benefits of work. The unions themselves often encouraged this view. The NFWW, for example, paid a marriage benefit to members on leaving their employment; its organisers regularly left their jobs on marriage. But not all did and Mary Macarthur made little change in her domestic life when she married, since she continued to live above the office of the WTUL and NFWW. Marriage and the career of a union organiser were rarely combined, and the personal cost was enormous, but such a counter-example was impressive, and was seen as such.

Low wages tended to lead to a similar difference in organisation among women unionists. Dues collection was important to all unions, but it was the single most regular contact most members had with the union at all. Oral evidence indicates that women, far more than men, continued to contribute their wages to a family pool, leaving less money under personal control. Many women also had regular commitments to clothing and shoe clubs, whereby a group of friends or workmates could pool slender resources for large purchases. Many branches reported difficulty with dues collection in the *Woman Worker*, the paper that Macarthur founded and edited for the federation from 1907 to 1908, and revived in 1916. The solution was to develop organisation by using someone on the job, the shop steward. Women's unions were using shop stewards in the decade before the war without the anti-leadership implications of the office often described in the case of the skilled men's unions.[46] There were implications involving the power and experience women could develop by performing this role. Oral evidence indicates that shop stewards were often the older, married women who had the authority to collect money and the experience to speak formally with management. The few local disputes recorded in the press that took place in organised shops (that is not to obtain recognition) were over shop stewards. There were distinct maternalistic overtones to workshop organisation among women. Margaret Bondfield exhorted a meeting of the Women's Co-operative Guild (WCG): 'Every mother should get her girl a union card'.[47] The principle of organisation was one of protection, of help for the weak rather than of self-activity, but that many of the leaders and their philanthropic supporters felt this way about their organisations did not mean that their members saw themselves in the same way.

There was certainly disagreement within organisations about both tactics and organisation as well as pay.[48] One union, for example, split over the question of organisation: the National Union of Boot and Shoe Operatives (NUBSO). The woman who remained in the NUBSO, Mary Bell, continued to believe in women officials for women members, but also believed in industrial unionism. She addressed a meeting thus:

> Men might think they could organise women but they could not do it as well as women. (Laughter.) Girls would be more frank about conditions in the factory than they would be with men. Women and men ought to be summoned to joint branch meetings so that the women could be educated in unionism.[49]

Women were excluded from some unions as they had always been. In 1918, one union excluded them for the first time. When the National Union of Railwaymen was formed, from several unions, it included the Amalgamated Society of Railway Servants (which had organised women). It then excluded these members on the grounds that 'although a woman might be a railway "servant"... she was not a railwayman and therefore ruled out by the title of the new body'.[50] Reorganisation could as easily mean the removal of women from a union in this way as it could the extension of their organisation. It was against this sort of disregard, or Will Thorne's view that women were not good trade unionists, that the women's trade-union leaders set their face.

The aim to demonstrate that women were as good trade unionists as any man increasingly tended to dominate the direction of the NFWW and WTUL. Hence their policies were tailored to the dominant voice in trade unionism, the craft unions, particularly the Amalgamated Society of Engineers (ASE) and the boilermakers. Those who saw the future for women as lying with general unions took a different line on pay and on organisation. The division was clearest in the war, but it was already evident before then. Julia

Varley's activities in the Black Country had led to a surge of activity in the engineering shops of the Black Country and a great growth of union membership in 1912 and 1913. The WU negotiated a general wages agreement with the employers' federation which raised the basic rate for all workers but, relative to previous wages, it was almost doubled for women. It was not, however, the rate for certain jobs that the ASE wanted, and it was scorned by both the ASE and the NFWW who regarded it as selling the pass to the employer for the sake of negotiating rights. The ASE was particularly angry because recent bitter battles within the union over local autonomy had meant their control over engineering processes had been slackened. In the context of a general growth in union membership for women, the question of which interest within trade unionism they should ally with became crucial. That women would act in unity with others was not questioned. Women were participating in a move towards unionisation in all types of occupations and union settings: co-operative workers, women working on poisons in chemist shops, printing workers. The separate women's unions merely articulated the position more clearly, and tended to stand in as representative of all women workers. The change in the working woman's perception of herself, and her capacity to organise in defence of her own interests was not fully recognised until the war, but in fact that change was revealed, and diverted and delayed, by war rather than created by it. Mrs Fawcett still saw women in industry with nineteenth-century spectacles when she wrote in 1918, 'The war revolutionised the industrial position of women. It found them serfs and left them free'.[51]

War

War did not find women serfs. They were already emancipating themselves by organisation and agitation. Nor did it leave them free. In the context of trade unionism, the war severely restricted the field of operation of women's unions and helped to institutionalise a position for women in trade unions that presumed their inadequacies in the labour market and in self-organisation. Women's initial reaction to war ensured that this was built in from the start. War caused unemployment for women as people reduced consumption and war cut off both supplies and markets.[52] Women's position as the disposable part of the workforce had never seemed more apparent; their defencelessness never more evident. There was also a moral panic associated with troop embarkation which added force to the speeches of people who argued that unemployed women should be provided for.[53] Mary Macarthur was particularly prominent in the campaign to provide for unemployed women. She was secretary for the Queen's Work for Women Fund which ran workrooms for the unemployed. Sylvia Pankhurst protested to Macarthur about the wages in the workrooms and the fact that they would neither train women nor compete with private manufacture; she argued that they were effectively sweating women to keep them off the streets and out of trouble. The workrooms did attempt to retrain women in domestic skills, and they were given second-hand clothes to remake for their children, or orange crates to make into cradles if their hands were 'too rough to hold the needle'.[54] Pankhurst appeared to think in her account of the meeting that Macarthur had been corrupted by mixing with royalty, but Pankhurst's account of the problem in her journal and memoir of the war is itself corrupted by her own self-advancement as someone who truly spoke for the working-class woman: Macarthur was exploiting royalty, but royalty was quite keen to exploit Macarthur too.[55] Macarthur did have an industrial motive. She was anxious to prevent women becoming what some male trade unionists had always said they were, desperate competitors in the industrial struggle who had neither the experience nor the organisations behind them to prevent them accepting low wages and thereby reducing everyone's wages and conditions of work. By 1915 the need for more armaments had changed the labour market utterly. Women had begun to demand the right to participate in the war effort. The women's War Register was set up, and women who wished to do war work encouraged to record their desire to serve.[56] Women were thereby reduced to units of labour power and all differences of experience, training or skill submerged in their gender. The fact that women who replaced men as dilutees (doing the work of a skilled man) would get equal pay was not discussed with the representatives of women at all: 'this was not in itself unreasonable as the women at the time had no *locus standi* in the matter'.[57] The agreement made was one for the men in the interests of the men but it was accepted, even policed, by the NFWW, which came to an agreement with the ASE that if the ASE would help them organise, they would be the union for women war-workers, and would withdraw their members from such work so that the men could have their jobs back. The WU, on the other hand, made no such commitment, on the grounds that they would not be the same jobs, that the women were as good as the men and deserved to be judged on the work not their gender.

The difference between the two principles of organisation showed in the way unions carried out their work. All took on organisers, but the NFWW had nearly 200 women, mostly unpaid volunteers, to the Workers' Union's 20 women. For example, the two unions competed hotly in the Woolwich Arsenal for the 27,000 munitions workers there. The NFWW employed Dorothy Elliott to work for the union as a part of her social work diploma at the LSE. She hardly went into the Arsenal, never sat on the shop stewards' committee and did not hold branch meetings. She was very dependent on her shop stewards, and they organised the two big demonstrations involving women in 1917 and 1918. Mary Macarthur, Margaret Bondfield and Susan Lawrence came down to speak, but did so at meetings organised jointly with the ASE. The WU organiser, Florence Pilbrow, relied less on big-name speakers, and certainly did not ring up her union general secretary at home as Dorothy Elliott was encouraged to do. She said she was left pretty much to do what she liked.[58] The implications of this organisational inertia are ambiguous. The WU did have meetings, many of which were socially directed, and the advertising for members emphasised the social side: 'All the handsome boys and all the beautiful girls are joining the WU'.[59] On the other hand such activity could be said to reflect a belief that these members were temporary ones, only there for wartime and therefore not to be taken, nor encouraged to take themselves, very seriously. Within the factory it does not appear to have made very much difference to which union (if any) women belonged. They demonstrated a formidable strength in the face of poor conditions, unequal pay and exacting supervision. Protest often borrowed the language of trade unionism but was as likely to be settled by union officers as by management. Two other factors accentuated the social work aspects of trade unionism for women. The first was the increase in the amount of welfare provision, for munitions workers in particular. 'No word is more hated by the women worker than welfare,' said Mary Macarthur. 'They object to being done good to'.[60] Yet many women did not object to welfare provision at all: they found it more salient to their working lives than their trade union. The competition for the workers' allegiance could result in the union becoming more like a welfare organisation, concerned with every aspect of its members' lives.

The second factor was the growth in arbitration. Wartime bans on striking meant that other means of dealing with disputes had to be found, and the experience of the trade boards provided a valuable basis for the special arbitration tribunal (for women) which dealt with increasing protests from women who realised that they were not getting equal earnings at all, and certainly not getting the equal rates for the job that the Government had promised. Mary Macarthur sat on most of the important committees of the Ministry of Munitions, the Labour Party and the TUC. She was increasingly seen as the voice of all women workers. As G.D.H. Cole commented, her views were not shared by all women workers or all trade unionists, but she did represent the dominant trend in British women's trade unionism.[61]

When the war was over

Arbitration procedure, union recognition and membership all melted away at the end of the war, however. The NFWW did talk bravely of 'old faces in new places', but they lost members even more dramatically than other general unions as their war-members were forced out of industry altogether. Macarthur said, 'The new world looks uncommonly like the old one rolling along as stupidly and blindly as ever, and all it has got from the war is an extra bitterness or two'.[62] War was the culmination of a long process by which women's union organisation was to compensate both for women's weakness at the workplace and society's inadequacies in dealing with motherhood. Women were seen as especially vulnerable not only because of their inexperience but also because of their short life in the workforce, their lack of commitment to work and their docility. Those who organised women in trade unions did so in order to prevent wider social evils, to provide British society with a model of female co-operation. Class differences between organisers and organised were most crucial in this respect: they tended to lead to too much direction from on high or too little democracy below. Women never gained the experience they needed to rise through their union organisation to the top from an occupational base within their trade. The social aims of unionism dominated the occupational ones. The relationship to male unionists varied widely, but the two main strategies, independent organisation as in the NFWW or general, mixed unions, as in the WU, both recognised the need to overcome male reluctance to allow women any place in trade unionism at all. To win that recognition, Mary Macarthur was prepared to accept the exclusion of her members from their war work, and even to enforce it. Julia Varley was not. The difference in principle was not that great, the difference in leadership style was, but ultimately it made little difference to the large numbers of women who joined trade unions in the period, developed shop stewards' organisations, struck for more pay and campaigned for mothers' pensions and maternity allowances within the trade-union movement. They were not the victims of employers or male trade unionists at all; they did not generally accept the description of themselves that their leaders were attempting to undercut. The chain-makers, the munitions workers, the Cornish clay workers' wives demonstrated that the help of a Julia Varley was invaluable in presenting their case to the rest of the world, but that the case itself was one that they organised and stated. Their leaders were far more inhibited by the history of previous campaigns and by their experience of the difficulties of organisation than they were.

The history of women's collective organisation has been dominated by the history of its leaders, and thence by their ideology of the weakness of working women. More work needs to be done on the way in which that organisation worked at a local level for us to make any sense of what it meant to be member of a trade union, and that must mean more use of the recollections of participants. For too long women have been the stage army of history, particularly labour history. We need less of seeing them as others saw them, more of seeing them as they saw themselves.

Notes on Chapter 5

This chapter first appeared in ed. John, A, *Unequal Opportunities*, (Blackwell, Oxford, 1986). I am grateful to the publishers and editor for permission to reproduce it here.

Full details of all publications mentioned here are in the bibliography on page 209.

1   Woodward, Kathleen, *Jipping Street*, 1983, pp 12-13.
2   Boone, Gladys, *The Women's Trade Union Leagues in Great Britain and the United States of America*, 1942; Miller Jacoby, R., 'Feminism and Class Consciousness in the British and American Women's Trade

Union Leagues, 1890-1925' in Carroll, B.A. (ed.), *Liberating Women's History,* 1976.

3   Hamilton, M.A., *Mary Macarthur,* 1925, for example; Lewenhak, S., *Women in Trade Unions,* 1977, following Drake, B., *Women in Trade Unions,* 1921.

4   Drake, B., *Women in Trade Unions,* 1921, table 1 (folded in at back).

5   Hartmann, H., 'Capitalism, Patriarchy and the Case for Job Segregation by Sex' in Eisenstein, Z. (ed.), *Capitalist Patriarchy and the Case for Socialist Feminism,* 1980; Braybon, G., *Women Workers in the First World War,* 1981.

6   *Official History of the Ministry of Munitions, A History of State Manufacture,* vol. iv, PRO, part L, p 57.

7   Thom, D., interview, Dorothy Jones, 1975; as Dorothy Elliott, she was an organiser for the NFWW and then an official in the GMWU when the federation merged with it; Thom, D., interview, Grace Robson, 1980.

8   Drake, B., *Women in the Engineering Trades,* 1917; Report of the War Cabinet Committee on Women in Industry, PP 1919, XXXI, Cmd 135.

9   Minutes of evidence to the War Cabinet Committee, PP 1919, Cmd 167; evidence of the Fabian Women's Group.

10 *Bradford Daily Argus,* 15 February 1907, DJV 6.

11 Obituary by George Horwill (though Sylvia Pankhurst does not mention her in her history of the suffragette movement).

12 Biographies by M.A. Hamilton.

13 Mudie-Smith, R. (ed.), *Sweated Industries: Being a Handbook of the 'Daily News' Exhibition* vol. 2, 1906, p 256.

14 Cadbury, E. and Shann, G., *Sweating,* 1907.

15 Cadbury, E., Matheson, H.C. and Shann, G., *Women's Work and Wages,* 1906, p 283.

16 DJV 6, *Daily Herald,* 23 May 1915.

17 Leaflet, GTC at the TUC; Hamilton, M.A., *Mary Macarthur,* 1925, p 40.

18 Salter, A., *Slave of the Lamp,* 1957, also cited in *DLB,* vol. 2, p 246.

19 See note 15; also cited in *DLB,* vol. 5, p 217.

20 *Workers' Union Record,* July 1914, p 7.

21 Thom, D., interview, Dorothy Jones, 1975.

22 Hyman, R., *The Workers' Union,* 1971.

23 GTC at the TUC 357 (i), no date but seems to be 1913.

24 *Daily Graphic,* 2 July 1914, GTC at the TUC 604.

25 Olcott, T., 'Dead Centre: The Women's Trade Union Movement in London, 1874-1914', *The London Journal,* vol. 2, 1 (May 1976).

26 Hutchins, B.L., *Women in Modern Industry*, 1915; Smith, E., *Wage-earning Women and Their Dependants*, 1915.

27 Cadbury, E. and Shann, G., *Sweating*, 1907; Hutchins, B.L., *Women in Modern Industry*, 1915.

28 See chapter 7.

29 Sells, D., *The British Trade Boards System*, 1923, p 2.

30 *Ibid.*, p 79.

31 Tuckwell, Gertrude, *A Short Life of Sir Charles Dilke*, 1925, p 13.

32 Woodward, K., *Queen Mary*, 1927, p 190; DJV 6, *TGWU Record*, December 1951.

33 Black, C., *Mamed Women's Work*, 1915, repub. 1983: see essay 8; Lewis, J., 'Labour and Love' in Lewis, J., *Women's Experience*, 1986.

34 Bornat, J., 'Home and Work: A New Context for Trade Union History', *Oral History*, vol. 5, 2 (Autumn 1977).

35 DJV 7, *Bournville Works Magazine*, June 1951, p 180.

36 Lady Dilke, 'Trade Unionism Among Women', pamphlet, 1891, GTC at the TUC 506.

37 *Reynolds News*, 25 April 1909, GTC at the TUC.

38 Drake, B., *Women in Trade Unions*, 1920, p 46.

39 *Morning News*, 27 March 1914, GTC at the TUC.

40 IWM.EMP viii, 471.

41 Bondfield, M., *A Life's Work*, 1951, p 58.

42 Drake, B., *Women in the Engineering Trades*, 1917, p 129.

43 *Railway Service Journal*, November 1921, DJV 6, p 145.

44 *TGWU Record*, December 1951, DJV 6.

45 Letter, Thorne to Hutchins, 30 March 1910, BLPES, Webb TU Collection.

46 Hinton, J., *The First Shop Stewards' Movement*, 1973; Cole, G.D.H., *Workshop Organisation*, 1923.

47 *Woolwich Pioneer*, 5 May 1916.

48 Drake, B., *Women in Trade Unions*, 1921, p 50.

49 *Ibid.*, pp 62-3; Fox, A., *A History of the NUBSO*, 1958, pp 312-3; *Daily Citizen*, 5 June 1914, GTC at the TUC.

50 *Evening News*, 8 June 1914, GTC at the TUC. This goes completely unremarked in the history of the NUR when the amalgamation is described in Bagwell, P., *The Railwaymen* vol. 1, 1963, p 330, though it is mentioned later, p 357.

51 Fawcett, M.G., *The Women's Victory and After*, 1920, p 106.

52 Chapman, S.D., 'War and the Cotton Trade', pamphlet, 1915, pp 8-9.

53 Fabian Women's Group, 'The War, Women and Unemployment', pamphlet, 1915.

54 Interim Report of the Women's Employment Commission, PP 1914-16, v.XXXVIII, Cmd. 7848, p11; Hamilton, M.A., *Mary Macarthur*, 1925, p 138.

55 Minute books of the ELFS, 1915, Pankhurst Collection, doc. 27; Pankhurst, E.S., *The Home Front*, 1932.

56 PRO.MUN 5.70.26, 11 August 1915, 28 August 1915.

57 Mary Macarthur in Drake, B., *Women in the Engineering Trades*, 1917, pp 111-12.

58 I am very grateful to Richard Hyman for the chance to see his notes on the interview with Mrs Pilbrow and other information from his thesis on the Workers' Union.

59 Advertisement, 1917, *Woolwich Pioneer*, several issues.

60 Transcripts of evidence to the War Cabinet Committee on Women in Industry, 4 October 1918, evidence of Mary Macarthur, IWM, pp 10-11; Thom, D., 'The Ideology of Women's Work in Britain 1914-24, with specific reference to the NFWW and other trade unions', unpublished PhD, ch. 6, has more details on this.

61 Mary Macarthur in Drake, B., *Women in the Engineering Trades*, 1917, p 109.

62 *West Sussex Gazette*, 11 December 1919, GTC at the TUC 324A.

Chapter 6

TNT Poisoning and the Employment of Women Workers in the First World War

with Antonia Ineson

At the end of the First World War, a new role was proposed for medicine, a role which arose from the experience of dealing with poisoning and toxic jaundice among shell-filling factory workers using tri-nitro-toluene, TNT. An article in the *British Medical Journal (BMJ)* described the wartime history of jaundice as 'an object lesson showing the grounds on which scientific medicine should be based in the future'. Observation and experiment, in the laboratory using animals and in medical practice using people, was to be the foundation of the new medicine.

> The medicine of the future will attain that perfect advancement and full knowledge which all desire by the association of the physician and the scientific worker, not only in the laboratory, but also at the bedside.[1]

The Health of Munition Workers Committee and medical staff at the Ministry of Munitions added the factory to the list. The new practice would encompass an alliance between doctors and factory managers grounded in the experience of the war. The success of the special work of the factory medical service, together with the help given by research during the war opened up a new field for co-operation between medical science and the factory management of the future.[2] In this chapter, we examine the response to TNT poisoning among filling-factory workers. About 50,000 workers were employed on filling at a time, and 100,000 during the course of the war. The vast majority of them were women. The role of medicine was very far from the image of scientific advance outlined above. TNT poisoning, in common with other aspects of munitions production during the war, was the site for a struggle for control. What was unusual was the extent to which medical and managerial interests became clearly combined. The responses to poisoning can be divided into two groups. One, originating with those organising the production of filled shells, included medical, technological and managerial responses. The other comprised trade-union action and individual or group responses among those working with TNT. The notion of what TNT poisoning consisted of was articulated through a wide variety of experiences, those of the people who became ill on the one hand, and of the efforts of factory managers and the Ministry of Munitions to organise and control the filling of shells on the other. The medical view of TNT poisoning cannot be separated from the incorporation of factory doctors into the management of filling factories, or from a laboratory research programme with the over-riding aim of efficient shell production.

Shell-filling using TNT was established on a large scale for the first time in the war. Previously, almost all filling had been done at Woolwich Arsenal, although a small amount for export was done elsewhere. TNT was being introduced to replace other explosives in the pre-war years, partly because it was thought to be less toxic than dinitrobenzene, and was less explosive than lyddite. At the beginning of the war, filling was carried out almost entirely manually. The work was physically hard, repetitious, and there was a constant danger and fear of explosion. The workers were subject to strict rules of behaviour, in addition to the new systems of management being introduced in munitions work in the war. The Ministry of Munitions described the work as particularly suitable for women, as they were not seen as minding its unskilled, monotonous and dead-end nature: it suited their temperament.[3] The ministry soon recognised that shell-filling was far more dangerous to the workers' health than any other munitions employment, but there was an almost-total lack of attention paid to the coincidence of a concentration of women workers with a singularly dangerous task. The connection between TNT and deaths from toxic jaundice reported among filling-factory workers in 1915 was quickly made, largely because of similarities with the action of other industrial poisons. Dinitrobenzene, used in the dyeing and explosives industries, had been known to be linked with toxic jaundice for some years, and tetrachlorethane, a constituent of aeroplane dope, was similarly linked with jaundice soon after the beginning of the war. Toxic jaundice was made a notifiable disease as a result of the dope case in January 1916. By this time, public knowledge of the effects of working with TNT was proving a problem for the ministry. Workers were refusing to take jobs in filling factories, those already employed were becoming 'disorganised through fear of contact,' and levels of absence from work on grounds of sickness were said to be high.[4]

The medical investigation of TNT

Some action had to be taken if the production of shells was to be kept up. The result was a combination of managerial and medical solutions to the problem. The Health of Munition Workers Committee, which covered all munitions work, issued a memorandum entitled *Special Industrial Diseases* in February 1916, including a section on TNT poisoning. The Ministry of Munitions produced regulations in September of the same year. Sir George Newman, as chairman of the Health of Munition Workers Committee, inspected women TNT workers at Woolwich Arsenal in July 1916, and found a high level of illness. 37% of the women experienced what he described as 'severe pains below the xiphisternum, associated with loss of appetite, nausea and constipation,' and 25% had dermatitis, 36% suffered from depression, 8% from irritability, and 34% experienced some change in menstruation.[5] In the following month, Christopher Addison, then Minister of Munitions, called a meeting of representatives of all departments of the ministry concerned with TNT, and a TNT Advisory Committee was appointed in October. Members included people from the Medical Research Committee, various sections of the Ministry, the Factory Department of the Home Office, and the Health of Munition Workers Committee. The TNT Advisory Committee produced a new set of regulations in February 1917, and issued recommendations on the duties of factory medical officers, the use of respirators and so on. These were largely based on research set up by the Medical Research Committee (MRC), which had begun a series of experiments of the absorption of TNT in August 1915. The TNT Advisory Committee discussed reducing the contact between workers and the poison by alternating employment on TNT with so-called clean work, mechanisation of filling, the use of respirators and other protective clothing, and exhaust ventilation of the atmosphere in factories.[6] It is extremely difficult to estimate the extent to which the recommendations and regulations on work with TNT were actually carried out, or the degree to which they were responsible for the reduction in deaths from TNT poisoning due to toxic jaundice in 1917 and 1918. Certainly the number of deaths did fall – from 52 in 1916 to 44 in 1917 and lower in 1918 – but it is arguable that this was not the result of the medical attempt to investigate and combat the disease, but of greater general public knowledge about the dangers of TNT.[7] However, this was not because people had been told directly. From 1916, information about the effects of working with TNT was censored in both public newspapers and in the medical press. The results of inquests could only be published in a brief, standard form because, it was argued, recruitment of labour should not be hampered.[8] The reports of medical research also had to pass the Press Bureau censorship, and this limitation seems to have been accepted without any objections from the medical profession. The aim was clearly to maintain the state of ignorance in which, according to the Chief Medical Officer of the ministry, munition workers began TNT work.[9] Factory doctors and those involved in managing the munitions factories accepted that the prime necessity was to produce shells as efficiently as possible. The effects of this on the nature and direction of the medical investigation of TNT poisoning were clear. Doctors concentrated on distinguishing between symptoms of poisoning which did or did not develop into toxic jaundice and possible death.

It was assumed that work with TNT was likely to lead to illness of some degree; the point was to keep those workers whose lives were not endangered filling shells and to remove the early cases of toxic jaundice. However, this was by no means a straightforward task. The list of early effects of work on TNT was long: it included drowsiness, frontal headache, eczema, dermatitis, loss of appetite, gastritis, constipation, cyanosis, shortness of breath, vomiting, anaemia, palpitation, yellow or orange staining of the skin and hair, depression and a metallic taste in the mouth. Attempts were made to divide this list into categories: for instance, two medical officers working among women filling-factory workers suggested, in an August 1916 issue of the *Lancet*, that there was one group of irritative symptoms which might lead, in time, to toxic symptoms.[10] Some of the effects were said to be positively or negatively correlated with the susceptibility of the workers to toxic jaundice. Dermatitis was said to be inversely related to poisoning of other kinds, due to variations in the ease of passage of TNT through the skin and into the blood, for instance.[11] The relationship between 'serious' and 'minor' effects remained unclear throughout the war; it was claimed by the Medical Research Committee that the reduction of deaths was evidence of the reduction in illness, and various ratios of one to the other were proposed.[12] Once the number of deaths had begun to fall, increasing attention was paid to the economic effects of 'minor' illness. Linked with this attempt to distinguish between serious, or life-threatening, and minor, or irritating, symptoms was the belief that certain people 'have an idiosyncrasy towards toxic absorption'.[13] This was the basis for the official guidelines issued by the Ministry of Munitions on TNT work, and many proposals were made by doctors as to the characteristics of the so-called 'susceptibles'. The latter included the young and the old, those who had gastric or liver illness, alcoholics, people with syphilis, those who sweated a lot, the malnourished and the over-fatigued, a long list which must have included most of the filling-factory workers. The ideal aim was to be able to identify and exclude 'susceptibles' at a pre-employment screening by the factory doctor, at the same time as establishing that the worker was in an adequately healthy state for the job. However, no reliable means of identifying 'susceptibles' was found, although eye colour and general health were used. The other function of this inspection was to identify existing illness, not necessarily, or even usually, for treatment, or to exclude the person from work, but often so that the illness could not be used to claim compensation as being caused by exposure to TNT.[14] The factory doctor was supposed to have no curative role. An MRC report published in 1921 concluded that 'It has been suggested at different times that alcohol, syphilis, adenoids, obesity and bad feeding are predisposing causes, but no evidence is available pointing in any of these directions'.[15]

The Health of Munition Workers Committee agreed, but continued to support the importance of some individual characteristic being responsible in the 'Final Report':

> The few affected are not always those who, owing to ill-health or malnutrition might be expected to be especially liable. Industrial conditions, though important, have perhaps less influence than personal idiosyncrasy.[16]

Once workers had been accepted for munitions work, factory doctors, appointed by the Ministry of Munitions, were supposed to carry out regular checks on TNT workers, and to withdraw poisoning sufferers from work. The problem was to differentiate between those who were in danger of becoming 'seriously' ill with toxic jaundice, and those who were merely suffering from 'minor' effects. In September 1916 a TNT 'facies' was described, as typical of those who should be removed from work:

> ... a pale face lacking in expression and like anaemia but peculiar in itself, lips that can hardly be described as cyanosed but of an ashen blue colour, similar gums, and perhaps a faint trace of yellow on the conjunctivae, the rest of the skin showing no icterus.[17]

The same writer later stressed that it was important that the doctor should observe people at work:

> The excitement of going to see the doctor – over which at present a great deal of munition time is wasted – tones up the patient and disguises the symptoms. The best way is to steal round the workshops.[18]

The worker's own experience of ill-health had little or no place in the diagnosis of early poisoning. No questions were to be asked. An article in the *Lancet* in 1916 claimed that even among those already affected, 'the history given by a patient is often very misleading. Many of the workers have no idea as to the nature of the substance upon which they are working.'[19] Medical examinations wasted time which could be devoted to shell-filling, some argued, but others stressed their importance in reassuring workers that care was being taken of them.

Allied to the problem of the definition of the seriously ill was the exclusion of some effects of TNT from medical consideration at all. The most obvious example was the yellow staining of skin and hair, which was of concern to the people affected, but to doctors was simply a sign that the person worked with TNT. The effect on menstruation, mentioned by Newman early in the war, was not studied in any of the later research. Although it would be impossible (and is probably undesirable) to attempt retrospective diagnosis, it seems quite clear from accounts by women workers that they experienced much more general slight illness than could be suggested by the level of reports of toxic jaundice as a notifiable disease. Proposed treatments of TNT poisoning (if jaundice was not present) consisted of some variant of bed rest, a milk diet, and keeping the bowels open. Jaundiced patients were to be given alkali-producing drugs, linseed and mustard poultices for the liver, and rectal and intravenous saline injections. It was generally admitted, however, that the prognosis was poor and that the treatment was not based on any great understanding of the condition. The medical workers said that even if the person survived, their health was likely to be permanently damaged.[20] The factory medical officers were not only responsible for inspections of workers before and during employment, but were also able to advise managers on working techniques from the point of view of health. They were supposed to be seen by workers as being responsible for protecting them against poisoning. The importance of limiting doctors' activities, and of ensuring their allegiance to management was recognised by the TNT Advisory Committee at its first meeting in 1916: 'Doctors should be paid by the Factory Managements, otherwise the highest factor in the authority of the Management would be removed'. The doctor had to balance losing 'a few lives in the manufacture of TNT' with the importance of maintaining the supply of shells.

If ten percent of the workers at a factory were knocked off because they were susceptible, there would be such a panic that the factory would probably lose its labour.

> Of 200 people recently engaged for Perivale Factory, only 21 came in when they found it was a filling factory. Leeds factory was already losing its labour at the rate of 200 a week. [Doctors] should work hand in glove with the management, and should not pull a single girl out, except with the consent and approval of the Factory Management. Panic should be stopped by convincing the operatives that the Ministry had 'got the thing under control'.[21]

The doctors' function was to remove workers who were particularly likely to die, as long as there were not too many of them, and to deal with deaths, post-mortems and compensation. In the latter case, the point was to reduce payment for 'unnecessary' compensation claims by excluding other causes of death at post-mortem, and to give evidence at the inquest 'as to the precautions taken in the factory to protect the workers'.[22] There are few records of the details of compensation cases, but in one example which does exist, the doctor changed his diagnosis from TNT poisoning to pneumonia once the man had died; a letter to the doctor from the staff superintendent at Chilwell, where the man had worked, suggested:

Perhaps your certificate (of TNT poisoning) was only tentative. You will readily appreciate of course that we imply no criticism whatever of your care of the patient, but this question of TNT poisoning is one of national importance and that is why we labour this point of diagnosis.[23]

Factory medical officers, therefore, acted as medical administrators governing the passage of workers in and out of contact with TNT, according to certain preconceptions about the nature of the action of TNT and about the relative importance of the health of workers and the production of shells. Their work was supported and informed by more basic research, mainly carried out from August 1915 by a group headed by Dr Benjamin Moore of the Applied Physiology section of the Medical Research Committee. This work was intended to elucidate the route of entry of TNT to the body, and from the start was closely linked with decisions about the use of protective clothing (such as gloves, aprons and boots), respirators and exhaust ventilation. Tests for the detection of TNT poisoning were developed, and systems of alternation of employment proposed. This example of the co-ordination of laboratory research with clinical medicine and factory management was coloured by the stress on maintaining output, if necessary, at the cost of the health of the individual. Moore was a major supporter of the theory that individual idiosyncrasy lay behind TNT poisoning, and claimed that, if enough workers were screened, exposed to TNT and selected according to their reaction, a naturally resistant workforce would result through the 'industrial selection of the fittest'.[24] The connection between the scientific research and the development of new techniques of working was close, although the major change from hand-filling to machine-filling of shells took place under the impetus of increased production rather than reduced contact between worker and TNT. Medical support for the use of respirators, for example, was privately admitted to rest on dubious evidence but publicly stressed as part of the workers' own responsibility for protecting themselves from poisoning.

Factory management

A similar alliance of doctors and management lay behind organisational changes in shell-filling: alternation of employment on and off TNT work was partly based on Moore's work, and could be controlled by factory doctors. It could also be controlled, unofficially, by women themselves, who were, for once, in a situation where their labour was in demand. Their attitude to their work in general, and their willingness to keep working on filling, affected their control over poisoning more than their beliefs about the dangers of TNT. Did munition workers in fact ignore TNT poisoning as an issue? They experienced it in the context of the first mass mobilisation for warfare in Britain which included women, and their involvement in war work was characterised as ancillary to male fighters. The slogans of recruitment posters added to 'Do Your Bit' the slogan 'Replace a Man for the Front'.[25] Male munition workers were released for combatant service as soon as they could be replaced by women or boys. Munitions work was perhaps the women's war work *par excellence*, and this has confused the records of the experience – so much so that there are no adequate contemporary figures for the relative distribution of substituted and diluted workers, since the interests involved in the compilation of such statistics were heavily loaded in defining the nature of the work, or the definition itself was subject to much negotiation. (A substitute replaces a man directly, doing the same work; a dilutee replaces a skilled man and does the same job but often has the work rearranged or uses adapted machinery). It is clear, though, that the majority of women on TNT were working in jobs newly created for war, and only extant for the duration; the majority were employed in government filling factories (only operational 1916-1918) and, therefore, on new jobs with largely female workforces, in areas of the country previously unindustrialised.

TNT workers

Most TNT workers were apparently new to industry, the majority from domestic service or agriculture (unlike women engineering workers).[26] They entered a new style of production that had been designed to accommodate inexperienced workers. Reorganisation of the work process involved increasing repetition. Payment systems were devised to keep output high and rising. Piecework and fellowship piecework contributed substantially to increasing the amount and speed of production, and therefore the risks in volume use of a highly toxic substance.[27] The initial protection of women workers was to prevent explosion, and involved clean and dirty sides in workrooms, the donning of overalls, overshoes and caps, body-searches to prevent forbidden matches or cigarettes entering the factory, and the removal of all personal jewellery.[28] All these had an effect on the worker's consciousness of self and notion of her role as industrial worker, as unit of production.

Factory welfare

By 1916, when TNT had become established as the major explosive in British armaments, the welfare system had been set up by the Ministry of Munitions, which ran the government factories and assisted the management in controlled factories. Welfare was originally aimed at women and the young, both for external reasons, concerned with their social role, and internal, as part of the management of production. The dominant motive was to keep the level of output rising. As the Gretna factory-unit welfare supervisor summarised it, 'The welfare of the women operatives was considered by the Ministry and factory management as second only to the production of cordite'.[29] The worker on TNT found herself with two main agencies through which she could deal with TNT poisoning. One was the welfare system, the other workers' organisations: locally this meant the trade union. Despite the high degree of centralisation in the Ministry of Munitions and the persuasive argument of the official history of the ministry (that their welfare system was an all-covering umbrella for war workers), recent evidence makes plain a wide variety of welfare procedures. In some places, the welfare supervisor was well established, highly visible, and supported by management, for example at the Royal Arsenal at Woolwich. In others, welfare supervisors were barely tolerated by management, ignored by most workers and unknown to many, for example at Armstrong Whitworth in Newcastle. They were most effective in government factories where workers lived and worked in the same place, but this is not always true as a contrast between North Wales and Gretna shows.[30] In general, welfare systems did not gain support from workers in all their activities: supervision outside the factory was condemned, body-screening resented and education classes unattended. Canteens and washrooms were popular, as were football clubs, dances and choral societies. The supervision of TNT workers to prevent poisoning seems to have been seen as an activity in which welfare supervisors were interested, or for which they were responsible, not as an occasion for the self-activity of women workers. TNT poisoning met with very little organised or spontaneous resistance. Why was this?

One reason might have been the mutual suspicion of workers' organisations and welfare supervisors. Mary Macarthur, secretary of the National Federation of Women Workers (NFWW) and ex-secretary of the Women's Trade Union League (WTUL), was the leading speaker for women's trade unionism. Her union and other general unions enrolling women grew hugely between 1915 and 1919. She said at a conference on welfare in 1918 that among women workers 'there is no word more hated than welfare'.[31] The Health of Munition Workers Committee issued emphatic instructions to welfare supervisors that they were part of management, neither workers' representatives nor antagonists of trade unionism. This could, and did, happen. The Armstrong-Whitworth unit welfare supervisor reported that welfare supervisors:

> ... appeared to the workers in the light of spies who were going to watch and report to management... or as goody-goody people who were going to poke their noses into the workers' private affairs and interfere with their liberty and independence.[32]

However, workers themselves often used the welfare system to express individual grievances. Several welfare supervisors reported excessive dependence by workers; one recorded frequent demands for wage-packet interpretation. Welfare workers at the lowest levels, the supervisors who gave medical checks, and the foremen who supervised the cloakrooms and did body-searches, would have been best placed to monitor severe deterioration in individual health. In practice, it was left to illness to make the point – welfare workers concerned themselves most closely with good time-keeping. Unexplained absence from work or excess lateness could be caused by illness – and often it was not until the poisoning had made the worker so ill that she felt unable to work that it was detected.

Yet other factors in wartime affected women's time-keeping too: badly-organised food supplies meant two-hour queues in 1917; there were shortages of soap and coal, so washing was hard; transport was overloaded and slow; there were few childcare facilities. Welfare did provide a rough-and-ready safety-net for the severely ill, but it did not do so in any consultation with the worker herself. This was a blunt instrument for dealing with TNT poisoning. In its management-led interest in the worker's health, the welfare system reflected the views of women's organisations. The latter distrusted welfare's attempts to replace trade unionism, but sought the same generalised protection for women's health as did the philanthropists who had developed welfare before the war. They exchanged personnel: both Isobel Sloan and Madeline Symons moved from the NFWW to goverment service. Trade unionists agitated for the protection of women's health in the interests of their central 'national service', motherhood. A speaker at the 1919 TUC summed up the demand for mother's pensions thus:

> If we have got to have an A1 nation we must protect the mothers. I honestly believe that the institution of pensions for mothers would go a long way towards checking the race suicide that is now going on.[33]

The language of fitness categories in military enlistment was transposed to the nation, and the rhetoric of degeneration was used to emphasise the demand. Race is here used as a synonym for nation.

Lead

It is not simply that trade unions did not agitate over industrial disease, or poisoning. Lead poisoning had been the source of disquiet for many years; after a successful campaign it was made notifiable; and a special sub-committee of the WTUL had been created to monitor its use, and any associated rise in the incidence of poisoning. Lead poisoning was taken very seriously, and attempts made in wartime to put women back into lead processes scrutinised.[34] The only explanation which seems plausible is that lead was known to be not only a killer but a major agent in gynaecological disorders and malfunction in childbearing. It was also not specific to war production.

A comparison between lead poisoning cases and TNT demonstrates the difference in severity in cases for women and men, although of course the history of lead meant that 'cases' were more likely to be recognised and recorded while TNT poisoning did not necessarily lead to toxic jaundice.[35]

Table 6.1 **Incidence of toxic jaundice**

Year	Men Cases	Men Deaths	Women Cases	Women Deaths
1916	48	23	122	34
1917	45	2	145	42
1918	7	2	27	8

Table 6.2 Incidence of lead poisoning

Year	Men Cases	Men Deaths	Women Cases	Women Deaths
1916	318	20	30	1
1917	272	19	45	2
1918	124	19	20	0

Why did lead, less likely to cause death, lead to intense public agitation while TNT did not? The publications of the women's trade unions were silent on TNT, except in two individual cases. They did protest about another toxic substance, aeroplane dope, which could cause death by accident through drowsiness as much as through jaundice. In 1917, dope was made safer by the removal of tetrachlorathane, its most toxic ingredient.[36] TNT could not thus be rendered harmless. Trade-union representatives did use TNT poisoning in argument in discussions at the Ministry of Munitions, but it was mostly raised as an example of the increased exploitation of women as an argument that they deserved war bonuses or wage rises. Nationally, they did not speak out on TNT poisoning at all, as far as can be seen in the trade-union press. Locally, of course, it was different. Again, though, TNT was used as a general example of the need for better wages and conditions for war workers, not as a cause of major negotiations in its own right; in one incident, Addison wrote in his diary:

> I had to admonish a deputation from the Federation of Women Workers this afternoon. They have been holding meetings in Coventry. One of their speakers, of an inventive turn of mind, has been giving a lurid account of the dangers of TNT saying, *inter alia*, that all their inside organs would turn yellow and that they would not be able to have children, etc.[37]

When seven women refused to return to work on amatol (a compound containing TNT) in 1917 they were prosecuted at an industrial tribunal and fined 15 shillings each. 'We are not labour conscripts,' they said. The NFWW commented cautiously in the *Woman Worker,* 'We do not recommend our members to refuse work on explosives'.[38] This fine, and many others for infringements of safety rules, was paid by communal whip-round. It demonstrates the new self-confidence among women workers, a new articulacy about their rights that was notable in wartime; these represented a general refusal to allow militarisation of industry. But women's trade unions owed much of their purchase on government to their power to discipline their own members. To agitate against TNT in any wholesale way would have been perceived as agitating against women's war work itself, logically plausible after the pacifist statements of 1914 but technically impossible after 1915 and their acceptance of dilution on terms dictated by the trade unions of skilled men.

Reactions among women munition workers

Oral evidence displays an ambivalent view among workers. Lack of written record should not be taken as lack of concern. The women who were yellow found the yellowing unpleasant. Some cafes would not serve munition workers, who added discoloration to the already low status of 'factory girl', supposedly rough and ill-mannered, and now instantly detectable. One interview describes officers in a first-class railway carriage looking at her, 'as if we were insects'. Another of her fellow-workers said, 'They used just to frown on the big factory because we were all yellow you see'.[39] One said very poignantly:

> They called us canaries you know, but it wasn't nice like that, it was a horrible sickly green colour. My boys said, they wouldn't kiss me goodnight... 'Oh mother, we don't like to see you green'.[40]

Yet none of the interviewees recorded fright at the prospect of TNT poisoning, only of accidents. The one worker who suffered any ill-effects from TNT resented not being allowed back on the work.[41] Another said she'd had TNT poisoning, but described work on cordite, which she had chewed, and had believed had had severe gynaecological effects.[42]

This unconcern may reflect ignorance. The first deaths from TNT were given some public notice, although they were not publicised, but they were few; they could be seen as exceptional and blamed on the idiosyncrasy of the individuals concerned. In 1916, when most died, the information was suppressed. By 1917, though, in some factories regular checks were given, and each girl had half a pint of milk a day, which indicated to the workers that Government was concerned about the problem, as did discipline over the use of gloves and respirators. One of the women who had refused to work on amatol in 1917 said that she had a further grievance, that she should have been given a mask since 'doctors had argued against respirators, gloves and veils for CE work since they resulted in more dermatitis than without'.[43] These women were aware of the correct procedures, and that management was not following them, but this perception did not result in any more generalised attempt to convey information to other workers; or any attempt to enlist others in the same cause. Evidence from interviews shows much greater fear of accident, particularly explosions, and greater experience of accident. The interview sample had some accidents: two broken legs and one broken arm because of bad lighting and poor workplace safety. One woman saw three severe accidents: one severed arm, one scalping, one crushed hand.[44] Accidents were quick, sudden and directly attributable to work; death from toxic jaundice was often slow and usually did not occur in public. But TNT was more complex an issue than even this contrast would imply.

The dominant notion in assessing perceptions of TNT work was the relation between war work and war service. Mrs Pankhurst changed the name of her march in 1915 demanding a Women's War Register from 'Right to Work' to 'Right to Serve', or so the discussion at the Ministry of Munitions would imply; certainly the posters and the newsreel caption emphasise war service.[45] Women's work fell into the service category pre-war; women on explosives wore uniform; they enlisted for war service. The deaths from TNT were recorded on a 'roll of honour' so that death from an industrial disease was translated into a death on active service.[46] Several interviewees commented spontaneously, 'We didn't go through what the men did at the Front'. They certainly saw then and say now that the odds were very uneven: life expectancy at the front was six weeks for much of 1915 and 1917. The ratio of dead to survivors of men on active military service was 1 to 7.5; while, as far as can be calculated, 0.1 per cent of women TNT workers died. (The figure is a difficult one to ascertain because people moved around a great deal, and may therefore have been counted several times in any tally of the numbers of women on specific war tasks.)[47] The contrast was extreme and, although not quantified as such, was recognised by women workers and, amid the rhetoric of sacrifice, it is not surprising that women should have felt that their war service did not put them much at risk.

Secondly, the war was a temporary phenomenon and so, therefore, seemed the production of TNT. It was a short period in a working life: hence it could be controlled by short-term stratagems rather than cured or rendered safe. Women did demand work after the war, but not the same work making instruments of death. For example, the prize-winning essay in a factory newsletter said of the writer's war work:

> Only the fact that I am using my life's energy to destroy human souls gets on my nerves. Yet on the other hand, I am doing what I can to bring this horrible affair to an end. But once this war is over, never in creation will I do the same thing again.[18]

Although women's labour was in short supply 1916-1917, for the rest of the war there were enough workers to keep production rising and supply the front – even if they had to be moved around from job to job.

The third reason for a lack of any general systematic attempts to prevent TNT poisoning by its victims was that it could be prevented in individual systematic ways of dealing with war production, that is, what management and Government called labour turnover and absenteeism. The War Register of 1915 had turned all women into potential war workers, reducing a variety of labour histories into a pool of labour. The new factories run by the Ministry of Munitions were based on this source of labour, and many women left areas of traditional female employment to work on munitions. Wages were much higher relatively. Women became more mobile and financially able to cope with short periods of unemployment. Witness after witness to the War Cabinet Committee on Women in Industry bemoaned women's bad time-keeping, lack of commitment to their work and lack of ambition, as well as their high rate of turnover. They had an interest in so doing – showing that women were incapable of replacing men and thus preventing retrospective post-war claims for equal pay or equal benefit – but it is the case that this high mobility was seen as a problem of management.[49] It was not a problem for the workers themselves. From 1916-1918, after the abolition of the leaving-certificate system, women could move freely within factories and between factories, if free of domestic obligations. Since ultimately the only remedy for the build-up of toxic material was to avoid taking in more, for the individual woman this was the most effective means of dealing with the problem. Change in the labour market and associated new independence among women were probably the major factors in reducing the incidence of TNT poisoning, as important as medical inspection and policing of the workforce in the interests of production.

A fourth factor in dealing with TNT poisoning was the other conditions affecting women's health. Some women's health improved, as civilian health was generally improving – as Jay Winter has argued – mainly because of rising household income.[50] Those on engineering processes or some skilled or clerical jobs in government factories benefited from higher wages than women had earned before, and from some aspects of welfare. Munition workers who ate in canteens got subsidised meat rations after 1917; TNT workers got half a pint of milk a day until 1917; simply eating away from home could mean a woman's first chance of eating a proper meal rather than what was left after others had eaten.[51] The Health of Munition Workers Committee's reports showed both improved stamina and output from attention to seating, light and lay-out, as well as from the provision of canteens, tea-breaks and medical attention.[52] The ministry claimed that milk was ineffective as a specific against TNT poisoning. They dropped the daily half-pint in 1917 since milk was in short supply, but the general state of nutrition may have been improved by the protein intake.[53] Here the concern for motherhood allied to the need to keep production high and rising did not work unambiguously together. The Medical Research Council could find no necessary connection between nutritional state and resistance to TNT, but felt the general improved level of nutrition among women could be justified as an indirect incentive to war production. It seems quite probable that more frequent investigation into TNT and its effects had the effect of revealing previously unrecorded conditions among young women in employment: anaemia, for example, could as equally have been attributed to war conditions as to TNT. The information we have is unreliable because of the short-term nature of the interest, the fears for morale and the mobility of the women themselves. The limitations of the state's knowledge of women's condition of health are shown by the nature of the discussion on TNT in Britain in 1914 to 1918. Oral evidence would also indicate a high level of death among workers who had been on explosives in the post-war influenza epidemic, but the relationship needs closer examination to achieve any certainty. Many interviewees told of friends who had got through the war only to die just after the Armistice, and the age-group of young workers was that most affected by the epidemic.

The nature of the medical research and accounts of the effects of TNT were deeply affected by the job that the medical profession was being asked to carry out. There was no core of 'scientific medicine'

Notes on Chapter 6

This chapter was written with Antonia Ineson, whose work provided most of the medical and scientific section of this chapter, and was first published for the Society for the Social History of Medicine in Weindling, P. (ed.), *The Social History of Occupational Health*, 1985. I am grateful to Antonia, the society and the publishers, Croom Helm, for permission to republish.

Full details of all publications mentioned here are in the bibliography on page 209.

1   Willcox, W.H., 'Lettsomian Lectures on Jaundice: with special reference to types occurring during the War', *British Medical Journal*, 17 May 1919, p 708; Medical Research Council, *Poisoning and the Fate of TNT in the Animal Body*, Special Report Series no 58, 1921, p 5.
2   *Official History of the Ministry of Munitions, A History of State Manufacture* part III, 1920-4, PRO, p 68.
3   Report of the Superintendent of HM Cordite Factory, Gretna, IMP.MUN 1/2.
4   Health of Munition Workers Committee, *Health of the Munition Worker*, 1917, p 97.
5   Newman, Sir George, report in Addison papers, box 2, Bodleian Library, Oxford.
6   Advisory committee minutes, Addison papers, box 2, Bodleian Library, Oxford; PRO.MUN 4/1782.
7   Medical Research Council, *Poisoning and the Fate of TNT in the Animal Body*, Special Report Series no 58, 1921, p 25.
8   Notice to the press, 1 November 1916, Addison papers, box 2, Bodleian Library, Oxford; TNT Advisory Committee instructions to the Press Bureau, 1916, PRO.MUN 4/154.
9   Medical Research Council, *Poisoning and the Fate of TNT in the Animal Body*, Special Report Series no 58, 1921, p 31.
10 Livingstone-Learmouth, A., and Cunningham, B.M., 'Observations on the Effects of Tri-nitro-toluene on Women Workers', *Lancet*, 12 August 1916, p 261.
11 'Trinitrotoluene Poisoning', *Lancet*, 16 December 1916, PRO.MUN, p 1027.
12 Medical Research Council, *Poisoning and the Fate of TNT in the Animal Body*, Special Report Series no 58, 1921.
13 Editorial, *Lancet*, 16 December 1916, p 1021; 'Trinitrotoluene Poisoning', *Lancet*, 16 December 1916, PRO.MUN, p 1026.
14 O'Donovan, Dr W.J., 'Circular to Medical Officer in filling Factories',

1916, Addison papers, box 2, Bodleian Library, Oxford; Gummer, R.H., 'Barnbow no 1 (Leeds) National Filling Factory', unpublished (nd), p 45.

15 Medical Research Council, *Poisoning and the Fate of TNT in the Animal Body,* Special Report Series no 58, 1921, p 16.

16 Health of Munition Workers Committee, final report, 'Industrial Health and Efficiency', 1918, Cd 9065, p 78.

17 Moore, B., *BMJ*, 4 August 1917, p 164.

18 Medical Research Council Special Report Series no 11, *The Causation and Prevention of Tri-Nitro-Toluene Poisoning*, 1917, p 47.

19 'Tri-nitro-toluene Poisoning', *Lancet,* December 1916, PRO.MUN p 844.

20 *Lancet,* 16 December 1917.

21 Minutes of the TNT Advisory Committee, PRO.MUN 4/1782

22 Ministry of Munitions, issues to medical officers in filling factories, 1916, Addison papers, box 2, Bodleian Library, Oxford.

23 PRO.MUN 4/4872.

24 Medical Research Council Special Report Series no 11, *The Causation and Prevention of Tri-Nitro-Toluene Poisoning*, 1917, p 59.

25 Recruitment posters, IWM.

26 *Labour Gazette*, December 1917, p 438.

27 Cole, G.D.H., *Trade Unionism and Munitions*, 1923.

28 Health of Munition Workers Committee, Memo no 4, *The Employment of Women*, 1916, Cd 8185, p xxiii.

29 Report from National Shell Factory Gretna, IWM.MUN 14, p 9.

30 Thom, D., 'The Ideology of Women's Work in Britain 1914-24, with specific reference to the NFWW and other trade unions', unpublished PhD for the CNAA at Thames Polytechnic, 1982, ch. 6.

31 Webb, B., cit. Dewar, K. (ed.), *The Crisis*, 1920.

32 IWM.MUN 19, Armstrong Whitworth.

33 TUC Congress Report, 1919, cit. Braybon, G., *Women Workers in the First World War*, 1981, p 199.

34 *Women's Trade Union Review.*

35 Anderson, A., *Women in the Factory*, 1922, p 307

36 IWM.MUN 342, roll of honour (those killed on munitions work). This records 76 deaths from TNT poisoning. PRO.MUN 2/27, 16 Sept 1916.

37 Addison diary, Addison papers, box 2, Bodleian Library, Oxford.

38 *Woolwich Pioneer*, 16 February 1917; *The Woman Worker*, March 1917.

39 IWM, recording, C. Renolds, 000566/07, reel 1; IWM, recording, E. McIntyre, 000673/09, reel 1.

40 Thom, D., interview, Mrs L. Robinson, July 1977.
41 Thom, D., interview, Mrs MacKenzie, June 1977.
42 Thom, D., interview, Mrs Cushin, June 1977.
43 Thom, D., interview, Mrs Bennett, July 1977.
44 Thom, D., interview, L. Robinson, July 1977.
45 PRO.MUN 5.70, 11 August 1915, 28 August 1915.
46 IWM.MUN 34/2.
47 Calculation based on figures from Dearle, N.B., *The Cost of the War*, 1924. My thanks to Dr Jay Winter for this reference.
48 IWM.MUN 28, Alexandria Filling Factory.
49 Report of the War Cabinet Committee on Women in Industry, PP 1919, Cmd 135, and evidence to the War Cabinet Committee on Women in Industry, Cmd 167.
50 Mrs Pember Reeves, *Round About a Pound a Week*, 1911, demonstrates the pre-war eating habits of mothers in low-income households.
51 Health of Munition Workers Committee Handbook, *The Employment of Women*, 1917.
52 PRO.MUN 2/28, 27 April, pp 918-9.

Chapter 7

Tommy's Sister: Women
in World War I

In 1915 women were asked to 'Do Your Bit; Replace a Man for the Front'. Thousands did, working on munitions. In Woolwich Arsenal itself there were 27,000 in 1917; in the Woolwich area 60,000 women in war work, where women had not been working before. The Health of Munition Workers Committee reported that some women had accepted 'conditions of work which, if indefinitely prolongeed, would ultimately prove injurious to health'. They ascribed this to patriotic exertions which overcame the factor, 'woman is the life-giver, not the life destroyer'. Trade unionists feared the patriotism of women because they saw it as a contributory factor in the risk war posed to established conditions of work. But, as Edith Cavell said in explaining her activities in wartime, which endangered her life while saving others, 'Patriotism is not enough'. It does not explain why women chose the work they did, why some stuck to it throughout, and why their comments on it are in the main enthusiastic. As an issue it demonstrates the need to look at war work bifocally, as work and as war service, and to recognise the particularity of both in these women's lives at this time. Women created their own allegiances to work in a work-related community, while appropriating or exploiting other evocations of group experience, as in class, race and gender, and accepting the formulations of patriotism or nationalism when expressed in personal terms.

The example of the experience of war work is Woolwich, which was a community dominated by war. The Royal Artillery Barracks up on the hill, the Royal Arsenal and the Old Dockyard by the river dominated the town. It was a prosperous town, and had a low proportion of working women, married or unmarried.[1] Women worked locally in a shirt factory, three hospitals, the cable works at Siemens or Henley's Telegraph Company over the river in North Woolwich; or did home-work, particularly tennis-ball-making in the summer; or commuted by ferry or train across or along the river. Women's usual work was little affected by war; men's was greatly, and Woolwich's level of male unemployment was high before the war, since the Arsenal factories had laid off many workers. The Labour movement was strong, well-organised and supported a weekly newspaper, the *Woolwich Pioneer*, a Labour MP, Will Crooks, and one of the biggest co-operatives, the RACS (Royal Arsenal Co-operative Society). Women's organisations in Woolwich were numerous: some quite large, especially the Women's Co-operative Guild and the Primrose League, but specifically feminist organisations tended to come in from outside, the Women's Social and Political Union (WSPU) and the East London Federation of Suffragettes (ELFS).[2] Local issues predominated in the press and in the reported proceedings of local organisations; war was, essentially, seen as a local issue. Pacifism was never absent from local labour, but no leading figures were truly pacifists: even the local Independent Labour Party had dissolved into the British Socialist Party in 1912 and swung behind the war effort.[3] Feminist pacifism, which was a very strong current elsewhere, did not really exist in Woolwich.[4] When war began, women were made unemployed in many parts of the country, and in Woolwich the same groups were affected as elsewhere: domestic servants, milliners and dressmakers.[5] But it was not unemployment among women as such that opened up the Arsenal to women, but Government's need for labour. Other local munitions factories had employed women before Government insisted that women go into the Arsenal, and that experience was to be used to convince employers of women's usefulness on monotonous work processes, their docility and tractability, their lack of knowledge or experience of industrial life.[6] The descriptions of women's nature as workers, spread by Government extensively through propaganda in newspapers and newsreels, aroused the fears of organised trade unionists about women's 'innate' power to upset 'time-honoured' negotiating procedures in the factory, doubly so because they were women and because they were dilutees.[7] In the Arsenal, though, organised workers in trade unions controlled the dilution process to a greater extent than elsewhere; they even had desks in the main factories for individual members of the shop-stewards' committee who could monitor the replacement of skilled men by the unskilled or semi-skilled.[8] In the Woolwich Arsenal they did this mainly for boys: both management and men remained resistant to the idea of women in the factory.[9] As late as May 1916 there were as many boys as women in the Arsenal (at 8,000). By the winter of 1917, when there were most women workers, there were 27,000 of them. Women hardly entered the Royal Gun Factory or the Gun Carriage Factory, and they comprised only just over 25 per cent of the workers in small arms ammunition factories.[10] Most women in Woolwich and elsewhere were doing new tasks which had been designated as women's work (therefore not subject to equal pay regulation) and they predominated in the mass-production, repetition factories. Women particularly made and filled shells, a task that was increasingly done elsewhere in private works or in temporary government-run filling factories. (The Arsenal gradually resumed its pre-war function as adjuster for everyone else's production.)

Why did women do munitions work in the Woolwich Arsenal? Were they driven by patriotic motives, a desire for self-assertion? Is there anything to distinguish their behaviour in war from peace-time, or from that of young men entering the factory or military service at the same time? Government propaganda, like the *Women at Work* pamphlets (with excellent photographs by, among others, Horace Nicholls), was directed mainly at employers.[11] The aim of this volume of publicity for women's ability to perform factory work was to persuade factory managers that women were not only able to perform many tasks they had not done before but that their labour offered positive advantages. The Ministry of Munitions recorded one factory manager's judgement: 'Girls are more diligent on work within their capacity than boys – they are keen to do as much as possible, are more easily trained'.[12] Feminists argued that women should be allowed to do men's work. Mrs Pankhurst organised a 'Right to Work' march, later renamed the 'Right to Serve' march, in London, which was a dramatisation of demand for women to enrol on the War register.[13] Women's trade-union representatives deplored the capacity of such feminists to ignore the need to maintain adequate or equivalent wage levels. Mary Macarthur of the National Federation of Women Workers

(NFWW) said, 'There were too many sister Susies sewing shirts for soldiers,' and that they were prepared to do so for little or no wages.[14] Women's introduction to newly-opened war employment was shaped by the fact that it took place when women were unemployed in large numbers, and the fact that it posited women's deficiency as workers. Government action added to this emphasis. After the Right to Serve march, Lloyd George announced all women would register their availability for war service by enrolling on the Women's War Register.[15] Historically, women had not been allowed to do the engineering tasks which were in such short supply, so the impression of inexperience was enhanced, and actual histories of work ignored.[16] All women became a stage army, to be wheeled on and off as the decision demanded, as if many of them had not been on the stage before.

Women described their own motives in going to the Arsenal in a variety of ways. Many were unemployed when the Arsenal opened its gates to women, domestic servants in particular. The wives of serving men got very low dependants' allowances. They had to wait some time for them to be organised and administered, and to go through humiliating processes modelled on the charitable assessments of the Charity Organisation Society designed to eliminate the demoralised from among claimants for charitable relief. They were required to demonstrate their status, not their need, even having to produce marriage lines.[17] In Woolwich, the Army's married quarters had been reallocated to soldiers *en route* for Dover and the Western Front, so a large group of women had been rendered suddenly homeless because of the war.[18] Woolwich was an area of London in which war work was already central to the local economy. It was both the major inspection institution in armaments manufacture and the headquarters of the Royal Artillery. In interviews, most women recollect economic need as a main motive, but for most interviewees not a new motive. Why did they go to the Arsenal, rather than any other local munitions factory? It was the best-known munitions factory, wages were supposed to be high and it was central to munitions production. It had both local and national drawing power. I estimate (and there is no extant registration information to check this, although memories tend to support it) that about one third of all women workers there came through local contacts. They often entered their jobs by way of a personal introduction to a factory foreman, often by a family member. In this way women followed the procedure current in the Arsenal for years. Young women who entered in this way had not usually worked in the factory before, and often, but not always, had to argue against father or brothers who were reluctant to help. One woman only went in on the understanding that she did not speak to anyone else at all, and only threw off family tutelage after a month of being escorted daily to the factory by a kinsman. She described her impression of factory life in the first month very vividly, demonstrating the persistence of family relationships even in this most organised and regimented workplace.

> The girls from the danger buildings... were laughing and joking with one another. Some of them came from the other side of the water, they were pretty rough. My brother didn't like me going in there to work. They were all annoyed about it. I had five brothers. They said, 'The men will think you're cheap'. And I said, 'Well they won't if you don't act cheaply'. 'Well,' my father said, 'If she can't look after herself now she never will. Take no notice of them.' Of course when I first went in there I was a real dumb Dora, I wouldn't speak to anyone. If they spoke to me I wouldn't answer; I began to think they must think I'm a bit queer. My brother-in-law went to work with me; he was a foreman in the cordite, 'Don't talk to them, take no notice'. Oh, dear, it was really funny. But eventually when I did get to know the men in there they were a fine crowd; it was only some of the nastier element in there that were a bit nasty to the girls and eventually they had to accept them. What they didn't like was being released for some of them to go in the army.[19]

Another third of the women came from the local labour exchange, which drew on a large area of South and East London. These women were processed collectively, enrolling for factories rather than as individuals. They often found the process frightening, partly because of the fear of explosions, or of danger-work itself, as it was known at the time, partly because of the alienating effect of being dealt with by numbers. One woman kept going, even though she did not want to work in the danger sheds (using TNT to fill shells), because she didn't want to admit cowardice to her neighbour.

> They wanted women for the Danger Buildings. I went down to the Labour Exchange... everyone was all lined up and they were all half afraid of the danger buildings. 'Danger buildings only, danger buildings only.' Well the woman in front of me, she put her name down and she got a job and I thought, well, I can't let these people behind me think I'm a coward.[20]

The last third of the women went through the factory's own admission procedure: interview by welfare superintendent followed by medical assessment for suitable work. Helen Bentwich was vetted by a doctor:

> Hearts, nerves, veins in the legs and eyes were what she looked at, and head [for lice]. The Doctor said, 'You shouldn't be here. Aren't you a public school girl?'[21]

The physical assessment was decisive, social considerations were in some respects clearly incidental, and levels of education were important. Women only predominated in one main process, filling shells, 11,692 women and girls to 9,103 men and boys.[22] Women were reduced by this process to units of labour power, slotted in by condition, not by their own wishes. Any attempt to challenge this placing met short shrift. One woman with seven children wanted to leave danger work to earn more money, and to do a different shift system, so she went anxiously to see Lilian Barker, chief welfare superintendent, and was told either to keep her job or leave altogether.

> I knew I was gaining; it was what I went to work for. What I couldn't understand was that we on the danger part were getting less money than the girls sitting down needleworking. They were getting more money than we were; that was what I couldn't understand. Because once you got in they wouldn't let you go anywhere else, they wouldn't. I tried it once. She said, 'Either that or you get your discharge'.[23]

Self-assertion in these circumstances was difficult; but what about joint assertion? Did the experience of factory work lead to any concept of a collective greater than the family? Joanna Bornat's account of textile workers in an area where women traditionally worked until motherhood rather than marriage provides the argument that trade-union membership is fundamentally related to the domestic context, and can only be interpreted by looking at domestic relationshiops and practices as well as workplace activism. This is born out by the women of Woolwich.

The *Woolwich Pioneer* editorialised, 'Both men and women must recognise their interests as workers are identical,'[24] but for women in the Arsenal in 1915 this was particularly difficult at work. Some conflict between the sexes was explicit. Some women met with physical violence, many encountered substantial verbal abuse in 1915 when women first entered the various Arsenal factories. Most women I've spoken to in interviews recognised an expression of class prejudice, they being the daughters or wives of skilled men, the men abusing them being labourers.[25] It was what they had expected of factory life, and they saw it as an expression of their difference from the rest of the factory workforce. A few were domestic servants, and they saw it as factory life as they had expected it to be, but their indignation at the grossness of language and behaviour was still evident after many years. Women who had directly replaced men who had gone to the front, as these substitutes did, tended to explain this hostility as caused by that factor alone – 'Well, what do you expect?' – and felt little individual antagonism for men who behaved in this way. Some did indeed see themselves as helping to 'send' the men away.

Indirect division of interest between men and women was little recognised by the women themselves. Most knew that their pay was not the same as the men they replaced, but they did know that it was larger than their own pre-war pay and than pre-war rates of pay for unskilled men. Women did not get equal earnings at all, because men and women were given different war bonuses, designed to compensate for the rise in the cost of living. Women who should technically have got equal pay because their jobs were identical to the men they had replaced usually had to fight for it through the procedures involved in claiming at the special arbitration tribunal set up after the dilution programme was in place to deal with the negotiation of wages after a no-strike agreement. In the Arsenal, the only women who were awarded equal pay after appeal were clerks, crane-drivers and inspectors.[26] Women on engineering were paid at equal rates (piece rates), but had to pay for the toolsetter, who assisted with the setting up and maintaining of the machines, at 10 per cent of their own earnings.[27] This was not recognised clearly as not being equal pay until late 1917, when women had begun to be discharged from the Arsenal following the closure of the Russian Front, and therefore had lost the little power to fight back gained in negotiating at a time of labour shortage.

At work, women were further reduced to units of labour, sometimes addressed by name, sometimes by number. They wore uniforms with caps, mostly made of khaki-coloured fabric, like the Army's, sometimes navy like the other military services. In filling work or in the bullet factories, all personal belongings were handed over as women passed from the 'dirty' side (the outside world) to the 'clean' side. Everyone had to leave behind everything personal for reasons of safety, no-one could keep matches, cigarettes, purses, hairslides, flowers or jewellery. This policing of the body was described by some women as a very intrusive process, although all recognised the necessity of excluding any risk of explosion:

> We used to have two women stand at each barrier and we used to step over it. We had to wear garters and we used to climb over there and before we got over she used to run her hands all over us, round our hair, all over our body, look at our hands and look to see we haven't got anything on, and then she would allow us to go over. We used to call her the policewoman.[28]

Outdoor workers had a much freer experience of war work than those in factories. Indeed this was made visible because they often wore trousers.[29] They were less subject to stringent safety rules, and did not have to be searched every time they went back to work.[30] Discipline in the Arsenal could be very strict indeed. One girl got six months' hard labour for taking a match inadvertently into an explosives site; however, since there were 172 buildings each with a ton or more of explosive in an area of three square miles, such care was needed.[31]

Workers were aware of the danger. Women, however, to whom such discipline was most applied, tended to see the social consequences: men viewed it more benignly. One woman described the poisoning of workshop relations by an incident when her friend was summoned before the factory manager and a policewoman because a lighter had been found in her pocket. She denied it. Her friend supported her claim that someone else had foisted her with it, acting, it seems, both in self-defence and malice. But the woman was dismissed without a character reference, and therefore could never resume her old service job, for which a 'good character' remained essential.[32] Most did not resent the discipline. One woman actually chose to work at the much more dangerous Vickers works at Erith – where she saw one scalping, one mangled hand and one severed arm – because she preferred the more relaxed atmosphere, but this was unusual.[33]

The apparent effects of labour organisation, work enrolment and official discipline on women workers was to reduce the differences between them and emphasise their common gender. They reacted to this by creating their own collective allegiances, many of which did base themselves on identity as women, but always with substantial qualification.[34] Class was one important locus for differentiation or identity, though usually acting negatively. A special hostel, Queen Mary's hostel, was built for 'lady' munition workers, and the Arsenal probably had most of these volunteers, supplementing their full-time workers at weekends and at times of extra demand.[35] There was also a large group working with Lady Londonderry running canteens for men at the beginning of the war. The first welfare supervisors were initially of a similar sort. Lilian Barker, chief women's welfare superintendent at the Arsenal, excluded them, as she told the canteen committee in a description which demonstrates very clearly how welfare work assumed a kind of paternalism, or maternalism with the description of all women workers as 'girls', and the way in which the assumptions lying behind management practices become explicit in time of war. Barker's evidence, presented in the typescript, though not in the published version of the minutes of evidence to the War Cabinet Committee on Women in Industry, summed up her robust rejection of some of the conventional pieties of factory welfare work, and rejected misguided amateurism:

Q Have you any workers?[36]
A None.
Q We ought to commiserate with you.
A I beg to differ. You ought to congratulate me. I do not think women like voluntary workers, they are such busybodies. They always sum up the girls into the nice girls and the rude girls and the nice girls get attention and the rude girls get nothing. It makes some girls who are not rude, rude.[37]

There were some 'lady' volunteers who managed to stay on as welfare workers, but most of the supervisory staff had become 'women with experience of controlling other women' by 1916. There were some 'ladies' who worked on the shopfloor. One witness said of the ex-suffragette she met working beside her in the Arsenal, 'You'd never have known it. They were so nice, such ladies.'[38] The factory environment did not overcome the difference between the employer of servants and the servant, since the difference remained visible. And there was a further difference among women of respectability: the nice girls and the rude girls. Helen Bentwich, Elizabeth Gore (Lilian Barker's niece and biographer) and Gabrielle West, who worked as a policewoman, all commented on the roughness of some of the women in Woolwich.[39] Some of my interviewees drew the same distinction, distancing themselves from swearing, sexual immorality and dirt (though the moral rather than physical components of that word are not clear). Several witnesses talked of geographical origin as the explanation for difference: 'girls from over the water' were Eastenders who differed from the inhabitants of respectable Woolwich. Other geographical, social and ethnic distinctions were made. Irish and Scottish girls were identified as speaking differently and being 'clannish'. Jewish girls were seen as noticeably different, but few specifics mentioned.[40] Both written sources and oral interviews show the repeated use of the word 'girl' to describe women who were mostly young but many of whom were mature. It is in itself an indication of proletarian status rather than age at this time and in the discourse of the factory.

The qualities of being nice or being rude were seen as being inherent in the person, not the worker brought to the workplace, not acquired there. One worker described her sense of social vertigo faced with a factory workforce after life in domestic service thus:

> They were [sic.] a bad lot in there; characters. Oh my god, of course coming out of service with the gentry, I'd only lived among gentry and to go in with that lot. I had to watch my Ps and Qs.[41]

The Arsenal itself was not at all nice. Even clean, sitting-down work such as that in the wages office took place in a filthy environment. The Arsenal was infested with rats. It was badly ventilated. Lighting was anyway inadequate, and frequent Zeppelin raids meant total blackouts, often without any warning; three people died in blackout accidents, six in road accidents.[42] The emergency medical system was one doctor and a shed at the start of war; by the end there were 12 doctors, but they worked mostly vetting applicants, and had a very limited therapeutic role.[43] There was also a simple division by age. Very young girls did not do filling work; they worked with the (male) invalids in the paper shop. Girls aged sixteen to twenty tended to be put to mass-production work, on cartridges for example. The optimum age for filling was twenty-four, and many of the fillers were older than this: the placing of women by capacity to behave responsibly was a factor in this.[44] Oddly enough, marital status for women, which is normally a crucial division between women, was relatively unimportant, partly because it impinged so little on factory life, partly because most married women had husbands who were absent on military service. Having children was a major division, simply because of the time

needed to look after them added on to a 12-hour shift, the usual
time spent working at the Arsenal until the Health of Munition
Workers Committee forced the factory managers to change onto
the more general pattern of three eight-hour shifts in 1917. The
arduous working day, allied to childcare, left hardly any time for
friendship or group activity at all.

The main unit of group identity in the factory was the workplace, not the work task nor the age group. This seems to be
because people met in the canteen and then had a chance to share
experiences about work there, rather than at the workbench or at
home. It was also the only place where most women had a chance
for voluntary activity of many sorts. Each shift organised concerts
for themselves (often performed by themselves) or for wounded
soldiers. They competed in sports competitions or, more popularly,
in hair-length or hat-making contests.[45] Each workshop had its
own song, usually loaded with *double entendres*. One, which was
for print and is therefore rather bland, shows a strong sense of
identity of purpose with soldiers, wounded and serving.

1   Way down in Shell Shop Two
    You'll never find us blue
    We're working night and day
    To keep the Huns away.

2   All we can think of tonight
    Are the shells all turning bright
    Hammers ringing, girls all singing
    And the shop seems bright.

3   To our worthy foremen here
    Give three good hearty cheers
    Our wounded heroes too
    We're mighty proud of you.

4   And the boys who're still out there
    Good luck be always their share
    And bring them all back
    Everyman Jack
    To their dear old folks at home.[46]

That was intended for public consumption. The one that began
'Old man sitting on the Arsenal wall, Just like his dad doing sod

all' was not.[47] The songwriter, Rubens, who wrote 'Your King and Country', sold 7,000 copies of a song in Woolwich called 'She works at the Woolwich Arsenal now'.[48] Women workers took this identification of themselves with their workplace very seriously. They differentiated themselves with coloured shoe-laces, hair-ribbons or flowers. Friends from the group would make shift-changes together, so that every fortnight when days changed to nights there was a thirty-six-hour gap in which a little rest could be obtained and they could, if childless, go out to the music-hall, the cinema (which ran frequent programmes between 1915 and 1918, mostly of the 'Perils of Pauline' type of film and newsreels)[49] or even to the theatre in the West End. Shoe clubs or clothing societies were less important than pre-war, since women did not need to save for their clothes, but some did exist, and again they were based on the shift-workplace-canteen group. This grouping was the basis of collective action too. If a workshop was unionised, the union concerned depended on which had got there first, and that depended in turn largely on the men in the factory or on individual women's history. Engineering shops tended to be NFWW, filling-shops were less unionised but also Federation; bullet-paper and tailoring shops tended to be Workers' Union (WU). The women's branches did not meet inside the factory, and the NFWW and WU women's branches were only occasionally represented on the Shop Stewards' Committee.[50] Most women unionists were older than the average, most stewards in fact being married women, although the two main union organisers were, at twenty and twenty-one, relatively very young by comparison with their male counterparts.

The unions battled for the representation of war workers. Both trade unions claimed to have had most members in the Arsenal. Such figures as do exist would indicate that the WU probably had most by the end of the war, the NFWW the most in 1915-16. The WU certainly put itself forward as the union for the young worker, though its propaganda met little response among interviewees; those who could remember which they had belonged to remembered the federation. Union membership was nearly always attributed to family connections, with the phrase used to describe family, 'We were (not) a union family'. Bornat's account of union dues being collected from mothers at the workers' homes is not quite matched here at Woolwich.

I think more or less we all were. We all wore these badges... brass three-corner badge or whether they were to signify we all worked on munitions: I don't know. But that's one thing I can't remember: whether or not I was. I have an idea I was because I think most of them did join a trade union simply and solely as a safeguard for yourself, because in those days you didn't get compensation for anything, or you weren't paid for being off work sick or anything and I think that's why most of them joined trade unions, as a form of backing.[51]

Women's collective protest tended to take different forms from that of men. There were frequent canteen protests about a variety of issues, ranging from unjust supervision by factory foremen, and poor canteen service, to 'speed-up' in the work-rate and equal pay. It was the former sort of issue – working conditions – that tended to cause most fervour and be most effectively resolved. There are several descriptions of Lilian Barker, chief welfare superintendent, solving the problem and organising the return to work single-handed. A vivid description comes from the biography by her niece, who was living with her at the time, and although a young child had a clear recollection of her attitudes:

> She was away recruiting and summoned back to hear that three shops were ready to go. She turned up and found 500 girls waiting in the canteen in grim silence. Standing on a chair her hands clenching and unclenching in her pockets she told them in a speech of steadily mounting emphasis, 'to strike in war time was like giving guns to the enemy'. The meeting ended with a ragged cheer for the Lady Superintendent and a 10 minute break before returning to work. She is reported speaking on output. 'Anyone who limits that is a traitor to sweethearts, husbands and brothers fighting. If a worker does not like her job she should give it up.[52]

In another incident, women covered two supervisors with pudding and pelted them with orange peel because they did not observe a canteen boycott the workers had set up. This was solved by a joint appeal from the male shop stewards' committee and Lilian Barker, using the same rhetoric she had used to such effect at other times and meeting with the same response. A personalised appeal did effect a return to work in the way that a general appeal to the nation or against the Hun never did. Images of welfare at Woolwich were greatly affected by the personal status of Lilian Barker, who provided material for many myths. Several interviewees reported their belief that she was actually a man in the guise of a woman, but distanced themselves from the joke in reporting it by using the formulation, 'Some people said...'. She was certainly of considerable physical presence, extremely capable of command. Some found her supportive and interested.

> A lot of people didn't like her but I did because she stood no nonsense. I got knocked over by a runaway horse in Woolwich and I was off work for six weeks, and, of course, you didn't get any pay. And she found out I was off work for six weeks, and I was only one among hundreds, and she sent a secretary to my home to see if I got any compensation. 'Of course,' she said, 'if you haven't, I'll take it up for you'. I thought that was a wonderful thing to do among so many people.[53]

Another woman found the same sympathetic hearing when Barker sent for her, and explained to her why she could not resume her old job after she had ben poisoned with mercury, because the risk of further poisoning remained. A cynic might simply interpret this as efficiency in regulating a large workforce on many dangerous and unhealthy work processes in a dangerous environment, but the point of the memories is the way in which the factory's welfare service was seen even by those not dealt with by Barker personally as a personal link between her and each individual worker.

Women themselves tried to personalise the war itself by putting messages in the cases of shells, though they don't appear to have wanted to think, then or now, what the shells were for at the other end. Comments on the war itself reflect an attempt to distance themselves from it, or to say in terms of great vagueness, 'I just wanted to end it quickly'. Here there is a difference: male Arsenal workers construct their history of the Arsenal in wartime by the chronology of the front or of national politics, women do not. Both their chronology and their rhetoric are to do with the personal, the domestic, the issues over which their behaviour and attitudes make a difference.

There were several major issues on which women workers could have been evidently patriotic for their locality or sex. On two subjects – food and rent – women were among the protesters, though not leaders of it, but these were women as consumers, as the mainstay of the household, organisers of domestic economy. On the food question there was nearly an Arsenal-wide strike because of shortages and lengthy queues. Rents were rarely generalised beyond the people who faced the issue.[54] Air raids were a grievance to workers, and featured in trade-union negotiations and, in retrospect, are often mentioned in interviews.[55] The commissioners of enquiry into working-class unrest commented on these issues in 1917 when waves of strike action, involving skilled and unskilled alike, swept through munitions factories and did, of course, include women among them. All these were examples of what people now describe as their being badly treated in wartime, but acceptably so, because their conditions were not as bad as those at the front and because they could act against them. They do not appear to have felt hopelessly victimised, even by the worst excesses of landlords, food traders or factory management. One munition worker who was living with her parents still had to contribute to the organisation of the household, together with her mother also working on munitions:

> We had to go out shopping before we went to work, and we used to go out all weather. We had to go quickly up, and she'd probably be at the fish shop or the grocery stall; that's how we were rationed. I probably used to go up to the meat shop, and then we'd go home and prepare dinner between us, and then we'd go to bed. We didn't hardly ever get a decent night's sleep.[56]

Another worker demonstrated the difference between the mother and others by saying that she used neither the factory creche nor the canteens. Especially startling was her assertion that she did not expect anything from her printer husband, in a comment which demonstrated starkly the difference between male and female labour. Despite the rigours of munitions work, she did all the cooking, washing and cleaning, leaving the shopping and care of the younger of her seven children to the two older girls.

> My husband wasn't a man who could do any housework, he wouldn't lift a cup and saucer off a table. Mind you he worked hard so I didn't bother him.[57]

On one issue women might justifiably have felt interested in discussion, but were (and I can't find out if consciously so) excluded. That is the discussion of venereal diseases, which was one of the rare issues on which the Arsenal management and the shop stewards' committee agreed and acted in concert.[58] The previous history of agitation against the Contagious Diseases Acts and the wartime hostility to the revival of them in regulation 40d might well have meant that locally women would have been prominent at the public meeting to discuss the issue, but there is very little sign that they were. Women were often excluded from sheer lack of thought that they might be interested. Dame Mabel Crout, then Labour Party agent in Woolwich, said that they didn't think it was their job to organise or in any way make connections with the women munition workers who came to live and work in Woolwich in this way.[59]

Women who were politically active in the town were not women workers, and the gap between women at work and at home was particularly wide, although it was overcome within the family context in which political organisation took place. People would say 'Oh, but we were always Labour you see,' and that unexplained 'we' was usually elaborated as 'our family' or 'my father'. If 'my mother' was mentioned it was usually in the context of the Women's Co-operative Guild, which was not an organisation to which women themselves [had] belonged until they married. Labour patriotism, if expressed at all, was usually with reference to a later period, when interviewees had themselves had a limited purchase on political power through Labour's long dominance of the Woolwich Borough Council. People do and did have a strong sense of loyalty. It is not something volunteered as an explanation for behaviour then or now (except negatively, in that people would use arguments of the 'Now, don't think I am not patriotic' sort). The loyalty, though, is to groups over which women can have some control, in which the way they exercise power can matter. For women of this time and in this place, adherence to the abstractions of military mobilisation or the nation-state had little part in the complex of loyalties which kept them going through a hard, dangerous and unhealthy war at work. One of the reasons that women refer to Queen Mary's visits so often in their recollections is that this personal contact did translate the notion of the head of state into a real person, and was thereby sustaining. The war itself was unpopular, although the chance to work with friends and be both decently paid and publicly approved of for it was not.

Although women did work long hours, they did not ever lose the sense that this was only for a short time, that it was unusual because it was war work, and that it was possibly directly helping some people they loved. Many interviewees talked of the 'boys' at the front, using and absorbing the rhetoric of war propaganda without irony. Each woman, though, had her own views about the factory environment, the benevolence of management, and the way in which work was organised, which prevented any ready acquiescence on work that was beyond her capacity. A woman acted collectively or individually against exploitation, depending on her situation, history and workplace. Some histories see these women as victims of man or of the state, particularly in accounts of their post-war lives. It seems more appropriate to see each one as an active and often conscious historical agent. The factory did not detach women from domesticity: it helped to reproduce a domestic ideology and extend it to the state. To talk of 'emancipation' or 'freedom', even of 'improvement', in this context is to blur the issues of class, race and gender by reducing them to too simple an abstraction. Women themselves did not abandon the distinctions that governed their assumptions about their own social identity in or out of the workplace, nor did they accept very readily some of the arguments of Government, particularly the primitive sort of work study that was produced by the War Cabinet Committee on Women in Industry. Both their motives for volunteering and their recollections of war work came from a differentiated notion of community, which was as much to do with home and family as it was to do with state and nation, but which centrally included the workplace in the sense they made of it afterwards.

Notes on Chapter 7

This chapter is based in part on two previously-published pieces, an article on women in the Woolwich Arsenal in *Oral History* 6, Autumn 1978, and 'Tommy's Sister' in Samuel, R. (ed.), *Patriotism and the Making of the National Identity* (London, 1988, Routledge). I am grateful for the opportunity to revise and republish them.

Full details of all publications mentioned here are in the bibliography on page 209.

1   Stone, G. (ed.), *Women War Workers*, 1917; Churchill, Lady Randolph (ed.), *Women's War Work*, 1916; Caine, H., *Our Girls*, 1916; Marwick, A., *Women and the First World War*, 1977; Braybon, G., *Women Workers in the First World War*, 1981.
2   Thom, D., 'Women Workers in the Woolwich Arsenal in the First World War', MA thesis, Warwick University, 1975, for general information. On this particular point the evidence is   negative. The women's organisations had no local speakers after 1910, and local activity, like interrupting the Minister for War in 1912, was carried

out by women from outside the area. Local activists were involved with the Adult Suffrage Association, and large groups attended their rallies and demonstrations. On occupations, PP 1913 Cd 7018, General Report of the Returns of the Census of England and Wales, p 404, shows what women were doing at the time of the 1911 census, as, slightly earlier, do some articles in the local Labour paper, the *Woolwich Pioneer,* January-February 1908.

3   British Socialist Party collection at the London School of Economics. Annual conference reports 1912-1914 and miscellaneous paper fols. 10-11; Kendall, W., *The Revolutionary Movement in Britain,* 1969, pp 49, 88.

4   Sylvia Pankhurst had open access to the *Woolwich Pioneer* as long as she wrote on maternal welfare or working women or suffrage, but not when she wrote on pacifism, particularly when, after 1917, she moved closer to communism. There were no local counterparts to the socialist pacifists described in Liddington, J. and Norris, J., *One Hand Tied Behind Us,* 1978.

5   Interim Report of the Standing Committee on Women's Employment, PP 1914-1916, xxvii, Cd 7848.

6   Braybon, G., *Women Workers in the First World War,* 1981; Thom, D., 'The Ideology of Women's Work in Britain 1914-24, with specific reference to the NFWW and other trade unions', unpublished PhD for the CNAA at Thames Polytechnic, 1982.

7   Cole, G.D.H, *Trade Unionism and Munitions,* 1923; Drake, B.; *Women in the Engineering Trades,* 1918.

8   Hinton, J., *The First Shop Stewards' Movement,* 1973.

9   Secret labour reports, comment on the particularly low figure for the Arsenal, PRO.MUN 5.55; PRO.SUP 6 records the number entering the Arsenal by Departments; Hogg, O.F.G., *The Royal Arsenal* vol. 2, 1963, p 977.

10   *Official History of the Ministry of Munitions, A History of State Manufacture,* vol. 8, pt 2, PRO, pp 16-17.

11   *Women at Work on Munitions and Women at Work in Non-munitions Industries,* 1916.

12   PRO.MUN 2.27, 16 October 1916, p 40.

13   *The Times,* 17 July 1915; PRO.MUN 5.90.17, negotiations over costs, 11.8.1915-28.8.1915; *Woman Worker,* April 1918, p 8.

14   Cited several times in the GTC at the TUC, file Mary Macarthur, 1915 (the collection consists mainly of press cuttings). The quote is *Daily Sketch,* 8 November 1915 and IWM 47.

15   Pankhurst, E.S., *The Home Front,* 1932; Addison, C., *Politics from Within,* 1924, pp 121-7; Wolfe, H., *Labour Supply and Regulation,*

p 18; Hammond, M.B., *British Labor Conditions and Legislation*, 1923, p 18.

16 Drake, B., *Women in the Engineering Trades*, 1918 (she also wrote the historical introduction to the Report of the War Cabinet Committee on Women in Industry, PP1919, Cd 136); Hutchins, B.L., *Women's Work in Modern Industry*, 1915. All these accounts of the traditional determinants of women's exclusion from certain trades reflect the FWG view, as expressed by Drake in her evidence to the Atkins' committee, that 'if anyone should be excluded from industry it had better be the women'.

17 Pankhurst cites several examples in *The Home Front*, 1932, pp 77-82; Pedersen, S., 'Gender, Welfare and Citizenship in Britain During the Great War', *American Historical Review*, vol. 95/4, October 1990, p 1001, records allowances in 1914 as 14s 7d for a woman with two children, 17s 6d for a woman with four children, at a time when a woman's wage (on non-munitions work) was 13s 6d, but a skilled fitter was earning 38s 11d.

18 *Woolwich Pioneer*, August 1914.

19 Thom, D., interview, Mrs Mackenzie, 1977.

20 Thom, D., interview, Mrs Robinson, 1977.

21 Bentwich, H., *If I Forget Thee*, 1973, p 80.

22 Hogg, O.F.G., *The Royal Arsenal*, vol. 2, 1963, p 977.

23 Thom, D., interview, Mrs Hewes, 1977.

24 *Woolwich Pioneer*, 7 July 1916.

25 Thom, D., interviews, Mrs Mackenzie and Mrs Fleming, 1977; BBC 'Yesterday's Witness' on the Arsenal (1977), directed by C. Cook and produced by S. Peet, had some examples of the same experience.

26 Thom, D., 'Women Workers in the Woolwich Arsenal in the First World War', MA thesis, Warwick University, 1975, ch. 5.

27 Drake, B., *Women in the Engineering Trades*, 1918, pp 1-7.

28 Health of Munition Workers Committee pamphlet 11, *Handbook for Overseers*, 1916.

29 Not that this made the difference in consciousness attributed by one male historian. Unfettered legs don't necessarily make unfettered minds or, put another way, to wear men's clothing is not necessarily to become free. Marwick, A., *Women at War*, 1977.

30 Health of Munition Workers Committee, 'The Employment of Women', PP1916, xxiii, Cd 8185.

31 Hogg, O.F.G., *The Royal Arsenal*, vol. 2, 1963, p 959.

32 Thom, D., interview, Mrs Ayres, 1977.

33 Thom, D., interview, Mrs Hansen, 1977.

34 I do not want to labour this point, but I do feel it important to make

it clear that, although no-one would expect men to react in the same way to a situation, they do expect this of women.

35 *Official History of the Ministry of Munitions, A History of State Manufacture*, vol. 5, pt 5, PRO, p 25.

36 The word 'workers' here means 'voluntary workers', an interesting semantic shift where, for women, work meant voluntary social work. This meaning had gone by 1918, and the National Union of Women Workers had become the National Council for Women.

37 IWM; evidence to the Atkins committee, PRO.MUN 18/2, 24 11.1916, p 25.

38 Thom, D., interview, Mrs Hansen, 1977.

39 Unpublished diaries of Gabrielle West, IWM documents.

40 The women who were most emphatic about this were those who had been domestic servants before the war, in rural areas, and who were new to both the city and the factory.

41 Thom, D., interview, Mrs McCaffery, 1976.

42 Statistics collected from newspapers of the war period. There may have been other such accidents for which the inquests were held elsewhere.

43 See chapter 6.

44 IWM.MUN has several reports for individual factories which list workers by age, task and pay.

45 'In Woolwich,' said the *Official History of the Ministry of Munitions, A History of State Manufacture*, PRO, 'girls were not very fond of educational classes and preferred to go dancing'.

46 *Woolwich Pioneer*, 16 February 1917.

47 Thom, D., interview, Tom and Mabel Biggs, 1977.

48 *Woolwich Pioneer,* 11 April 1917.

49 Programme adverts in the local press, and interviews by the author.

50 I am grateful to Richard Hyman, who let me look at his file on Florence Pilbrow who, as Florence Lunnon, was Workers' Union organiser. Thom, D., interview, Dorothy Jones, 1975;

51 Thom, D., interview, Mrs Loveland.

52 Gore, E., *The Better Fight*, 1975, p 90.

53 Thom, D., 'Women Workers in the Woolwich Arsenal in the First World War', MA thesis, Warwick University, 1975, chapter 4.

54 PRO.SUP 6, 54; PRO.MUN 2.15, 13.4.1918, p 8; 2.28, 23.6.1917. *Woolwich Pioneer*, 22 March 1918.

55 *Woolwich Pioneer.*

56 Thom, D., interview, Mrs Mortimore.

57 Thom, D., interview, Mrs Hewes.

58 *Woolwich Pioneer.*

59 Thom, D., interview, Dame Mable Crout.

Chapter 8

The Mother Heart: Welfare and the Underpinning of Domesticity

To leave the mother heart out of account, as we have so long done, is to retard progress.[1]

Women's domestic lives became an object of intense public interest during the war in ways which were reflected in the administration of life in the factory. Motherhood was emphasised, described as their primary activity, whether they were actually engaged in it or not. It was both the discipline of women's behaviour outside the home and the lure to make the home seem more desirable. War reinforced eugenist notions and, since many working-class fathers were absent, increased responsibility for working-class women. A shift in explicit ideology was made permanent in practice by the establishment of a new machinery of employer and state-welfare provision. Post-war, the welfare of women at work became a very subordinate issue due to the decline of the female industrial work-force and the withdrawal of many married women from industrial occupations. Working-class women's organisations seem to have learnt from the war experience to exploit general pro-natalist fears to their own immediate advantage, but these fears were in fact ones they shared. As the Health of Munition Workers Committee (HMWC) report expressed it, there was a tension at the heart of any argument based upon notions of women's natural role.

Upon the womanhood of the country most largely rests the privilege of creating and maintaining a wholesome family life and of developing the higher influences of social life. In modern times however many of the ideals of womanhood have found outward expression in industry and in recent years hundreds and thousands of women have secured employment within the factory system.[2]

The state did not explicitly confront the issue of the employment of married women. It had been hoped that they would be able to avoid it, but some clear-thinking officials at the Ministry of Munitions raised the issue in 1916, in the secret reports of the Labour Supply Committee, and the exigencies of labour shortage ensured that, in practice, married women were welcomed.[3] Women's unions did not discuss the issue in principle at all in the first three years of the war, and tended to assume that all their members were single and young, hence the repeated use of the word 'girl'. General unions tended to degender members when addressing them directly, using the gender-neutral language of workers, occasionally even comrades, and therefore implicitly ignored gender distinction. To admit in practice that there were problems in being wife, worker and mother was to lend weight to descriptions of women as inherently deficient workers. Hence responses to the provision of welfare and demands from women themselves were often muted, despite demonstrable difficulties for women who combined both activities. Married women were to be found in almost all trades, but appear to have predominated in heavy trades and outdoor work: chemicals, gas-stoking, navvying, agricultural labour and municipal services.[4] Paradoxically, these trades were those where formal welfare provision was very slight. Married women in fact tended to have specialised forms of welfare to prevent domestic obligations limiting output.

Welfare provision was initiated by people who had been advocating it on general principles of amelioration for years pre-war. The War Office began a correspondence with the North American National Civic Federation which they passed to the newly-formed Ministry of Munitions in 1915. The American organisation drew up a twenty-point plan for welfare provision which the Ministry appears to have used as a broad general guideline for its own schemes.[5] Seebohm Rowntree came from private industry, Isobel Sloan from the National Federation of Women Workers, Miss Symons from the Home Office inspectorate.[6] Some large factories initiated their own welfare programmes: in the Woolwich Arsenal,

for example, Lilian Barker's appointment as woman welfare superintendent predated the establishment of the Ministry's team; many
textile mills had supervisors who fulfilled a welfare supervisor's
role. The ministry's innovation was not so novel as is sometimes
argued.[7] Where it did innovate can be seen in the publicity given to
the reports of the HMWC, and thence the recognition that welfare
paid for itself, with demonstrable effects upon output.[8] It also
affected the attitudes of workers to it, so that their organisations
began by being hostile but ended the war with a predominantly
sympathetic view. Women workers themselves varied widely in
their response because welfare provision impinged upon them in
very different ways. The most visible provision was the one to which
they were most hostile, the pressure on time-keeping and home-
visits to ensure reasons given for absence were true. Women had
initially fulfilled traditional expectations (and the fears of skilled
trade unions) by being apparently more conscientious than men, particularly over time. Kirkaldy's team of investigators from the British
Association noted some complaints of bad time-keeping among
women in 1915, but they argued, with convincing detail, that these
cases were isolated, to be found only among groups where women
were completely new to the factory, whereas, as the Glasgow inves-
tigator noted, there was general agreement that the women are, on
the whole, better time-keepers than men. It was not possible to test
this opinion satisfactorily; but the returns for one factory for one
week, as far as they go, support this view.[9] The HMWC dealt with
time-keeping frequently, but usually with other general concerns. It
argued forcefully that time-keeping was not an individual moral
quality among workers, but one that was affected by welfare
provision assessing the situation and confusing opinion with an
objective stance, as Kirkaldy noted:

> The employers moreover, in many ways, simply voice the general view
> uncorrected by any accurate observation on their own part. His inves-
> tigators eventually summarised a multitude of local differences by
> saying that, 'women had better time keeping on day work, on night
> work not so good'.[10]

Unfortunately the Atkins committee, which should have taken the
same scrupulous care, had to a certain extent prejudged the issue.
One of the common questions asked to nearly all witnesses was
over the issue of time-keeping, usually put in terms of assuming a
deficiency, that is, 'were women as good at time-keeping as male

workers?' As on output and productivity in general, Atkins did not compare like with like. Female war workers were compared with their pre-war male counterparts, not those of wartime, yet in many ways the reasons for poor time-keeping lay in wartime, not the gender of the worker. In fact Atkins demonstrated that where factory work was an accepted feature of women's lives they made adequate arrangements for childcare and household tasks, and this major cause of poor time-keeping was removed. The textile industry witnesses demonstrated this in their evidence, in which women were portrayed as better time-keepers than men. The other witnesses failed by any standard to give objective judgments, and were quite open in conforming to Kirkaldy's low opinion of their observational powers.[11] Where the problems were associated with being a wife and/or mother, wartime accentuated them. The practical difficulties of running a household were immensely worsened by war. There was no suggestion, anywhere that I have looked, for redistribution of household tasks among family members, although indirectly there were some socialising effects, in that many young workers, of both sexes, contributed more to household labour than they had before the war, or so they record in taped interviews.

The first problem for household maintenance was food. There were severe shortages in some working-class areas of many staples of working-class diet: bacon, tea, sugar and bread. Shortages were most severe in the overcrowded areas of troop embarkation, and munition works, where fluctuating populations and poor supply mechanisms made the problem worse. Queuing in shops became commonplace, and averaged two hours in some munitions areas in 1917. Submarine warfare 1916-1917 interrupted supplies of other fresh commodities, as did requisitioning of the men and vessels of the fishing fleet. In the end, rationing was introduced for the consumer by fixing supplies to regular customers at the point of sale.

By 1918, four items had been controlled in this way, by rationing consumers: bacon, butter, meat and bread. But food shortages and the difficulties of overcoming them remained a feature of life throughout the war, and were seen by the Commission of Enquiry into Working Class Unrest as a major cause of discontent.[12] Certainly munitions workers began to agitate over the issue of food in 1917, but only in Glasgow and Woolwich, and then because, they argued, men were being made late at work by having to spend so much time in queues. Any more sympathetic approach to the problems of housewifery lay with women's organisations, for the women at home, rather than the workers, who were not absorbed into local institutions unless they were from local families.

The other area of control that created a strong public reaction was that of alcoholic drink. In 1915, liquor control had been introduced under DORA. Initially only eleven areas were chosen, because they were areas of munitions production or armed-forces embarkation; later this was extended to others. People were not allowed to 'treat' (buy drinks for others), or to buy spirits by the bottle. Drink was restricted in quantity, reduced in alcoholic content and only served at restricted times. Lloyd George admitted privately that excess drinking had little effect on production, 'It's all fudge,' he said. Women drank less than men and used pubs less too but this did, indirectly, increase domestic work because it reduced the number of places available to workers for meals away from home. There was a widespread belief, fostered by temperance campaigners, that liquor control was helping to prevent a decline in public morals by preventing increased drunkenness among women.[13] The Women's Advisory Committee of the Liquor Control Board rejected the suggestion that special legislation should be introduced for women because, they argued, 'The undoubted increase in excessive drinking among women is mainly among those who drank before.' They pointed out another benefit of liquor control, in that it was seen as reducing domestic violence; in Greenock a greatly-reduced number of offences were committed in the homes.[14]

Working-class organisations of 1914 were ambivalent about drink control. They resented the limitations on their consumption, which left alone the wealthier spirits market, but they had many temperance campaigners in their midst, and no wish to be seen to condone drunkenness. By 1917, drink was seen as an acceptable component of working-class recreation. Witnesses to the enquiry into working-class unrest were prepared to blame watered beer and inadequate supplies of it as one of the main instigators of revolt. Women did not by-and-large play much part in these discussions since their canteens and clubs were all unlicensed.

Canteens were the original focus of factory welfare work, and they were first provided for men workers. The organisations running them were often motivated by a mixture of idealism, usually including temperance, but also patriotism. The Women's Legion, Young Men's (and Women's) Christian Association (YMCA/YWCA) and the Red Cross provided the middle-class married women's most likely form of war service in 1914-1916. Such war work fell in public esteem as the voluntary mechanisms proved inadequate to cope with mass industrial production. This was characterised by contemporaries as 'unreliability' among middle-class volunteers.

> It is the hardness of the work. It is work which would not fit anyone else but charwomen. These women have done it for eighteen months for the sake of the country in an emergency until someone else could take it over. I reckon that the time has now come when it should be done by paid labour.[15]

So said Mrs Burnes in her evidence to the Women's Service Commission. This body investigated wartime social provision in 1916, and marked clearly the transition towards professionalism in welfare provision which is so noticeable in memoirs of the volunteer workers and the institutional histories of organisations which assumed a more permanent form because of it.[16] It was not accidental, nor because of a confusion with trade unions, that the National Union of Women Workers changed its name to the National Council for Women, but because the word 'Worker' could no longer be applied unambiguously to women doing social work. Lilian Barker, in charge of the welfare of all women workers at Woolwich Arsenal, expressed the new point of view perfectly, in her evidence to the commission, cited earlier when she argued for professionalisation in welfare.

> Q Have you any workers?
> A None.
> Q We ought to commiserate with you.
> A I beg to differ, you ought to congratulate me. I do not think that women like voluntary workers, they are such busy-bodies.[17]

Less vividly but more specifically another witness explained the practical effects of the volunteer who extended her voluntarism to her duties:

> I think a certain number are probably incapable because they cannot realise it is a business concern and that they cannot give big helpings to some girls and small to others.[18]

The middle-class women's experience of housekeeping and philanthropy could no longer be seen as naturally extending into welfare work, but the working-class women's could into domestic war work. So that the Women's Legion argued for replacing men in the army, 'in the cooking, anything to do with housekeeping, which is women's sphere naturally'.[19] Women, however, retained along with this a humanising role which meant that the word welfare was associated with women inextricably.

> They give sympathy to the soldiers and are absolutely above them. They are a great support to the soldiers; they are guardian angels to them, and they may help them in every sort of way.[20]

So said Lady Bessborough on YMCA volunteers running a canteen for soldiers.

The distinction here implicit is between welfare as humanising influence and welfare as asset to industrial production, for which even the propagandist Women's Legion becomes much less confident in advocating a voluntary solution. It was impossible to envisage soldiers' recreation clubs and canteens being staffed by men; those for women industrial workers often were. Although the rhetoric of national unity fudged the distinction between combatant service and war work, it was one that was intrinsic in every facet of the administration.

The provision of meals outside the home did further emphasise the separation of home and work, but commuting patterns had begun to make such a separation commonplace before the First World War. The development of new domestic equipment – ovens and coppers built into new houses – meant that the housewife's lot was improved physically, but that expectations were higher. Most of the women interviewees did not use canteens anyway, preferring to eat at home or lodgings and take sandwiches in the day-time; the men all did use canteens. Wartime only temporarily reduced domesticity for the unmarried woman worker. Advertising assumed independence in the war worker, particularly the Bovril series which appeared in most women's publications of the period, a different war worker and her need for Bovril in each advertisement. But it may not be correct to envisage this as directed at the worker herself, since it is likely that they were aiming for the worker's landlady or mother. Most advertising addressed women as housewives using unchanged templates for advertisements throughout the war years. In the *Woman Worker* Allinson's flour and Glaxo milk for babies are the commonest advertisements; again, this is not clear evidence, since the placing of such advertisements may indicate political sympathy, misplaced understanding of the magazines' circulation or a true understanding of a potential market. The only truly war-related advertisement that I have found that addresses women war-workers directly is one for corsets designed for war-weary backs and general posture.[21]

Post-war advertisements were likely to be more specific about their constituency; they explicitly approached the single woman as worker, usually in an office, or the woman at home, usually assumed to be a mother. The Labour press tended to have a majority of the latter, although the volume of advertising aimed at women diminished. This may well reflect a realistic assessment of women's spending in and out of wartime. Fry and Allinsons had specifically addressed women with advertisements assuming both household control and independent income, but with demobilisation – both of armed forces and war munition volunteers – independent incomes contracted once again to a single-wage household budget. Far more important than the imperfectly-realised social ideal of the advertisement or the literature of exhortation and advice were the attitudes of philanthropists and the state.

The Queen's Work for Women Fund, which became the Central Committee on Women's Employment, saw its job as retraining women for domesticity. It did so in 1915 with unemployed workers who were set to work making baby cots from orange crates, baby clothes from old shirts and meals out of leftovers or the cheapest ingredients. Some failed to sew because 'their hands were too rough to hold a needle'.[22] This concern disappeared in 1915, submerged by labour shortages, but re-emerged in 1917 when the first women war-workers on munitions were laid off. The Ministry of Reconstruction suggested training schemes for women factory workers who had not learnt to run a home, and these were set up, run by the Ministry of Labour. The committee that vetted such schemes was composed entirely of men, of the serviced class, except for Lilian Barker, who had been experienced in running a home when she nursed her mother through the six years of her last illness, but had more experience with industrial workers than household management.[23] Women were not by-and-large enthusiastic about such schemes, and several failed to run for lack of takers. The successful ones were those with a genuine specialised domestic skill – cooking and needlework – which would assist a worker to get a job.[24]

Factory life itself was seen as good training by some trade unionists, as Margaret Bondfield of the NFWW said to a meeting of new federation branches:

They might think because they were in industry only six or eight years after which they would go to a home of their own it was not worth putting their backs into it because it would not benefit them in after life... It would benefit them all their lives, if during their wage earning years they tried to build up a decent standard of life. Women want to learn to stand together loyally.[25]

An anonymous welfare worker shared the view, reporting from Small Arms Factory 4 at Woolwich Arsenal:

The future mothers of England through their factory experiences will be more broad-minded and self-reliant and with a determined spirit, gives greater hopes of a splendid future generation.[26]

Many contemporaries eschewed such excesses of biologised moralising, but used arguments of the same sort to express disquiet on the poor training factory life was for domestic skills. As G.A.B. Dewar said, 'To assemble fuses or to cool shell forgings is easier than to cook a dinner or to rear a child'.[27]

In 1918 some expressed anxiety that the will to acquire domestic skills at all was lacking. The 'natural' skills of housekeeping and mothering were being posited as less innate than had been thought, or anyway subject to the dehumanisation of factory life. The solution of the post-war years was twofold: to make women competent by training them, and to make them want to acquire competence by incentives. The first need was partly met by the conversion of factory welfare supervisors into instructresses in domestic economy. Many societies and charities ran retraining schemes additional to those run by the Ministry of Labour.[28] The second need was met by increasing the support for the home-working mother, although in practice the married woman was seen automatically as a mother, since birth control had not yet made much numerical or public impact upon working-class women, that is most wives were mothers, and so were many widows; and there were more of them than before.

Although there were eugenic anxieties about the quality of births, the more common pro-natalist view of the social reformers, like the Webbs and Eleanor Rathbone, was that all motherhood should be supported to take mothers away from the labour market and increase the general health of the population by improving the condition of children.[29] In wartime the consensus about the importance of biological function for women was greater than pre-war.

172

The unofficial National Birth Rate Commission pressed for the restoration of population numerically, and in general eugenic notions were submerged by the demand for quantity. The replacement population could be nurtured in such a way as to improve its quality, rather than bred for it. In 1916 the discussion of 'war babies' became a commonplace of Parliament and the national press. 'Involuntary motherhood', as it was called, did increase. Illegitimacy rates do not necessarily inform the historian of a rising rate of conception out of wedlock, but may reveal a decrease in abortion or infanticide which, because they take place outside the law, is impossible to quantify at all. The climate of sympathy for women who had anticipated a legal ceremony that death prevented from ever taking place was much greater; some young women were unsuccessful at abortion or infanticide because they were away from home or friends; a very few women felt more able in the upheaval of wartime to act unconventionally; but women like Sylvia Pankhurst cannot really be said to reflect a trend. It does appear likely that rising illegitimacy rates did probably reflect more sexual relationships, but more as an anticipation of the registrar than a rejection of monogamy. The physical mobility of wartime and the new life of lodgings or hostels for war workers, often away from home or domestic service for the first time, meant that many courtships were more speedily sexualised. Despite contemporary perceptions of factory life (and that of outdoor workers like those on transport) it was not by-and-large among factory workers that illegitimacy rates appear to have risen most sharply, but among domestic servants.[30]

Children born out of wedlock were better supported than ever before, as were those of married mothers. (In some cases the discrimination between the two was abandoned.) Voluntary associations concerned with infant welfare merged their forces to run National Baby Week in 1916, and annually thereafter until 1921, when it was felt that new state provision was doing the task of caring for the nation's children which had been supported by it; its effects were mostly at the level of political rhetoric.[31] The Children's Jewel Fund collected £70,000 to provide for poor children between 1917 and 1920. The monthly magazine *Maternity and Child Welfare* began to appear in 1917. Local authorities began to revive the infant welfare centres, many of which had had to close down after 1911 for reasons of economy, and many new ones were built. From six clinics in 1914, there were 120 in 1918, 1,417 by 1933. Milk depots opened up again, so that women could easily feed a young child on pasteurised, clean, fresh milk. In 1919 the new Ministry of Health generalised the notions of a few innovatory local authorities by recommending such practices for all and providing funds to assist in providing them.[32] Mary Macarthur argued in her 1918 election campaign leaflet preserved in her papers at the Trades Union Congress (TUC), 'The great force in politics is going to be the baby,' and as if to match her words, Glaxo began their campaign using 'King Baby' as an advertising slogan and symbol of the new centrality of infancy to the public mind.[33]

The war removed fathers (as such) from the public mind, since they were so often physically absent, but also because it elevated motherhood. Yet it is not clear how far this rhetorical commitment affected the policies and practices of industrial management in war factories. The idea that mothercraft was a skilled task acted upon advertisers and the producers of baby books, as did some of the presuppositions of industrial welfare. TNT poisoning, however, did not let maternal welfare overwhelm production, and it is as much the needs of the worker as those of the mother that appear to have been given impetus by the war itself. The emphasis on women's physical health was not new, but what was intensified was the reduction of that health to the childbearing function. Prewar concern for the health of working-class mothers was reflected little in wartime increases in provision. The Women's Co-operative Guild had long campaigned for a maternity allowance, which was given by law in 1913 to all women whose husbands were in the national insurance scheme.[34] Although it was small, only 30s, it represented a major step away from the insurance principle proper, since the payment was not directly to those who contributed to the fund, many of those men paying being ineligible as unmarried. This national support of motherhood predates the post-war demobilisation and its more sustained and widespread abandonment of the insurance principle.

One major piece of protective legislation that was not abandoned in wartime was that which offered four weeks' absence from work after childbirth; another was the exclusion of women from coalmines, although a few women did return underground in Scotland. In other words, although pro-natalist arguments and practices were not completely dominant in wartime, they did continue to affect general perceptions of the married woman worker and her needs, construed as the same as the national need for healthy motherhood.

How far did workplaces make it easier to be a mother in practice? One factory developed a scheme for the support of its workers during childbirth – the National Ordnance Factory at Leeds – in April 1918. The scheme was carefully worked out, from no heavy work after confirmation of pregnancy, day work only at four months, to work in the clothing department for the seventh month, where the last hour of the day was given up to the making of clothes for the baby under the help and guidance of the sewing-department forewoman. After the birth, mothers returned to the sewing department and worked hours compatible with breast feeding. This comprehensive scheme was not copied elsewhere, and was anyway of short duration, reflecting an acute local labour shortage, as did a weaker scheme at Aintree.[35]

The official history and later historians have tended to exaggerate the support for working mothers in wartime.[36] In practice, special needs of mothers were provided for reluctantly, only when it became apparent that childcare was a major factor in women's difficulties in working the hours needed for production at maximum level and throughout a factory's continuous operation. Nursery facilities were unevenly distributed throughout the country. In general, they existed either because an area was used to working women, as in Leeds, or where war industries competed with other employers of women, as in London, Glasgow or Newcastle. The national factories did not often provide them because many such factories were sited well away from large towns, and relied on mobile, childless workers housed in hostels for their workforce (as at Gretna and Carlisle). The Ministry of Munitions had to be pressed considerably to get the grants allocated in 1916 for nurseries, and they were awarded reluctantly at all times, only provided when no other organisation was assisting with crèche facilities. It did provide 75% grant of capital costs and 7d per baby payment for each 12 hours of care.[37] Other organisations did provide nurseries, but from the different motives than had created existing nursery provision: that is to compensate for perceived motherhood deficiencies, either in maternity care or of income. Unmarried mothers sometimes found it easier to place their children, as Charlotte Haldane explained in 1927 of the war baby:

> Although it was recognised that to leave the two together was the best way to ensure her future virtue, this was hardly practicable. Again, outside help came to her aid, and while mother earned large wages in the munition factory, baby was well cared for in a beautifully managed nursery for him and his like.[38]

In fact babies were not always segregated according to the marital status of their mothers by voluntary organisations, and factory crèches rarely did so (as far as I can ascertain). There is very little extant information about the methods of running wartime nurseries. A film, 'The Mighty Atom', which is preserved at the Imperial War Museum, gives a small piece of evidence, and photographs of Margaret McMillan's nursery at Deptford (which was described as having gone over to caring for munition workers' children because of the grants) survive in the Greenwich local history library. Representatives of care committees giving evidence to the Women's Service Commission expressed grave doubts about the quality of care in factory nurseries because they were staffed very badly.[39] The visual evidence shows about two adults to about 40 babies, which is very low, but obviously not necessarily the case, and advertisements for staff in Woolwich nurseries imply one to ten rather than one to 20. No witness that I interviewed used a nursery or knew of anyone who did. It does appear that new war nurseries were not exceptionally popular.

Post-war, the Ministry of Health empowered local authorities to take any measure:

> ... for attending to the health of expectant mothers and nursing mothers, of children who have not yet attained the age of five years and are not being educated in schools recognised by the Board of Education.

The model scheme in the accompanying circular includes:

> Provision in day nurseries, crèches or otherwise for the children of mothers who go out to work.

By 1933, one account says, there were only 100 day nurseries of which 18 were run by local authorities, 82 by voluntary associations, accommodating 3,550 under-fives. By my calculation, one in 1,113 children had access to a nursery place, and regional differences meant that apart from London and textile areas the ratio was much higher.[40] This inadequacy of provision is perhaps not surprising when looking at the beliefs of contemporaries about nurseries. In 1918, Dr Janet Campbell sent out a survey from the Ministry of Reconstruction to local medical officers of health (MOH) asking for views on nurseries and a draft report on them by the MOH Sheffield. The replies demonstrate clearly that only in areas where nurseries were a feature of life before the war were they viewed with any approval, despite the experience of war. Other MOH disapproved most strongly, on the grounds that they were 'a makeshift for lessening the bad effects of mothers having to leave their little children,' and that there was:

> ... a danger that new day Nurseries established for patriotic reasons to meet a temporary emergency will become permanent institutions.

Objections to them included the high rate of infection, the discouragement of breast feeding, the dual responsibility, the difficulties of control, and (this in most detail) the cost. Sheffield and Birmingham both espoused boarding-out as cheaper, safer and more controllable means of dealing with childcare difficulties, through the infant-life protection officers of the Board of Guardians. But MOH in Leeds, Blackburn, Halifax, Liverpool, East Ham and Willesden were in favour of them, and in Swansea the MOH argued that the:

> Working class mother who has to live without a maid or other assistance does at certain times need to be relieved of the care of the children and to feel that they are under proper care.

Those who opposed nurseries saw them as inadequate substitutes for the care of a child's own mother or somebody else's, a child minder. Another factor was the effect on mothers, as reported the MOH for Preston, noting that mothers found the separation from their babies quite difficult:

> Day Nurseries are especially difficult to manage on account of the desire on the part of many of the mothers to interfere with the arrangements.[41]

Even during favourable conditions, their support for mothers was in most cases inadequate, grudgingly given and rarely done for the sake of the mother, but for her child, or to maintain high levels of production. When the war was over, it was hoped that the normal state of affairs would return; fathers would take their place again. As the care committees noted from their branches around the country:

> I think the absence of the fathers is a more serious thing than we anticipated. The father seems to have had more to do with the home than we all thought before.[42]

Wartime did little to expose such notions to public scrutiny and, in placing the blame for poor social conditions on temporary alterations due to war, Government and social reformers could evade fundamental questions about families and childcare. They could believe that wartime problems could be solved by the restitution of pre-war life. There was no-one by the end of the war arguing publicly for the right of mothers to work, although there were many who recognised that they did need to work or have some other means of support.

Feminist thought had tended to follow two paths on the issue of motherhood. The first was to attempt to remove all handicaps from single women wishing to work and to assume married women could be supported through dependency or the state if they were widows. The Women's Industrial League (WIL), for example, was the only group to demand the removal of all protective legislation, or argue for the endowment of motherhood, but this was almost an afterthought, and not dwelt on in their leaflets.[43] The reconstruction of domestic life was put forward by campaigners for reform of the urban slums, and Utopian visions of a future in which the productive forces revealed by war could be harnessed for peace were very evident in Labour's reconstruction rhetoric.[44] The fit occupation for women, in the context of demobilisation, was being presented as housekeeping both in their own homes and in society at large. Women's humanising capacities were to be turned to the home away from the factory. This general argument was not contradicted by the experience of factory welfare schemes, which might be said to have made factories more like homes. The absence of direct effect on post-war women's employment lay in the wartime nature of such welfare schemes and the way in which they were introduced, that is to compensate employers for women's deficiency as workers and to compensate society for removing them from the domestic sphere.

The guidelines given by the National Civic Federation to the Ministry of Munitions were carried out to greater or lesser degrees in factories producing armaments. Those under the ministry's direct control, the national factories, had the best schemes, whereas the royal arsenals and privately-owned 'controlled factories' varied from the good to the appalling. The motive initially was production. As the Gretna supervisor said, echoing the comments of many supervisors, 'In short the welfare of the women operatives was considered by the Ministry and factory management as second only to the production of cordite'.[45] It was not only secondary to production but ancillary to it, in that rising production levels, initially thought to be due to inexperience allied to enthusiasm, turned out to go on rising if certain welfare facilities were provided. As the HMWC argued in their report on 'The Employment of Women', 'Cleanliness and good order contribute to discipline and output as well as to increased morale within the factory'.[46]

Output was not raised only through the provision of seats, clean clothing, ventilation and lighting, although these played a major part, because, as the HMWC argued, they greatly increased women's physical fitness and therefore prevented sickness. Women's output did seem to be directly affected by the effectiveness of a good welfare system. It was also raised by the extension of supervision itself. This entailed, as the handbook for ministry welfare supervisors described, a wide range of duties which included keeping a check on time-keeping, hiring and firing workers, encouraging thrift and dealing with wages, especially on piece-work.[47] The final report of the HMWC admitted, 'the confident support of the workers has yet to be obtained,' and, in view of the opportunity for a new style of management that their wide brief provided, it is not surprising that the people who received their administration did not always approve.

The reports of their work filed by welfare supervisors form the bulkiest part of the Imperial War Museum's collection on women's work on munitions, and they reflect the diversity of interpretations of the general brief that factories were to provide welfare for women and the young. They also differed in that welfare workers came from different social classes in different factories: at Dudley National Projectile Factory they were, according to the supervisor's report, 'Not especially trained but they were the wives of police constables and soon picked up their work'.[48] At two national shell factories they reported that inadequate 'ladies' had been replaced by 'women used to dealing with girls', 'forewomen and schoolmistresses', with much greater success.[49] Some factories used women police patrols, which emphasised the disciplinary function of the job, though as Gabrielle West found out in Wales, the uniform was not a guarantee of success.[50] The instructions issued by the Admiralty to the NUWW showed how police patrols were seen as working in the vicinity of ports anyway:

> Their duties were to make friends with the girls and gain their confidence, to warn any girls seen speaking to men on duty or behaving in any way unsuitably.[51]

Women, it was argued at the time, were particularly suited to welfare or police patrol work by this author because, 'being their own sphere,' it was something they could do naturally.

What were workers' reactions to welfare? Some of its provisions were warmly welcomed, and brought hidden talents to light. At Cardonald, for example, there were three football teams, a newspaper, *The Shield*, a Pierrot troupe and a theatre group, the 'Merry Magnets', as well as an institute running classes, although the only really popular event was dancing.[52] Gretna had less home-produced amusements but two institutes and a girl's club which 'appealed more warmly to the girls'.[53] One of the middle-class war workers who did relief shifts at weekends at Vickers Crayford said, 'The whole life was a happy recovery of one's schooldays'.[54] The areas totally devoted to munitions production did provide the sheltered atmosphere of fun with discipline, reminiscent perhaps of the lack of responsibility of a middle-class youth, but other areas did not see the same relationship between welfare workers and war workers at all.

> At Dudley, workers went to welfare supervisors about their wages. They often came to us to have their wages explained. This was often a very complicated matter and it is not surprising that workers were often in doubt as to what they should receive.[55]

Some workers saw welfare as on their side, others perceived it as another arm of management, all the more suspect for being apparently benevolent. The HMWC *Handbook* was very firm about a supervisor's relation to trade unions:

> Supervisors ought not to interfere with the work of the Trade Unions. They are, after all, the servants of the employer, and cannot as such be accepted as the authorised and official representatives of the workers even as regards matters which affect only the conditions in the particular factory in which they are employed. They are not intended and cannot replace Trade Unionism.[56]

Women in the factory did sometimes treat welfare workers as though they were there for their benefit alone, but this reflects more on the weakness of trade unions in some workplaces than it does on the quality of welfare. In some factories welfare was viewed with deep suspicion because the trade unions were very successful in recognising and remedying the workers' grievances.

Supervisors were introduced in Armstrong Whitworth's Elswick works after a strike, along with canteens, tea-breaks and improved lavatory facilities but, said the chief welfare supervisor at the factory:

> Supervisors appeared to them in the light of spies who were going to watch, and report to management, the ring leaders in Trade Union organisation and endeavour to weaken this influence, or as 'goody goody' people who were going to poke their noses into the workers' private affairs and interfere with their liberty and independence, which the majority of women are tasting for the first time as industrial workers on the same footing as men.[57]

Oddly enough, Gladys Robson, who was one of those ringleaders, said in her interview that she thought they had no welfare supervisors at all: she remembers only being searched by a woman police patrol at the gate.

The 'official' view of most women's trade unions was rather similar to that of the militant NFWW members in Newcastle. Mary Macarthur said at a conference on welfare in 1918:

> There is no word in the English language more hated among the women workers of today than that of welfare. The chief objection they have to recent developments is that they find it difficult to understand the position of the welfare worker who tells them that she is looking after their interests yet they know she is paid by their employer. Besides welfare workers often interfere outside factory hours, and such interference with home, life, leisure and liberty undermines the workers' independence and self-reliance, and tends to make them forget it is more important to be a good citizen than a good machinist. The workers have a right to the best conditions obtainable, Trade Unions are necessary to claim and maintain these conditions and, having secured them... the workers can look after much for themselves which welfare workers undertake to do.[58]

Mary Macarthur said her members particularly resented the undignified interference in personal life most welfare workers tended to provide:

> They object to be being lectured on their dress... They object to being visited in their homes and they object to organisation of amusements and so on as counter attractions to their meetings. She finished her

speech quoting one munition worker saying, 'We object to being done good to'.[59]

This last, less-considered view probably represents the actual response of some workers more directly than the defence of trade-union interests in Macarthur's speech. There were serious conflicts of interests. As Madeline Symons of the NFWW pointed out over the provision of hostels, there was a danger of reviving the hated 'truck' system by including goods and services as any part of wages. This was avoided by ensuring that all hostels and hutments were paid for through rental, but there remained the tied cottage aspect of dependence on one employer for both home and wages. The trade unions argued for self-government in hostels, and so eventually did the ministry, since allowing workers to regulate their own domestic arrangements actually meant hostels were full instead of remaining unpopular and empty.[60]

Trade-union leaders and the women they represented disliked the disciplinary part of welfare, but approved of many of the material improvements brought about by welfare schemes. They approved in principle of the support of motherhood through nurseries and cash endowment. Of the latter, Jessie Stephens, then working for the Domestic Servants Union, said in 1919:

> One way of solving the female labour problem is to get the married women out of the labour market by providing mothers' pensions. This would not only make more room for the single girl but also reduce the number of juvenile delinquents.[61]

Others argued for the nursery as the way to ensure an adequate supply of labour and successful parenthood. Lilian Barker proposed a 'national crèche' scheme in 1916, enthusiastically endorsed by Mary Macarthur:

> Think of a great summer camp of happy healthy children taken care of in the best and most simple fashion and under proper direction – regular military discipline as it were. A splendid scheme.[62]

The implication of a utopian vision of alternatives to conventional patterns of household labour also raised aspirations for the home, briefly, when women's labour was in short supply. As Marion Phillips wrote in her account of the home of the future, as part of the Labour Party's plans for reconstruction:

We have been told that a woman's place is in the home. If women are to accept their position, they must also claim the right to have that home built to their own desires.[63]

If the humanising of the workplace was responsive to the conditions of the labour market then the demand for women's labour could be shifted elsewhere in reconstruction, but there were few who shared the views of the historian of the Women's Co-operative Guild in the 1920s:

There need be no unemployed women in the country, if only the work could be well planned and suitably organised. Slums might be cleared, the homes of the poor cleansed and repainted, greater attention given to the needs of children and to the improvement of public health.[64]

This survival of a wartime ethos of extensive social reform was to be unusual in the period of demobilisation and reconstruction, but it was a response learned in part by the observers who had seen that women war-workers could benefit from life in the factory, that the provisions of factory welfare could provide lessons for a post-war world. Unfortunately, few retained these insights into the years after the war was over. The effect on production of adequate seating, lighting, food and hours of work was evident, but so too was the stimulus provided by competitive rate-fixing through the premium bonus payment system. The one lesson that was not carried into the post-war world from the war factory was the desirability of including an assessment of the workers' own views in patterns of factory management. Women had demanded a limited amount of workers control through the contests over welfare, but they had not succeeded in enforcing the demand in a post-war industrial world.

Notes on Chapter 8

Full details of all publications mentioned here are in the bibliography on page 209.

1   Macarthur, M. in Dewar, K. (ed.), *The Girl*, 1920, p 96. This chapter is based on Thom, D., unpublished PhD for the CNAA at Thames Polytechnic, 1982, ch. 6.

2   The Health of Munition Workers Committee, memo 4, 'The Employment of Women', PP 1916 xxiii, Cd 8185, p 4.

3   See chapter 3.

4   Cmd 135, p 233 makes the same point negatively, that the better kind of factory was only for the single woman.

5   IWM17/9, correspondence between Isobel Sloan and Mrs Young of the National Civic Federation, list of recommendations approved, 6 November 1915.

6   MMOH vol. V, pt III, pp 1-8.

7   N. Whiteside.

8   21,000 copies of the Health of Munition Workers Committee reports were circulated in industry, PP 1918, xii, Cd 9065, Final Report of the Health of Munition Workers Committee, p 5.

9   Kirkaldy, A.W. (ed.) *Labour, Finance and the War*, 1916 (an enquiry for the British Association), Glasgow report, p 113. These were the only enquirers to ask whether women were better time-keepers than men, rather than worse.

10 Op. cit. pp 81, 84.

11 Transcripts of evidence to the War Cabinet Committee on Women in Industry, evidence of Mr Blain, general manager of the LGOC, day 11, IWM.EMP 70 TE, p 529; Umberto Wolff, day 1, p 61, day 39, p 1; whereas good time-keeping was reported by David Shackleton, day 3, p 23, Mr Crinion, Cardroom Operatives, day 25, p 48 and J. Thomas of the NUR, day 27, p 16.

12 Report of the Commissioners into Industrial Unrest, Cd 8666 pp 2-3.

13 PP1916, xii, Cd 8243, second report of the Control Board, Liqor Traffic, pp 8-9.

14 Report of the Women's Advisory Committee, IWM.MUN 18/8, pp 8, 31.

15 IWM.EMP 18/2, 24 November 1916, p 50.

16 A point taken up in Woolacott, A in 'Maternalism, Professionalism...' op. cit.

17 IMW.MUN 18/2, 24 November 1916, p 50.

18 IWM.MUN 18/2, 23 November 1916, p 8.

19 IWM.MUN 18/3, 28 November 1916, p 4.

20 IWM.MUN 18/4, 1 December 1916, p 48.

21 *Woolwich Pioneer*, 9 May 1917.

22 Interim Report of the Women's Employment Committee, PP 1914-16, xxxvii, Cd 7848, p 4.10.

23 Minutes WTUAC, 6 December 1917, PRO.MUN 5.52.78; Gore, E., *The Better Fight*, 1975, pp 94-99.

24 Ministry of Labour Weekly Report, 4 Jan 1919, IWM. EMP 80, p 12;

25 January 1919, p 7; 1 February, 1919, p 12 and instances record until July when they begin to close courses down.

25 *Rugby Advertiser*, 18 December 1915, GTC at the TUC.

26 Report from factory manager, Woolwich Arsenal, SACF4, IWM.MUN 29.

27 Dewar, G.A.B., *The Great Munitions Feat*, 1921, p 317.

28 Training schemes for women, IWM.EMP 79.

29 Land, H., 'Family Allowances, an Act of Historic Justice' in Hall, Land *et al.* (eds) *Choice and Conflict in Social Policy*, 1972; Macnicol, J., *The Campaign for Family Allowances*.

30 Wimperis, V., *The Unmarried Mother and her Child*, 1967.

31 National Baby Week: Sylvia Pankhurst organised a counter demonstration in 1917, minutes 18 June, IWM Welfare (Wel) Box 1, 16.

32 McCleary, G.F., *The Maternity and Child Welfare Movement*, 1934, pp 19-20, 55-7, 216.

33 *Woman Worker,* May 1917.

34 Women's Co-operative Guild, *Maternity Letters from Working Women*, 1915, was the book they produced in support of their demand that the new allowance, although dependent upon a husband's insurance status, be paid to the woman herself.

35 IWM.MUN 20 Leeds, IWM.MUN 21 Aintree.

36 MMOH vol. V pt III, Welfare; Whiteside, N., 'The Ministry of Munitions and Welfare Institute of Historical Research' paper 1977.

37 IWM.MUN 18/9, report on intra-mural welfare work in national factories, p 8.

38 Haldane, C., *Motherhood and its enemies*, 1927, p 11.

39 IWM.MUN 18/5, evidence of Miss Moreton, 5 December 1916, pp 40-1.

40 McCleary, G.F., *The Maternity and Child Welfare Movement*, 1934, pp 20-22, 108, ratio calculated on population statistics from Halsey, A.H., *Trends in Modern British Society*, 1972, pp 31-3.

41 BLPES, reconstruction papers, box 4, document 90.

42 Evidence of Miss Moreton, IWM.MUN 18/5, p 44.

43 Objects and aims of the WIL mentions this in a report of a speech, not as a central platform, IWM.EMP 71/5.

44 Caroline Rowan.

45 Report from the National Shell factory, Gretna, IMW.MUN 14, p 9.

46 Health of Munition Workers Committee, Memorandum no 4, 'The Employment of Women', PP 1916, xxiii, Cd 185, p 7.

47 Health of Munition Workers Committee *Handbook*, p 4.

48 Dudley national projectile factory, IWM.MUN 21, p 5.

49 Intra-mural welfare in national shell factories, IWM.MUN 20.

50 Diary of Gabrielle West, IWM.
51 Cit. Dewar, K. (ed.), *The Girl*, 1920, p 93.
52 Report of welfare at Cardonald, IWM.MUN 9.
53 Report on welfare at Gretna, IWM.MUN 9.
54 War volunteers, IWM.MUN 17.
55 Dudley NPF, IWM.MUN 21, p 6.
56 Health of Munition Workers *Handbook*, 1917, p 13.
57 Armstrong Whitworth, IWM.MUN 19.
58 Macarthur, M., *Women's Trade Union Review*, July 1917, p 11; cit. by Webb, B. in Dewar, K. (ed.), *The Girl*, 1920.
59 Evidence of Mary Macarthur, IWM.TE 4 October, p K10-11.
60 Evidence of Madeline Symons to the Women's Committee of the Liquor Control Board Canteens Committee, 15 December 1916, IWM.EMP pp 61-2; *Woman Worker*, December 1918, p 6.
61 *Empire News*, 9 March 1919, GTC at the TUC, 654.
62 Unfortunately I have found no other reference to this and it may rest upon journalistic exaggeration. *Weekly Despatch*, 28 February 1916, GTC at the TUC, 603.
63 Phillips, Dr M., *The Working Woman's House*, 1918.
64 Webb, C., *The Woman with the Basket*, 1927, p 138.

Chapter 9

Passengers for the War

Demobilisation and reconstruction

> Reconstruction has been for some time our favourite shibboleth. Shall I be accused of faintheartedness if I say that, at this moment, the new world looks uncommonly like the old one, rolling along as stupidly and blindly as ever and that all it has got from the war is an extra bitterness or two?[1]

Mary Macarthur had good reason for personal grief in 1919. She had been very ill, her husband had died and she had failed to win a seat in Parliament.[2] But her bitter words reflected a general disenchantment felt by industrial women with the post-war world. Heidi Hartmann has blamed men for this phenomenon:

> Man's ability to organise in labor unions – stemming perhaps from a greater knowledge of the techniques of hierarchical organisation – appears to be the key in their ability to maintain job segregation and the domestic division of labor.[3]

Mary Macarthur blamed no-one, but did see the loss of wartime openings as a concerted and ideological attack on working women:

> Now she, 'woman', is being turned out of her war employment and it is explained that she was never really as satisfactory as she might have been.

The vital part, though, in the changing role of women in industry was played by women's own unions, expressing in many cases the wishes of women themselves. The unions went through a rapid succession of sudden changes in industry and state policy, and responded by a process of amalgamation and change. Some aspects of the ideology of women's work had been changed little by the war years. The belief that social forces of a general kind were the primary agent of control over women's labour was one held by most trade unionists, male and female. Women trade-union leaders continued to see their main task as winning acceptance for working women within trade unionism. Labour politics, now open to women over thirty, absorbed some of the campaigning energies of social reformers who had previously worked through trade unions as agents of social change.

Susan Lawrence and Ellen Wilkinson, along with Barbara Drake, either went into educational politics at local or national level or into a new life as a member of parliament. Both Margaret Bondfield and Mary Macarthur stood for election as MPs in 1918 and the former succeeded in 1923.[4] Sheila Lewenhak sees a division between the two in terms of their commitment to national politics, but the only difference seems to have been not on the principle of political action, since both supported state regulation of wages and conditions through the growing trade board system and the revival of protective legislation, but on the personalities or practice of political action. The question was who should go into politics rather than whether these measures should be taken.[5]

The struggle for entry into national politics matured in 1919, at the same time as other trade unionists' struggles in the streets over the 40-hour day, the right of policemen and soldiers to organise, and some major rent strikes. It was a period of political readjustment, and one in which women's demands tended to be taken less seriously since they were made less urgently. The report of the War Cabinet Committee on Women in Industry 'was about as effective as driftwood on the tide'.[6] Women gained some legal rights in 1918. Middle-class women found the way to the professions more accessible through the Sex Disqualification (Removals) Act; older working-class women now had the vote, but they were more affected at work by the Restoration of Pre-war Practices Act, which removed dilution agreements from industry and hence excluded dilutees from all the jobs they had taken 'for the duration of the war'. Under this act, the male trade unionists laid claim to aircraft-making, as it was analogous to engineering, and to the technique of arc-welding. As a result, women who had literally 'made' the trade found themselves excluded from it. The Society of Women Welders enlisted feminist writer Ray Strachey on their side, and she mounted a strong campaign against this by writing to the press on their behalf.[7] (The Women's Industrial League used this case as the main feature of their campaign for equal access to all occupations for women.) Mary Macarthur dismissed the league as 'an organisation of former dilution officers of the Ministry of Munitions'[8] who did not express the real aspirations of working-class women, and part of the reason for her organisation's support of the AEU, rather than the arc-welders, was the class background of the members of the Society of Women Welders, who were all of the middle class; but far more important was the continuing need, as she saw it, to integrate women trade unionists with the trade-union movement as a whole. Thus the Women's Trade Union League (WTUL) supported the principle they should ensure that jobs given to women in wartime be given back to the men after the war was over. In this case, the National Federation of Women Workers (NFWW) was prepared to sacrifice this small group of women workers in order to maintain the credibility of its wartime stance into peacetime. On aeroplane work, union organisation was much more limited, so the AEU had less success in enforcing the exclusion.

The whole process of demobilisation was affected by the dual pressures of state policy on the labour market and the need of women's unions to preserve their membership and extend into a peacetime, reorganised economy. War workers were very quickly sacked from munitions production, but the wholesale winding down of the national factories kept the Ministry of Munitions occupied and in existence until March 1921. Women were discharged, though, and men were kept on to dismantle and reprocess metal and machines. The aspirations of the Hills Committee, that the factories could be used to remedy the main deficiency of women workers, namely their lack of training, were never seriously considered. The only concern was that state manufacture should be shown not to have created a massive debt, but come out slightly in profit. When Winston Churchill, retiring as Minister of Munitions, said that the ministry was the 'greatest argument for State socialism that has been produced'[9] it was probably this he was thinking of, although the welfare work which helped keep output high may have been one of his reasons. Trade unionists persistently argued for alternative peaceful uses of the war production machinery, but consistently found that their proposals went unheard since they were for products already supplied by private industry.[10] Women's organisations did not oppose the processes of demobilisation as such, but they opposed the manner in which they were carried out, often without adequate arrangements for travel for demobilised women or for an overnight stay. They complained that there was class favoritism, as the well-off were being kept on and the poor discharged; that women were being sacked while men worked overtime; that women were being forced to go into the WAACs or the Land Army.[11] The Ministry of Munitions ordered a system of discharges in the general instructions of November 1918 but it is clear from these complaints and the record of individual factories that they were widely ignored in practice. Many women, especially married women, were impatient to leave anyway. They reported that they wanted to leave the war factories if family members were on leave or demobilised from the armed services.[12] The Ministry of Labour had laid down a hierarchy of discharges for women. Women without industrial experience went first; second went those readily absorbed into previous occupations; then bad time-keepers, those with short periods of service and lastly the skilled and those in training.[13] These strictly industrial criteria were speedily super-seded by the Treasury announcement on 11 December 1918:

> In present circumstances, the continued production of munitions involves a waste of money and of labour and material which it will be impossible to justify to Parliament save in wholly exceptional circum-stances, such as the temporary continuance, for brief periods, of production in order to avoid too great a simultaneous discharge of labour.[14]

By June 1919, the Ministry of Munitions had discharged 90 per cent of its women employees and 48 per cent of men in the national factories.[15] Winston Churchill and Christopher Addison, who had both been Minister of Munitions, used similar metaphors to describe the industrial army of munition workers. Addison complained that the Ministry of National Service officials were careless about the way in which they dehumanised their workers. '[They] appear to think that you move labour about in blocks of hundreds or thousands,' he wrote disapprovingly,[16] while Churchill said of the War Office, under criticism for hanging on to reluctant soldiers:

They are blamed like Pharaoh of old because they will not let the people go. Our difficulty is that we cannot let the people stay... we have actually succeeded... in discharging nearly three quarters of a million persons from munitions production the bulk of whom did not want to go.[17]

More war workers, though, did not want to leave, and if they did have to go, felt that equal rates for the job should also mean equal unemployment benefit. This demand was raised by all unions representing women war-workers and supported by the trade-union movement as a whole.

In March 1919, a huge meeting was organised at the Albert Hall to make the demand for equal unemployment benefit, following a series of demonstrations in Trafalgar Square particularly from London munitions workers demanding this as a fair reward for the time they had spent doing war work. Under the National Insurance (Part II)(Munition Workers) Bill of 1916, any worker on munitions and associated trades could enter the national insurance scheme of 1911. But many trades, most notably cotton, wool, and boot and shoe got exemption orders excluding their workers from the scheme. The result was that of the new entrants into the insurance scheme, 1,100,000 people in all, about three quarters were women and girls, and these were nearly all working on the direct production of armaments, paying and getting pre-war rates of contribution and benefit.[18] The attempts by reconstruction officials to extend the scheme to all civilian war-workers went unheeded and, as a result, war workers were given unemployment benefits even though they had not paid into the scheme for long enough, in its initial form, to qualify for extended periods of benefit. The government's panic reaction to demobilisation actually gave most of these women more money than a straightforward insurance scheme, and, by removing the insurance principle, made it more clearly a reward for war service. Women were demanding, therefore, equality of reward and equality of need in unemployment, but the women who could most legitimately do so, war workers, were those who had least claim on existing jobs. Hence the politics of the campaign on unemployment muddled the issue of any general right-to-work demand.

On 4 April 1919 out-of-work donation was extended for women war-workers and members of the services, partly in response to demands from trade unions.[19] The public meeting in the Albert Hall on 17 February 1919, organised by the *Daily*

Herald with the NFWW, had put forward the slogan 'The Right to Work; the Right to Life; the Right to Leisure'.[20] The report of it in the *Woman Worker* said:

> They do not ask their country to maintain them in idleness. They ask to be set to productive work... They merely plead for a minimum of security, comfort and leisure; not for any distant Utopia, but for a means of escaping from the grinding poverty, the overwork and the desperate uncertainty of their pre-war lives.[21]

This report sums up the issue of demobilisation. The maintenance of wage levels was allowed for in the Wages (Temporary Regulation) Act, which only allowed a wage cut with trade-union agreement. No women sat on the tribunal which was set up to deal with any contested wages issue.[22] No women were on the Select Committee on the 'out-of-work donation'. The result was that many employers laid off large numbers of experienced women workers and took on young trainees to evade the wages schemes.[23] Many women were refused out-of-work donation because they had not been employed before the war, irrespective of whether the reason for that was family circumstance or age, so that although 500,000 received the donation by March 1919, 150,000 more women were excluded from it by these two factors.[24] Eighty-seven per cent of all women's appeals against withdrawal of donation (for not being prepared to take work offered) were refused, as a refusal was not accepted by March 1919 on any job in domestic service.[25] The separation between categories of unemployment was made, quite simply, one of gender. The Ministry of Labour's instructions went:

> Every effort should be made to minimise unemployment utilising employees for a short period on labouring and clearing up work. In allotting this work preference should be given to workpeople who are ordinarily dependent on industrial employment.[26]

Most women war-workers had not been industrial workers before the war, although many had some industrial experience. The first group who were discouraged from remaining in the workforce were married women. In February 1919, the Labour reports of the Ministry of Labour said that many out-of-work donations had been claimed and were finished, and more men than women were being placed in job vacancies: 'These facts tend to show that as soldiers

return to their homes their wives are reverting to housewifery'.[27]
How free this choice was must be open to doubt. Married women
were not allowed to participate in training schemes for employment
if they had children.[28] By 1920, the Ministry recorded the difficulties in placing married women, 'since employers generally, as
before the war, are showing preference for unmarried employees'.[29]

Yet the Ministry of Labour chose to retrain people in traditional
women's trades. They explicitly disassociated their policy from
attempts to undermine the sexual division of labour. In March
1919, they said:

> Industrial training will for the present be confined to normal women's
> trades, for example clothing manufacture, in the processes known as
> women's processes before the war in which recent inquiry has shown
> there is a need for skilled workers and a good prospect of employment.[30]

By June, the courses were only for women's processes where there
was a demand for labour. There was large demand for clerical
courses, and a persistent refusal by clerical workers to shift into
another form of employment. Courses at Rotherham for fuse-
makers to retrain on clocks and watches were also very popular.
Employers were subsidised at 12s 6d a week per worker to employ
women on silk, straw hats, gloves and beading, but workers found
their wages, at 25s in all, often as unattractive as the dole, which
had been raised to 25s for women, 29s for men.[31] Trade unions
were in general uninterested in training. The exception was the
WTUL, which was happiest in an educative role, and exhorted its
supporters to encourage the use of these courses.[32] The male trade-
union movement was much exercised by the plight of ex-servicemen.
The shop stewards' movement particularly took up their case and
argued, 'Not one war-hand should remain while ex-service men are
dismissed'.[33] A conference on the demarcation of men's and
women's work raised the ex-soldiers as an example of the necessity
to ensure that work should return to its original 'owners'. The ASE
speaker argued:

> There was a tendency in industry for women to sort themselves into a
> particular trade or process, and he was of the opinion that if this ten-
> dency was encouraged, the men would not feel so much as they are
> today that the women are taking their jobs.[34]

History in 1918 and 1919

Women in war has been the subject of much writing, both cele-bratory and pessimistic, which mirrors, just as the books on literary modernism have done, debates about the war itself. Between 1918 and 1920 there was a short publishing boom which, like the eco-nomic boom, included some women. Mrs Fawcett herself looked to a future without exclusion in writing *Woman's Victory and After*. Ray Strachey was to write *The Cause* in 1927, which saw the war's end and the franchise as marking a victory for women's politics and for women in politics. The language of militancy and the assumption of battle and antagonism as characteristic of the women's part of the fight for the vote and thence of the war effort has been much criticised, because these writings are seen as flawed by male assumptions about the nature of politics, allowing negoti-ation and compromise, nurture and gentleness to be overwhelmed by a violence constructed out of deformed male models of the political.[35] Similarly, some have pointed to the way in which the trade unions organising women entered and vanished into the General Federation of Trade Unions as a loss of a distinctively female political representation of the working woman.

In the 1920s there was also a revival of sexual antagonism which some had seen as characteristic of the years before the war. The survey of women's employment published in 1919, the report of the War Cabinet Committee on Women in Industry, had set the trend, in a way, by debating so vigorously the relationship between men and women to the detriment of the latter. The secret labour reports of the Ministry of Munitions had cynically reported that the trade unions in munitions supported women's demand for equal pay because they believed that this would ensure the return of men to their jobs; employers would, they believed, always prefer men.

> Equal pay is demanded in order that the inequality – such is the judge-ment of the men - in the value of the two types of labour may become effective towards the ultimate expulsion of the women from the indus-trial regions into which they have penetrated during the war. Curiously enough the women do not seem to see this.[36]

Despite substantial debate at the time, the women never did alto-gether see this. Barbara Drake identified the cause for their refusal to resent the exclusion when she argued:

Male trade unionists were determined to reimpose their restrictions on female labour. Nor was the decision opposed by industrial women, who were quick to acknowledge the common justice of the men's claim that pledges given by government and the employers must be redeemed in full. This necessity seemed, indeed, so plain to men and women trade unionists that the only matter for surprise was that they should have had to insist upon it.[37]

One of the reasons for women's difficulty in perceiving the cynicism of this view was that many of them were swept up in the months when war ended in finding new jobs and fighting unemployment, and because, as Drake said, the war's end was a time for good faith and behaviour, in which ideas of solidarity and sacrifice had been entrenched in war for munition workers as well as soldiers.

Yet the first post-war history of women's work was the report of the War Cabinet Committee on Women in Industry, which concluded that a woman's work had been the equivalent of two-thirds that of a man. They had met 53 times between 3 October 1918 and 1 April 1919. The committee was chaired by Mr Justice Atkin, who had made the landmark legal decision to include railway wagons in the category of munitions for the purposes of introducing dilution, the prohibition of strikes and regulation of the whole wartime labour market. Beatrice Webb had accepted her invitation to serve despite, as she recorded in her diary, the fact that she was 'not in the least interested in the relation between men's and women's wages' because she was initially invited (as were all members, because of a clerical error) to be chairman.[38] Two other professional arbitrators sat on the committee, Sir Lyndon Livingstone Macassey and Sir William Mackenzie, although Beatrice Webb believed that only the secretary, Lt Col. the Rt Hon. Sir Matthew Nathan, did any work before the sittings. She also recorded that the committee only met once after February 1919, to sign the report, so that although the report did not come out until the September, time for deliberation was extremely short. The Government was very clear about what it expected to come out of the committee's investigation. Barnes invited Webb to lunch with Nathan at the War Office because they did not want her to produce a minority report:

> Barnes wanted to persuade me to acquiesce in the Committee acting as a cloak to the Cabinet in their refusal to carry out their pledges (the pledges to give equal pay).[39]

She refused, arguing that the Government must discuss the question in public. The committee had not even finished hearing evidence at this time, so it is not surprising that Webb assumed that the sittings were far more a palliative for the striking munitions workers and tramworkers, whose cases had brought the committee into existence, than a serious attempt to analyse the principles upon which payment was allocated. Although, in the end, both the two minority reports and the main report concluded that there should be equal pay for equal work, their interpretations of what this meant were very divergent. The Women's Industrial League (WIL) argued that the right to work should dominate over the right to equal reward, but the majority were with Webb in arguing that equal pay should overwhelm equal opportunity. At least there was an attempt to come to terms directly with the efforts and contribution of munition workers as part of the first writing of a history of the war. Other industries outside the protected munitions area showed that some lessons of the history of war were to demonstrate more fully the revival of simple prejudices about women's capacities, productivity and nature.

Employers varied as to whether they argued for equal pay or equal opportunity, and the complexity of the issue is shown by some evidence to the Ministry of Reconstruction which argued, for example, that arduous manual work could show differences of output of as high a ratio as 2 to 1 in heavy leather work or bleaching and dying; warehouse work, one employer said, showed so significant a difference that though women were only a quarter as productive as men, there was 'None, if leggings or other suitable dress is worn'. What was meant here by 'suitable' was complicated by the working conditions of manual labourers in the factory, where comments about the 'experience of war' were made which were directly reminiscent of the debate over women working underground 70 years before. One soap manufacturer said he was very doubtful, 'of the wisdom of mixing the sexes in any part of the building; it is very hot and the men wear very little'.[40] Yet even this denial of women's capacity to learn how to work and to deal with social difficulties was recognised by such comments as 'Inferiority diminishes with experience'.[41] Others had learned lessons about women's physical capacities and natures which worked differently.

Dr Janet Campbell wrote the medical section of the final report of the War Cabinet Committee and she concluded:

The whole experience tends to show that light sedentary work is not by any means always the most suitable for women, that operations involving a change of posture are preferable and that, given adequate nutrition, many women would have better health and greater vigour of they followed more active occupations.[42]

However, there was a great fear that the history of the experience of war might be inscribed on the bodies of mothers and thence onto their children:

The stunted physique and poor health of many of our industrial workers suggests there may also be the graver and more fundamental injury to the germ plasm itself and so to the future of the race.[43]

Campbell herself believed that the history so ably outlined by Barbara Drake in her historical chapter was being undermined by the reduction in differentials of strength, but that the most fundamental cause of difference between men and women was:

Less remediable. It must always involve some dependence of women on men's support in connection with her essential service to the race.[44]

Since this history of women and war was, unusually in observations of labour, actually documented in terms of what the workers produced and how fast they produced it, it all became a question not of output *per se* but of ancillary costs. Campbell pointed out that lifting tackle introduced to maximise the output of women in fact improved male productivity also, Webb that employers were anxious to recover as much wartime cost as possible, so they tended to attribute all innovation as part of the history of the women introduced in wartime rather than of the war itself. Transport is an interesting example of the way in which these many factors accumulated to make an indictment of the woman war-worker.

Women were said to generate more complaints, be unreliable, physically incapable of collecting all the fares. Clerks substituting for men on the railways could not sometimes deal with knotty examples of railway etiquette like handling dogs or racehorses: 'It requires someone with a good deal of strength to maintain the railway point of view sometimes'. Some transport workers were seen as endangering social order:

Some of the girls wanted to go in for low blouses and that sort of thing and we had a good deal of trouble with them cutting their uniform about to suit themselves.[45]

Others distinguished between the innocent and virtuous novice worker and the old hand who had flourished in wartime because of labour shortage. Mrs Blanco White gave evidence about the 'Old hands in the rope trade who sat on the newcomers and drove them out of the factory and refused to allow any but the same type of slum labour as themselves'.[46] Extra costs of the introduction of women are given a 'natural' status in the report of the war cabinet committee along with the evidence upon which it is based, the costs being supervision, reduced output, welfare supervision, separate accommodation (especially lavatories) and special mechanical appliances.[47]

The process of reconstruction of women in the labour market was therefore taking place when a history of women's work was already being written. Women's wartime work was fast becoming seen as a demonstration of their nature; yet factors peculiar to war which affected productivity adversely were ignored in favour of a broad general, numerical assessment of their contribution. They themselves were weary of war and, apart from a few who occupied the war factories and demanded the right to stay on at work, and another few who demanded the right to stay on living at their war hostels, most women gladly resumed a life outside the factory of wartime. What they could not do was either reconstruct a new sort of work or return to the work they had done before the war. The former was precluded by the absence of formal or informal means of representation, evident in trade unionism's speedy renunciation of any special interests in war workers and the failure of women to achieve parliamentary seats in England in the first election including a female electorate: the latter was demonstrably impossible, after four years when much had changed in family life, location and work skills. Many women had lost the chance to return to pre-war training, been 'spoiled' for their pre-war aspirations by the physical consequences of arduous manual labour. Domestic servants, for example, often found that factory work excluded them from specialised domestic skills such as cooking or nursery work, and they were only considered eligible for general service jobs. Education deferred for four years could not easily be resumed. The emphasis in retraining on domestic skills was to demonstrate the wider assumptions that women had gained no general expertise from war work and, on the contrary, that they were lacking in what they most needed to build a post-war society.

Notes on Chapter 9

Full details of all publications mentioned here are in the bibliography on page 209.

1   *West Sussex Gazette*, 11 December 1919, GTC at the TUC, 324.
2   Hamilton, M.A., *Mary Macarthur*, 1923.
3   Op. cit. p 233.
4   Cole, M., *Women of Today* (1938); Bondfield, M., *A Life's Work*, 1951, p 1.
5   Lewenhak, S., *Women in Trade Unions*, 1977, pp 164, 174, 187.
6   Anthony, S., *Women's Place in Industry and the Home*, 1932, p 83.
7   File on the Society of Women Welders has an extensive collection of press clippings on this debate, GTC at the TUC, 504 G; Drake, B., *Women in Trade Unions*, 1920, p 82; *Common Cause*, 23 January 1920.
8   IWM.EMP 71/5; IWM.MUN 5.55, 24 February 1918.
9   Address, 19 March 1919, PRO.MUN 5.52.78; PRO.MUN 2.21; *Official History of the Ministry of Munitions, A History of State Manufacture*, vol. VIII.
10 *Woman Worker*, December 1918, p 5; *Workers' Union Record*, January 1919, p 3.
11 PRO.MUN 5.52.78; 6 December 1917 meeting WTUL; MUN 5.52.78, 20 December 1917; 3 January, 4 March 1918.
12 *Ibid.*, 4 March 1918.
13 PRO.MUN 2.17, 16 November 1918, p 2.
14 Letter from Robert Chalmers of the Treasury to the Secretary of War, 11 December 1918, PRO.MUN 1.16.
15 PRO.MUN 2.19, 14 June 1919.
16 Addison, C., *Politics from Within*, 1924, 22 March 1917.
17 PRO.MUN 1.17, 13 January 1919.
18 Beveridge, W.H., 'Unemployment Insurance' in Beveridge (ed.), *War and Insurance*, 1927, pp 232-3.
19 IWM.EMP 80, April 1919.
20 Lewenhak, S., *Women in Trade Unions*, 1977, p 165.
21 *Woman Worker*, February 1919, p 6.
22 *Woman Worker*, January 1919, p 10.

23 WTUL Annual Report 1919, p 8.
24 *Reynolds News*, 30 May 1919, GTC at the TUC. This figure is claimed by Dorothea Jewson of the NFWW, but it is impossible to check because benefit refusals are not separated by gender until 1925; see Deacon, A., 'The Politics of Unemployment Insurance in the Twenties', in Briggs, A. and Saville, J. (eds), *Essays in Labour History*, 1977, p 21.
25 Anthony, S., *Women's Place in Industry and the Home*, 1932, p 82.
26 *Labour Gazette*, October 1918, p 438.
27 Weekly labour reports, 1 February 1919, IMW.EMP 80, p 7.
28 IMW.EMP 80, 19 July 1919, p 24.
29 IMW.EMP 80, 22 May 1920, p 571 (pagination cumulates after 1 January 1920).
30 IMW.EMP 80, 15 March 1919, p 24.
31 IMW.EMP 80, 22 February, 1919, p 20, 30 August 1918, p 22, 6 September 1919, p 18.
32 WTUL Annual Report, 1919, p 8.
33 IMW.EMP 80, 21 February 1920, p 105.
34 *Woman Worker*, April 1919, p 3.
35 See discussion of Ray Strachey in *Women's History Review* 3.1, 1994.
36 PRO.MUN 2.16, 31 August 1918, p 12.
37 Drake, B., *Women in Trade Unions*, 1920, p 106.
38 Webb, B., Diary at the BLPES (BWD), 1 September 1918, p 3,618, records the invitation, and again 3,624 and 3,652 from which entry the comment quoted comes.
39 BWD, 1 November 1918, p 3,631.
40 Tabular reports by HM Inspector of Factories, January 1917, for substitution in industries other than munitions, BLPES, reconstruction documents, box 1, doc. 63.
41 *Ibid.*, p 3.
42 Cmd 135, p 238.
43 *Ibid.*, p 253.
44 *Ibid.*, pp 220-1.
45 Transcripts of evidence, evidence 19 October 1918, S27, also 29 October 1918, IWM, p 23.
46 Evidence of Mrs Blanco White, women's wages section, Board of Trade, Cmd 167, p 5.
47 Cmd 135, pp 6, 27, 34, 238.

Chapter 10
Conclusion: The History of the
History of Women and the War

Hence the history of a group of novice wartime workers has been turned into the natural history of women's work itself. Subsequent histories have, from different political perspectives, tended to do the same thing. Initially the war was seen as a means to an end: the entry of women into citizenship through the acquisition of the parliamentary franchise, coincident with the war's end. The causal relationship between the two dates has often been assumed. David Mitchell wrote a book about suffrage called *Women on the Warpath* in 1957 which looked at outstanding individuals rather than large groups. This story emphasised achievement, drama and novelty rather than the minutiae of economic policy or the labour process. In so doing, they were faithful to their sources which were the more celebratory aspects of the Imperial War Museum's collection and newspapers and memoirs. This process was continued in the 1960s and 1970s by historians who began to look critically at the war and its relation to social progress. Arthur Marwick's many studies outlining an anatomy of war and social change, forces which he believed were central to the creation of modern Britain, includes the most upbeat of all the books on women and the Great War, his contribution being the book accompanying the exhibition of 1976 which first celebrated the Imperial War Museum's holdings in the Women's Work Collection.[1] This book, like Mitchell's, used the photographic record to excellent effect, but, as I have argued, did not always ask the critical question of why the pictorial record took the form it did.

Another development of the 1970s was the rise of women's history. In the United States, this was particularly successful in generating theoretical accounts of the material conditions of women's lives with a theory of the labour market which gave an ideology of sexual division great explanatory power. Heidi Hartmann has seen the exclusion of women from war work after the war as a classic example of patriarchy under capitalism when male power is used against women as a sex. This strand has tended to discuss the sex war in industry as the central historical legacy of the period. In wartime, sexual divisions are particularly stark. Conscription's primary category is gender, with age and occupation coming far behind. Government and the professions address the state of gender relations explicitly, and organise the workplace around them, explaining what they are doing in ways which have previously been far more occluded. Hartmann's account of the trade unions of skilled men accepted their rhetoric of 1917-1919, but ignored the similar emphases of the unions representing general workers and women. The assumption of a simple gender divide, men depriving women, thus limited her explanation of the ease with which women left their wartime occupations and ignored the wider social assumptions that were as important a determinant of women's behaviour as the occupational exclusion she was explaining.

Oral historians, with their emphasis on experience, also began to look to the survivors of the period and use their testimony to comment, often critically, on the more upbeat published sources, and the museum holdings which had been designed to show the especial nature of the war experience rather than its continuities. Women's history using testimony began to contribute those emphases on home and family which women themselves used in explaining the 'experience of war'. Paul Thompson, one of the main promoters of oral history, put the war centrally in his explanation of generational change, in which he wanted to argue that the social change of the period is made by people of all social classes.[2] Joanna Bornat, describing the relationship between home and work for textile workers, particularly emphasised the integrated nature of domestic life and the workplace, calling into question the segmented nature of 'dual sytems' theories as explanations of women's secondary workplace status.[3] However, this emphasis on experience also created problems. The problems were those in part of history itself. Vera Brittain's *Testament of Youth* was serialised on television in the United Kingdom; her second volume of memoirs was called *Testament of Experience*. In both these, her account of war was of loss, of bereavement, sacrifice on the one hand, and of a growing consciousness of the potential of women to prevent their repetition on the other. Histories of the war increasingly looked to its negative aspects, not least because the learning experience of war seemed easily forgotten.

At the same time, the war itself was coming under scrutiny by historians alert to its cultural significance. Jay Winter wrote *The Great War and the British People* in 1985; ten years before a book had been called *War and Economic Development*. In both these early works, the war was quantified as an economic incident and as a shaper of demographic change. Women were seen not as losers but beneficiaries of war as their health and mortality rates improved, their relatively higher wages and better physical health only being undermined by the effects of the 'flu epidemic and geographic mobility, which led to more respiratory disease. In these accounts, experience was seen in the averages of demography, the vast numbers of deaths, pensions claims and labour market statistics. These valuably called into question some contemporary impressions. Women had thought that they were less healthy during the war; many had thought that they had been better off, some that they were worse off. The juxtaposition of subjective and objective measurement of well-being was illuminating, but historians seeking to assess experience still had the problem of concluding which measure was most historically significant.

At the same time, a group of British women scholars were investigating these records with a feminist project on the experience of women's war work. Marion Kozak investigated the munitions workers in a PhD for the University of Hull, Antonia Ineson looked at the medical history of munitions work, and Gail Braybon looked at male attitudes to women war-workers. I started in Woolwich and then became fascinated by the particular role played by working women's own organisations. These works of the late 1970s shared a belief in the power of ideas to determine behaviour, and were an investigation into the quality of the lived experience. Gail Braybon's *Women Workers in the First World War* in 1981 was followed by *Out of the Cage* in 1987. The move from ideas of progress and the centrality of work to a more cultural history is evident in the titles of these books about the women of wartime. The second placed the question of how people had felt about the war as centrally as the attitudes and practices of Government towards them.

More literary accounts of the discourses of femininity and masculinity followed in the 1980s, particularly evident in the work produced in the United States and collected in *Behind the Lines*.[4] This shift represented the linguistic turn in feminist history quite as much as did the more evident shifts in the historiography of the British male working class. Deconstruction could find a lot to say about men and guns, but very little about women and lathes or milling machines, and the question of female sexuality tended to over-ride the phenomenology of work, as indeed it was doing in feminism on both sides of the Atlantic. Literary scholars Sandra Gilbert and Susan Gubar, and Elaine Showalter, looked to sexuality, madness and politics to assess the impact of war on gender relations. They found mysogyny, hysteria and paternalism in the discourses which policed boundaries. Yet assessing these histories of mental distress and literary creativity speaks little to the histories of women of the working class whose breakdowns in wartime were far more likely to come from overwork or impossible domestic situations than they were from social control of sexuality.

Discussion of sexuality rather than work had the effect of emphasising the sexed nature of gender in ways which undermine the complexity of gender relations. When women were described as rude, it was their general insubordination, a crudity of language and a resentment of managerial authority that was in question, and it encompassed relations of power between women as much as it did between women and men. One of the most striking changes of wartime was the development of a cadre of female organisers or administrators as welfare supervisors, WAAC officers and factory inspectors. There were more of them, and they had more capacity to change institutions. However, their power was almost entirely exercised over other women. Their history demonstrates the enduring significance of social class in British Government and civil society. Women who worked in war factories were often faced with new relations of power which demonstrated the intersection between the places where they held it. The healthy worker would produce guns or children better if she continued to enjoy better health in the post-war world, but the ways in which she interpreted and changed her activities in production or reproduction were very different. If we collapse the world of the woman war-worker into any one of her component parts, we lose a vital recognition that she retained these parts, always in tension, through the four years of war. Although fewer women worked on munitions than popular histories have sometimes assumed, the fact that the popular history exists in the imagination of many is itself an historical fact of great interest. Women workers' own experience of war may contradict some of the myths, but the myths were as instrumental in constructing the post-war labour market as the facts. Women's own representations of the war experience need to be read in the light of the discursive texts which addressed them at the time.

If I have argued in these chapters for a recognition of the historical specificity of different phases of the war and a profound scepticism about the official records, it is in the attempt to argue that the sense of significance of nearly all participants in the 1914-1918 war was an important part of the way it was organised at the time. The novelty of public attention paid to women workers was extremely important for their placing in work, their representation by trade unions and the political impact of their contribution. My pessimism about the gains made by women during wartime comes from the same history. In the end, women were able to argue for, and get, better working conditions, some support for domestic labour, relatively improved wages and much greater recognition. But, also at the end of war, these things turned out to be dependent on a necessarily contingent need for high output producing something that was little needed after 1919. Full citizenship was not based on the contribution to society made by their work, however productive, but on the crudities of power relations. Their entry into war work had been negotiated on the presumption of their place as secondary, 'meantime' workers; that presumption remained unchallenged by war.

The culture of the war factory was a rich one, showing that people have endless resource in humanising even the most uncongenial workplace environment. Trade unions similarly showed a fertility of invention that is rare in British labour history. But, to paraphrase Marx, women make their own histories but not in circumstances of their choosing. The circumstance of war was not for the choosing of most women at its outset, even less so at its end. The histories of women's contribution to the war that emphasise its nature as opportunity 'to show what women can do' seem strangely detached from the evidence offered by women who lived through the experience. They already knew that they could do many tasks involved in manual work, they enjoyed, more or less, contributing to the war effort, but they did not, and were rarely allowed to, take the arguments generated in war work into the post-war world. Historians, however, must ask whether the fact that they did not want to is not as important a determinant of the peacetime labour market as working men's attempts to get back a world they too felt they had lost, or as the power of social norms to recuperate. Discursive histories do not question who is speaking and out of what interests they speak, but the history of a cultural change in ideas of women and work must include an assessment of authority. Women were heroes of their own lives, to quote Linda Gordon's title of her history of family power relations.[5] The material circumstances of those lives did change, but they need to be looked at in the context of much longer a view than that of 1918. The testament of experience relayed through oral history conveys very powerfully the importance of looking at the war as an episode in the history of the woman worker, not its essence.

In the 1990s, women's history was called into question by those who pointed out that to assume all women experienced the same oppression was to ignore the real differences of social power between women. To speak of a woman's history of the war, as some did, was to demonstrate that many were excluded; their experience of marginality was redoubled by the assumption that they shared it with all women. The history of women's war work particularly raised this problem. Women of the middle class had benefited from replacing men and keeping some of the new jobs thay had done in war. Women of the working class had less power to retain their work, less enthusiasm for doing so, and had often suffered more adverse consequences from it. The debate over deconstructionism and experience between Joan Wallach Scott, Denise Riley, Susan Kingsley Kent and others on one side, and Linda Gordon, Joan Hoff, Laura Lee Downs on the other, took place largely in American journals and collections, the *Journal of Women's History* and *Signs*, but entered the pages of British-based journals too: *Women's History Review*, *Gender and History* and *Women's Studies International Forum*.[6] Deconstructionists argued that there was no category of experience separable from representation, no real material truth lying behind texts.

They called into question a singular 'women's' experience, arguing that when women were defined in general in historical texts, they were a fluctuating, not a fixed, entity. This recognition of the mutability of gender relations is absolutely central to my arguments, as is the significance of reduction in ascribing to all women qualities or experiences which only some share. However, I part company with some of the writings about discourses on womanhood because they too are reductive. Mary Louise Roberts, *Civilisation Without Sexes: Reconstructing Gender in Postwar*

France, 1917-1927 published in 1994, and Susan Kingsley Kent, *Making Peace: The Reconstruction of Gender in Interwar Britain*, published in 1993, both use the methodology of deconstruction to propose that, in France and Britain respectively, the war was followed by a conscious and deliberate attempt to redefine womanhood which could be seen in popular fiction, journalism and professional literature. Both tend to assume a unitary feminism which is problematic for both countries, and both tend to collapse profound differences of class and material opportunities in looking at the effects of such discursive formulations. Both see sexuality and motherhood as primary, which they clearly are, but ignore the effects of social class and economic inequality. Ironically, there is in these two books a return to the issue of liberation or emancipation with which many writers wrestled in the 1970s. By suggesting that sexuality was as much about control as freedom, they end up precisely where discussions of power began 20 years ago. Work as an experience constitutive of gender identity needs to be included in any assessment of improvement or loss, and needs to be built in to the history of the history of women and war as much as sexuality, home, family and consumption.

The question with which this book started was that of how far women had created a new world for themselves in the factories of the First World War. In the end, the circumstances of war work were so circumscribed that although there was change and women made a substantial contribution to the war, the change did not endure, nor was it seen as changing women's nature as workers or as citizens. Some new models of the woman worker were created and given dramatic visibility by photographs, posters and demonstrations, but they tended to show novelty, and disguise the limits of power obtained as a result of wartime administration. Workers were still being described either in relation to men – as Tommy's sister – or in relation to their moral economy, as nice or rude. These ascriptions could be exploited, and were, by organisations representing working women, but such an exploitation carried risks which became only too evident in the labour market after the war. Profound cultural change in the world of the woman worker or the 'girl', the 'mother' or the woman citizen awaited the changes in society and economy of the next world war, expansion of education and the development of a welfarist politics that could begin to create institutions in the interests of women.

Notes on Chapter 10

Full details of all publications mentioned here are in the bibliography on page 209.

1   Marwick's book actually has two titles, one on the cover of my copy, another inside. It is mostly cited as *Women at War 1914-1918*, but it is also called *Woman at War.*

2   Thompson, P., *The Edwardians*, second edn, 1977.

3   Bornat, J., 'Home and Work: A New Context for Trade Union History', *Oral History*, vol. 5, 2 (Autumn 1977).

4   Higonnet, M.R., Jenson, J., Michel, S. and Collins Weitz, M. (eds), *Behind the Lines, Gender and the Two World Wars*, 1987.

5   Gordon, L., *Heroes of their Own Lives*, 1989.

6   Scott, J., *Gender and the Politics of History*, 1988; Riley, Denise, *'Am I that Name?' Feminism and the Category of 'Woman' in History*, 1988; Kingsley Kent, S., *Making Peace: The Reconstruction of Gender in Interwar Britain*, 1993; 'Theoretical and Methodological Dialogue on the Writing of Women's History', *Journal of Women's History*, 2/3, 1991, pp 58-108; Scott, J. and Gordon, L., in *Signs*, 1991; Hall, C., 'Politics, Post-structuralism and Women's History', *Gender and History* 3, pp 204-210; Stanley, L. (ed.), special issue on British feminist histories, *Women's Studies International Forum*, 1995; Purvis, J., 'From Woman Worthies to Post-structuralism' in Purvis (ed.), *Women's History: Britain 1880-1945*, 1995; forum on methodological issues, *Journal of Women's History* 5, 1993; Hoff, J., 'Gender as a Post-modern Theory of Paralysis', *Women's History Review* 3, 1994, and debate in *Women's History Review*, 5/1, 1996. These debates have invigorated the discussion of how historians write about subordination, and how far we can rank the comments on their lives in terms of their representativeness or validity.

Bibliography

Sources with Abbreviations Used

Public Record Office (PRO)
Records of the Ministries of Munitions (MUN);
Records of the Ministries of Labour (LAB);
Records of the Ministries of Supply (SUP) and Works
Official History of the Ministry of Munitions, A History of State Manufacture, 8 volumes.
Collections of documents are classified by main number, followed by file number.

Imperial War Museum, Women's Work collection (IWM)
This is classified by subjects:
Munitions (MUN);
Employment (EMP);
Army (ARMY);
Medical Services (MED);
Welfare (WEL).
The IWM also holds Documents: Diary, Gabrielle West, 'The Spark', Leeds 1917 and photographs which each have an individual index number; and an oral archive.

British Library of Political and Economic Science (BLPES)
This contains the Beveridge collection in 6 volumes, which includes documents from Beveridge's stint at the Labour Supply department at the Ministry of Munitions. The archive also includes the Webb collection Reconstruction documents (Recon), in four boxes, the Webb Trade Union collection and the manuscript of Beatrice Webb's Diary.

The Library of Trade Union Congress (TUC)
TUC Annual Reports, 1914-1926;
National Federation of Women Workers (NFWW) Annual Reports, 1914-1921;
Women's Trade Union League (WTUL) Annual Report 1914-1921;
The Gertrude Tuckwell Collection (GTC), a collection of press clippings collected for the WTUL with pamphlets and photographs, and handed over when the WTUL disbanded.
GTC references are quoted with the file number when the whole file is used.

Trade Union records
 General and Municipal Workers' Union;
 Executive Committee minutes, gasworkers, 1916-1921;
 Journal of the National Union of General Workers, 1920-25;
 Executive Committee minutes, GFTU, 1916-1919;
 Amalgamated Union of Engineering Workers;
 ASE Monthly Journal and Report, 1915-1919;
 Transport and General Workers Union;
 Workers' Union Record, 1913-1920;
 Workers' Union Annual Reports.

Other organisations
Labour Party:
 Minutes of the SJCWIO, 1916-1917 (the rest, unfortunately are lost);
 WEWNC;
 Leaflets, correspondence of the WLL.
Fawcett Society:
 Reports of the Women's Industrial Council.
London Borough of Greenwich, local history library:
 Annual reports of the Medical Officer of Health, Woolwich, 1913-15, 1917-26;
 John Martin photographic collection;
 Sales leaflets GLC, RACS and private estates;
 Miscellaneous ephemera, Woolwich Labour Party;
International Institute for the Study of Social History, Amsterdam:
 Sylvia Pankhurst papers (SP), Postgate collection.

Government publications
 War Office, Women's Work on Munitions, 1916;
 Women's Work in non-munitions industries, 1916;
 Parliamentary Papers (PP);
 Annual Reports of the Registrar General:
  1914: PP 1916, v, Cd 8206;
  1915: PP 1917-8, v, Cd 8484;
  1916: PP 1917-8, vvi, Cd 8869;
  1917: PP 1919, x, Cmd 40;

 Census reports:
  1911 census, PP 1912-13, cxi, Cd 6258 cxii, Cd 6343;
  PP1913, Lxxvii, Cd 6910;
  Lxxviii, Cd 7017, Cd 7018.

Annual Reports of the Chief Inspector of Factories and Workshops:
   1914, PP 1914 16, xxi, Cd 8051;
   1915, PP 1916, ix, Cd 8Z76;
   1916, PP 1917-18, xiv, Cd 8570;
   1917, PP 1918, xi, Cd 9108;
   1918, PP 1919, xxii, Cmd 340.

Reports on Conciliation and Arbitration:
   PP 1919, xiii, Cmd 185, twelfth report on conciliation and arbitration;

Reports of the Health of Munition Workers' Committee:
   Interim Report, PP 1917-l8, xiii, Cd 8511;
   Final Report, PP 1918, xii, Cd 9065;
   Industrial Canteens, PP 1914-16, xxix, Cd 8133;
   Sunday Labour, PP 1914-16, xxix, Cd 8132;
   Welfare Supervision, PP 1914-16, xxix, Cd 8151;
   Memorandum on the Employment of Women, PP 1916, xxiii, Cd 8185.

Reports of the Central Committee for Women's Employment:
   Interim Report, PP 1914-16, xxxvii, Cd 7848;
   Report of the Hills Committee, PP1918, xiv, Cd 9239;

Commisssioners' Reports:
   Report of the War Cabinet Committee on Women in Industry, PP 1919, xxxi, Cmd 135;
   Summaries of evidence to the above, PP 1919, xxxi, Cmd 167;
   Report of the Women's Advisory Committee on the Domestic Service Problem, PP 1919, xxix, Cmd 67;
   A study of the factors which have operated in the past and are operating now to determine the distribution of women in industry, PP 1929-30, xvii, Cmd 3508;
   Commission of Enquiry into Industrial Unrest, PP 1917-18, xv, Cd 8666.

Newspapers and Journals

Common Cause
Co-operation
The Daily Herald
The Engineer
The Kentish Mercury

Solidarity
The Times
The Woman Worker
The Women's Trade Union Review
The Woolwich Pioneer
The Women's/Workers' Dreadnought

Pamphlets

Fisher, V., *The Babies' Tribute to Modern Moloch*, 1909, SDF
Fabian Women's Group, No 178, *The War, Women and Unemployment*, 1915
Hutchins, B.L., *Women in Industry after the War* (a Social Reconstruction pamphlet), 1917
Maclean, J., *The War after the War*, Glasgow 1917, repr. 1973
Murphy, J.T., *The Workers' Committee*, Sheffield 1917, repr. 1972
Phillips, M., *The Working Woman's House*, 1918 (WLL)
Gallacher, W. and Campbell, J., *Direct Action*, Glasgow 1919, repr. 1972
Hines, N. and V., *Birth Control and the British Working Classes*, 1929

Films

'Everybody's Business/Don't Waste', 1917, Ministry of Food, 1777VB
'Heart of the World', 1918, dir. W.G. Griffiths, 2594H
'The Girl Who Stayed at Home', 1919, dir. W.G. Griffiths, 2204F
'Topical Budget Newsreels', 2S June 1916-21, March 1918, 2140A-C
'Women's Work on Munitions', 1917 compilation, War Office, 1124B

Reference numbers are to British Film Institute, 1977-8

Secondary Sources

Books (all published London, unless otherwise stated)

Anon., WAAC, *A Woman's History of the War*, 1930, T. Werner Laurie Ltd
Adam, R., *A Woman's Place*, 1975
Addison, C., *Politics from Within*, 1924
Anderson, A., *Women in the Factory*, 1922, John Murray
Andrews, I. and Hobbs, M., *The Economic Effects of the War Upon Women and Children*, New York, 1921, OUP
Anthony, S., *Woman's Place in Industry and the Home*, 1932
Askwith, G., *Industrial Problems and Disputes*, 1920

Bagwell, P., *The Railwaymen*, 1963

Bax, G., *Thought Rhythms of a Munitioneer*, 1915

Bentwich, H., *If I Forget Thee*, 1973

Beveridge, W., *Unemployment, a Problem of Industry*, 1909

Beveridge, W., *War and Insurance*, Oxford, 1927

Beveridge, W., *British Food Control*, Oxford, 1928

Black, C., *Married Women's Work*, 1915, G. Bell

Blainey, J., *The Woman Worker and Restrictive Legislation*, 1928

Bondfield, M., *A Life's Work*, 1948, Hutchinson

Boston S., *Women Workers and the Trade Unions*, 1987, Lawrence & Wishart

Bourke, J., *Dismembering the Male*, Reaktion, 1996

Bowley, A.L., *The War and Employment*, Oxford, 1915

Prices and Wages in the United Kingdom, Oxford, 1927

Braybon, G., *Women Workers in the First World War*, 1981, Croom Helm

Braybon, G. and Summerfield, P., *Out of the Cage*, 1987, Pandora

Brittain, V., *Women's Work in Modern England*, 1928, Douglas

Brittain, V., *Testament of Friendship*, 1940, Macmillan

Brittain, V., *Testament of Youth*, 1933, Gollancz

Brown, K., *Labour and Unemployment*, Newton Abbott, 1971, David & Charles

Buxton, N.K. and Mackay, D., *British Employment Statistics: a Guide to Sources and Methods*, Oxford, 1977, Blackwell

Cable, B., *Doing Our Bit*, 1916

Cadbury, E., Matheson, H.C. and Shann, G., *Women's Work and Wages*, 1906, T. Fisher Unwin

Cadbury, E. and Shann, G., *Sweating*, 1907

Caine, H., *Our Girls*, 1916

Cathcart, E.P., *The Human Factor in Industry*, Oxford, 1928

Chapman, S.J., *The War and the Cotton Trade*, Oxford, 1915

Chapman, S.J., *Labour and Capital after the War*, Oxford, 1919

Churchill, J.R. (ed.), *Women's War Work*, 1916, Pearson

Clegg, H.A., *General Union*, Oxford, 1954

Clegg, H.A., *General Union in a Changing Society*, 1964

Clegg, H.A., Fox, A. and Thompson, A.F., *A History of British Trade Unions since 1889*, Oxford, 1964

Clay, H., *The Post War Unemployment Problem*, 1929

Cole, G.D.H., *The World of Labour*, Oxford, 1915, G. Bell & Sons Ltd

Cole, G.D.H., *Trade Unionism and Munitions*, Oxford, 1923, Clarendon

Cole, G.D.H., *Workshop Organisation*, Oxford, 1923, Clarendon

Condell, D. and Liddiard, J., *Working for Victory? Images of Women in the First World War 1914-1918*, 1989, Routledge & Kegan Paul

Cunnison, J., *Labour Organisation*, 1930, Clarendon

Dearle, N.B., *Dictionary of Official Wartime Organisations*, 1928

Dearle, N.B., *Economic Chronicle of the Great War*, 1929

Dewar, G.A.B., *The Great Munitions Feat*, 1920, Constable & Co.

Dewar, K. (ed.), *The Girl*, 1920, G. Bell

Drake, B., *Women in the Engineering Trades*, 1917, George Allen & Unwin for the Fabian Society

Drake, B., *Women and Trade Unions*, 1920, George Allen & Unwin

Dwork, D., *War is Good for Babies and other Young Children*, Tavistock, 1987

Ewing, E., *Women in Uniform*, 1975, Batsford

Fawcett, M.G., *The Women's Victory – and After*, 1920, Sidgwick & Jackson

Fischer, H.G. and Dubois, B., *Sexual Life During the Great War*, 1937

Ford, P. and G., *A Breviate of Parliamentary Papers, 1917-39*, Oxford, 1957, Blackwell

Fox, A., *A History of the NUBSO*, Oxford, 1958

Fraser, H., *Women and War Work*, New York, 1918, G. Arnold Shaw

Fulford, R., *Votes for Women*, 1958

Fyrth, H.J. and Collins, M., *The Foundry Workers*, Manchester, 1959

Gallacher, W., *Revolt on the Clyde*, 1936

Gollancz, V. (ed.), *The Making of Women*, 1918, George Allen & Unwin

Gordon, L., *Heroes of Their Own Lives: The Politics and History of Family Violence*, 1989, Virago

Goodrich, E.H., *The Frontiers of Control*, 1920

Gore, E., *The Better Fight: The Story of Dame Lilian Barker*, 1965, Geoffrey Bles

DeGroot, G., *Blighty: British Society in the Era of the Great War*, 1996, Longman

Haldane, C., *Motherhood and its Enemies*, 1927

Halsey, A.H. (ed.), *Trends in British Society Since 1900*, 1972, Macmillan

Hamilton, M.A., *Mary Macarthur*, 1925

Hammond, M.B., *British Labor Conditions and Legislation*, New York, 1923

Hinton J., *The First Shop Stewards' Movement*, 1973

Higonnet, M.R., Jenson, J., Michel, S. and Collins Weitz, M. (eds), *Behind the Lines, Gender and the Two World Wars*, Newhaven USA, 1987, Yale University Press

Hogg, O.F.G., *The Royal Arsenal: Its Background, Origins and Subsequent History*, 1963, OUP

Horne, J.N., *Labour at War: France and Britain 1914-1918*, Oxford, 1991, Clarendon

Howe, E. and Waite, H.E., *A Centenary History of the London Society of Compositors*, 1948

Hutchins, B.L., *Women in Modern Industry*, 1915

Hutchins, B.L., *A History of Factory Legislation*, 1926

Hyman, R., *The Workers' Union*, Oxford, 1971, Clarendon

Jefferson, E.F.E., *The Woolwich Story*, Woolwich, 1970

Jefferys, J.B., *The Story of the Engineers*, 1946

John, A., *By the Sweat of Their Brow*, 1980

John, A. (ed.), *Unequal Opportunities*, Oxford, 1986, Basil Blackwell

Kendall W., *The Revolutionary Movement in Britain*, 1969

Kingsley Kent, S., *Making Peace: The Reconstruction of Gender in Interwar Britain*, Princeton, 1993, Princeton University Press

Kingsley Kent, S., *Sex and Suffrage in Britain 1860-1914*, Princeton, 1987, Princeton University Press

Kirkaldy, A.W., (ed.), *Labour, Finance and the War*, 1916, British Association

Kirkaldy, A.W., (ed.), *British Labour 1911-1921*, 1921

Lewenhak S., *Women and Trade Unions*, 1977, G. Benn

Lewis, Jane (ed.), *Labour and Love*, Oxford, 1986, Basil Blackwell

Lewis, Jane (ed.), *Women in England 1870-1950*, Brighton, Wheatsheaf

Liddington J. and Norris J., *One Hand Tied Behind Us*, 1978, Virago

Llewellyn Davies, M. (ed.), *Maternity Letters from Working Women*, 1915 and repr. 1978, Virago

Lloyd, E.H.M., *Experiments in State Control*, Oxford 1924

Lloyd George, D., *War Memoirs*, 6 vols, 1933, Odhams

Lovell, J. and Roberts, B.C., *A Short History of the TUC*, 1968

Macassey, L.L., *Labour Policy – False or True*, 1922, Thornton Butterworth

Ramsey Macdonald, J., *Socialism after the War*, 1921

Mansbridge, A., *Margaret McMillan*, 1932, Dent

Mappen, E., *Helping Women at Work: The Women's Industrial Council*, 1985, Hutchinson

Martin, A., *The Married Working Woman*, 1911

Martin, A., *The Mother and Social Reform*, 1913

Martindale, H., *Women Servants of the State*, 1938

Marwick, A., *The Deluge*, 1965, Basingstoke, Macmillan

Marwick, A., *Women at War*, 1977, Fontana

McCleary, G.F., *The Maternal and Child Welfare Movement*, 1935

McKibbin, R., *The Evolution of the Labour Party*, Oxford, 1974

Mess, H.A., *Factory Legislation and its Administration*, 1926

Middleton, T.H., *Food Production in War*, Oxford, 1923

Milward, A.S., *The Economic Effects of Two World Wars on Britain*, 1984, Macmillan

Mitchell, D., *1919: Red Mirage*, 1965

Mitchell, D., *Women on the Warpath*, 1966, Jonathan Cape

Moran, J., *NATSOPA: Seventy Five Years*, 1964

Newman, G., *Infant Mortality*, 1906

Pankhurst, E.S., *The Home Front*, 1932, Hutchinson

Pankhurst, E.S., *The Suffragette Movement*, 1932, repr. 1977, Virago

Passerini, L. (ed.), *International Yearbook of Oral History and Life Stories* vol. 4, Oxford, 1996, OUP

Playne, C., *Society at War*, 1930

Playne, C., *Britain Holds On*, 1933

Pollard., S.H., *The Development of the British Economy 1914-1967*, second edn, 1969

Pribicevic, B., *The Shop Stewards' Movement and Workers' Control*, Oxford, 1959

Rathbone, E., *The Case for Family Allowances*, 1944

Reilly, C. (ed.), *Scars Upon My Heart: Women's Poetry and Verse of the First World War*, 1981, Virago

Riley, D., *Am I That Name? Feminism and the 'Category of Woman' in History*, Basingstoke, Macmillan, 1988

Roberts, Mary Louise, *Civilisation Without Sexes: Dismantling Gender in Postwar France, 1917–27*, Chicago, 1994, Chicago University Press

Ross, E., *Love and Toil*, OUP, 1993

Rowbotham, S., *Hidden from History*, 1973

Rowntree, B.S., *The Human Needs of Labour*, 1918/9, Thomas Nelson & Sons

Rowntree, B.S., *The Responsibility of Women Workers for Their Dependants*, Oxford, 1921, Clarendon

Saville, J. and Briggs, A. (eds), *Essays in Labour History, 1918-1939*, 1973

Saville, J. and Bellamy, J. (eds), *Dictionary of Labour Biography* vol. II, 1974, vol. V, 1979

Searle, G., *Eugenics and Politics in Britain*, Leyden 1976

Scott, J., *Gender and the Politics of History*, New York, 1988, Columbia University Press

Scott, J.D., *Vickers: A History*, 1956

Scott, J.D., *Siemens Bros, 1858-1958*, 1958

Sells, D.M., *The British Trade Boards System*, 1923, P.S. King

Shepherd, E.C., *The Fixing of Wages in Government Employment*, 1923

Smith, E., *Wage-earning Women and their Dependants*, 1915, Fabian Society

Snell, H., *Men, Movements and Myself*, 1936

Stedman Jones, G., *Outcast London*, Oxford, 1971, Clarendon

Stewart, M. and Hunter, L., *The Needle is Threaded*, 1964

Stone, G., *Women War Workers*, 1916, Harrap

Stopes, M., *Married Love*, 1918, Putnam

Stopes, M., *Radiant Motherhood*, 1920

Strachey, R., *The Cause: Our Freedom and its Results*, 1928, G. Bell

Stucke, R.B. (ed.), *Fifty Years History of the Woolwich Labour Party*, 1953

Swanwick, H., *Women and War*, 1915

Swanwick, H., *I Have Been Young*, 1935

Thompson, P., *Socialists, Liberals and Labour*, 1967

Thompson, P., *The Edwardians*, second edn, St Albans, 1977, Routledge 1993

Wall, R. and Winter, J. (eds), *The Upheaval of War*, Cambridge, 1988, Cambridge University Press

Watson, W.F., *Machines and Men: An Autobiography of an Itinerant Mechanic*, 1935

Webb, B. (ed.), *M. Cole: Diaries*, 1952

Webb, C., *The Woman with a Basket*, Manchester, 1927

Webster, C. (ed.), *Biology, Medicine and Society*, Oxford, 1981

Winter, J., *The Great War and the British People*, Basingstoke, 1986, Macmillan

Woollacott, A., *On Her Their Lives Depend*, 1994, University of California Press

Articles

Abrams, P., 'The failure of social reform, 1918-1924', *Past and Present*, 1963

Beaufoy, R., 'The Well Hall Estate', *Town Planning Review* xxi, 195

Beechey, V., 'Women and Production', in Kuhn, A and Wolpe, M. (eds), *Feminism and Materialism*, 1978

Bland, L. 'In the Name of Protection: Policing Women in the First World War' in Brophy and Smart (eds), *Women in Law*, 1985, Routledge & Kegan Paul

Bornat, J., 'Home and Work: A New Context for Trade Union History', *Oral History*, vol. 5, 2 (Autumn 1977)

Breugel, I., 'Women as a Reserve Army of Labour', *Feminist Review* 3, 1979

Davin, A., 'Imperialism and Motherhood', *History Workshop*, Spring 1978

Deacon, A., 'The Politics of Unemployment Insurance in the Twenties' in Briggs and Saville (eds), *Essays in Labour History 1918-1939*

Hartman, H., 'Capitalism, Patriarchy and the Case for Job Segregation by Sex', in Eisenstein, Z.R. (ed.), *Capitalist Patriarchy and the Case for Socialist Feminism*, New York, 1979

Hiley, N.P., 'The British Army Films "You!" and "For the Empire"', *Historical Journal*, 1985

Hoff, J., 'Gender as a Post-modern Theory of Paralysis', *Women's History Review* 3, 1994.

Land, H., 'The Introduction of Family Allowances, an Act of Historic Justice?', in Hall, P.K., Land, H., Parker, R.A. and Webb, A., *Change, Choice and Conflict in Social Policy*, 1975

Mayes, F., 'Local Government in Woolwich', *Proceedings of the Woolwich and District Antiquarian Society*, 194-197, 1958

Milkman, R., 'Organising the Sexual Division of Labor, Historical Perspectives on "Women's Work" and the American Labor Movement', *Socialist Review*, New York, 1980

Olcott, T., 'The Women's Trade Union Movement in London, 1874-1914', *London Journal*, 1976

Pugh, M., 'Politicians and the Women's Vote', *History*, 1974

Purvis J. (ed.), 'From Women Worthies to Post-Structuralism' in Purvis (ed.), *Women's History: Britain 1880–1945*

Stanley, L., (ed.), special issue on British feminist histories, *Women's Studies International Forum*, 1995

Thom, D., 'Women Workers at the Woolwich Arsenal, 1915-1918', *Oral History*, 1978

Woollacott, A., 'Maternalism, Professionalism and Industrial Welfare Supervisors in First World War Britain', *Women's History Review*, 3.1 1994

Woollacott, A., '"Khaki Fever" and its Control: Gender, Age, Class and Sexual Morality', *Journal of Contemporary History*, 29.1994

Television Programmes

Boston Sarah, 'The Chainmakers of Cradley Heath', BBC Network, 1977

Cook, Christopher, 'The Woolwich Arsenal', BBC Yesterday's Witness, 1978 (included 'The Mighty Atom')

Theses

Lewenhak, S., 'Trade Union Membership Among Women and Girls in the United Kingdom, 1920-1965', University of London, 1972 PhD

Kozak, M., 'Women Munition Workers During the First World War, with Special Reference to Engineering', University of Hull, 1977 PhD

Thom, D., 'Women Workers in the Woolwich Arsenal in the First World War', University of Warwick, 1975 MA

Thom, D., 'The Ideology of Women's Work, 1914-1924, with Special Reference to the NFWW and Other Trade Unions' for the CNAA at Thames Polytechnic

Index